NARROW GAUGE PANORAMA

To my wife who has been hugely and unfailingly supportive, both at home when I've been hiding behind the computer, and on expeditions to new railways where she has always kept cheerful even when she often had little idea about what awaited her. Without all her help this book wouldn't have been possible.

Very much an international machine! 700mm gauge 0-4-0T no 4 (KM 3175/1895) is the oldest steam loco in Luxembourg and on 12 September 2010 posed for her photo at Fond-de-Gras station on the Minièresbunn Doihl in the south western corner of the country. She is one of three steam locos at the railway to have been built at the Munich factory and first worked on the Collart steelworks' 700mm gauge railway at Steinfort. In 1941 she moved to Tannerie de Cuir Ideal at Wiltz and was rebuilt to run on their 800mm gauge line. She was withdrawn in about 1960 and after a close shave at a scrapyard near Steinfort was bought by Hubert Bauldauff, an enthusiast from Luxembourg City. For the next forty years she was stored in the garage at his home. The country's Service des Sites et Monuments Nationaux recognised her historic importance and bought her in 2001, after which she was restored to working order at Meiningen loco works in Germany. She first steamed again at Fond-de-Gras in 2004, now as a 700mm loco once more. Much of the railway runs in tunnel and its far terminus is at Saulnes, just over the border in France.

NARROW GAUGE PANORAMA

STEAMING ALONG THE RUSTIC AND NARROW

JAMES WAITE

PEN & SWORD
TRANSPORT
AN IMPRINT OF PEN & SWORD BOOKS LTD.
YORKSHIRE - PHILADELPHIA

First published in Great Britain in 2021 by
Pen and Sword Transport
An imprint of
Pen & Sword Books Ltd
Yorkshire - Philadelphia

Copyright © James Waite, 2021

ISBN 978 1 52677 621 1

The right of James Waite to be identified as Author of this work has been asserted by him in accordance with the Copyright, Designs and Patents Act 1988.

A CIP catalogue record for this book is available from the British Library.

All rights reserved. No part of this book may be reproduced or transmitted in any form or by any means, electronic or mechanical including photocopying, recording or by any information storage and retrieval system, without permission from the Publisher in writing.

Typeset in 11.5/14 Palatino
Typeset by SJmagic DESIGN SERVICES, India

Printed and bound in India by Replika Press Pvt. Ltd.

Pen & Sword Books Ltd incorporates the Imprints of Pen & Sword Books Archaeology, Atlas, Aviation, Battleground, Discovery, Family History, History, Maritime, Military, Naval, Politics, Railways, Select, Transport, True Crime, Fiction, Frontline Books, Leo Cooper, Praetorian Press, Seaforth Publishing, Wharncliffe and White Owl.

For a complete list of Pen & Sword titles please contact

PEN & SWORD BOOKS LIMITED
47 Church Street, Barnsley, South Yorkshire, S70 2AS, England
E-mail: enquiries@pen-and-sword.co.uk
Website: www.pen-and-sword.co.uk

or

PEN AND SWORD BOOKS
1950 Lawrence Rd, Havertown, PA 19083, USA
E-mail: Uspen-and-sword@casematepublishers.com
Website: www.penandswordbooks.com

CONTENTS

Preface	6
Acknowledgements	8
Locomotive and carriage builders	11
Canada and the USA	14
México	41
Guatemala	42
El Salvador	44
Costa Rica	45
Colombia	48
Brazil	52
Argentina	61
France	64
Norway	83
Sweden	85
Ireland	93
Wales	97
England	123
Portugal	127
Spain	131
Luxembourg	142
Germany	144
Switzerland	154
Austria	160
Hungary	168
Czech Republic	173
Slovakia	176
Ukraine	179
Russia	181
Italy	183
Serbia	185
Bosnia	189
Greece	195
Romania	200
Eritrea	204
Kenya	208
South Africa	213
Syria	217
Jordan	221
Pakistan	223
India	227
Burma	242
Thailand	247
Cambodia	256
Vietnam	258
Malaysia	261
The Philippines	266
China	272
Taiwan	276
Japan	280
Australia	287
New Zealand	293

PREFACE

Welcome to my second album of photos of the narrow gauge around the world. There can be few happier and more peaceful sights than that of a small train going about its business. Compiling these pictures has brought back many happy memories of travels to see the little lines, usually in beautiful countryside and always in the company of friendly and helpful people, both professional railwaymen and fellow enthusiasts. This friendship is one of the enduring pleasures of the narrow gauge as I hope will be apparent from many of the photos.

As I did in my first book *Twenty First Century Narrow Gauge*, I've laid out these photos to present an imaginary journey around the world, starting with Alaska and finishing in New Zealand. They are mostly of steam locos or scenes around them, generally as heritage attractions, though there are some from railways where steam was still in everyday service. I've treated everything that runs on track narrower than 4ft 8½ins as being eligible and so there are photos of enormous Garratts in Kenya and South Africa, far larger than any standard gauge locos in many other countries, as well as trains which are much smaller. I've tried not to repeat information which appeared in my first book and have done so only where I thought it was needed to give a coherent account of what the photos portray.

With heritage railways, I've concentrated on scenes which look at least something like they did when the trains were running for real. In addition to action photos there are also some of non-working locos where I thought they looked attractive or had an interesting history, and also a couple of miniature ones. There is even one railway which appears only in a tiled wall painting!

I've also included some First World War military locos. There's something uncomfortable about enjoying anything closely associated with the killing and suffering which were inseparable from a war in which the slaughter became a strategic objective for both sides and was carried out on an industrial scale. On the other hand, the trains weren't directly involved and the sight of them must have provided brief moments of relief for some of those facing the daily horrors of life on the front. The military light railways developed into huge systems with locos and rolling stock of considerable technical interest, and they went on to have a major influence on many narrow gauge lines throughout Europe and beyond for the remainder of their existence. I've placed these photos with those from France as the greatest concentration of military railways was there.

Place names have often changed to reflect different political or cultural realities. For the most part it seemed sensible to use the versions current when the railways I've described were working in their pre-heritage days, particularly those which I visited back then. This is particularly relevant in Catalonia and I intend no disrespect towards the reawakening of its culture which lies behind more recent changes of name. Perhaps perversely, I've used the Welsh versions of place names where the Anglicised versions have completely dropped out of circulation, partly because many of the events about which I have written have taken place only in recent years.

I've been asked about cameras. Since 2003, I've mostly used Fuji's products, its DSLRs until 2013 and more recently its mirrorless X-series which are less bulky and produce a sharper image with the back of the lens being closer to the sensor.

Between 2005 and 2007, I also sometimes used a Nikon D70. I'm not on Fuji's payroll (!) but while all makes of digital camera are excellent, I particularly like Fuji's colour balance. There are occasions when a small point-and-shoot camera is useful, even in the smartphone age, and mine is another Fuji product.

The UK's many heritage railways, especially narrow gauge, are rightly the envy of enthusiasts around the world but now face a period of great uncertainty. In recent years, visitor numbers from mainland Europe to our traditional holiday districts have grown exponentially, thanks to increased prosperity and a growing awareness of a shared European identity. The Welsh lines in particular have benefitted greatly and foreign visitors now account for a significant amount of their business. It remains to be seen how Brexit will affect this and we can but hope that our guests will continue to feel welcome and will enjoy the hospitality that awaits them. Now that we have turned our backs on our principal trading partners, even the most ardent Brexiteers accept that we enter a period in which the country's economy will suffer and with it personal disposable income. It's hard to see that UK-based visitors to our heritage railways are likely to increase significantly in the foreseeable future.

I happen to be writing this on the weekend that the UK has formally left the EU and we must also hope that those in charge of our country's affairs will now set aside the pursuit of political dogma and instead will concentrate on policies designed to benefit the people who live here, not least the development of tourism from overseas. In recent years, the biggest engineering project by far on the UK's narrow gauge scene has been the reconstruction of the Welsh Highland Railway. EU grants running into millions of pounds were involved. These, of course, are no longer available and schemes such as the extension of the Corris and the Lynton & Barnstaple lines will need to look elsewhere for funding. It is not clear how the loss of money from the EU can be made good. This is not the place to discuss Brexit more generally other than to say that it's always better to build bridges between people rather than walls.

Hard on the heels of Brexit the COVID-19 outbreak in Spring 2020 could not have come at a worse time for heritage and tourist railways, not only in the UK but right across the northern hemisphere. Many have wage bills, interest liabilities on loans and other expenses which accrue all year round and rely on ticket sales during the spring and summer, but in 2020, much of the summer season was lost and even when the trains began to run they have only been able to carry a much smaller number of passengers than usual. Even before the outbreak, many lines were struggling to attract volunteers in the numbers they need and it's not clear just how, or when, those they have will be able to return. The plight of these railways, of course, is just a minor aspect of a devastating worldwide tragedy, but many of those in charge are desperately worried about the future. We can only hope that things will have improved for them by the time this book is published.

On a happier note, I've continued to receive an unfailing welcome on railways everywhere I've visited, both in Europe and beyond, even if some of my European hosts have found Brexit to be incomprehensible and even bewildering. I hope this book will provide encouragement to go and visit them as well as lines at home once our public health issues are behind us, and that in the meantime it's as much fun to read as it has been to write.

ACKNOWLEDGEMENTS

I've received immense help, friendship and kindness from many people throughout my travels. I've named some of them in the captions to these photos. Of the others, special thanks go to Bernd Seiler from Berlin, whose FarRail Tours operation arranges visits to railways and the use of steam locos, often against seemingly insurmountable odds. Bob Turner has shared his immense knowledge of the railways of North America and has been a splendid travelling companion in many countries. In the US, Bill Shechter at Fairbanks, James Bane at the Sumpter Valley, Wendell Huffman at the Nevada State Railroad Museum in Carson City, Dan Markoff and Brian Norden who looked after *Eureka* during her visit to its sister museum at Boulder City, Ted Rita at the Hesston Steam Museum, Chris Robbins at Tweetsie and James Patten at Wiscasset were all most helpful as was Doug Cummings both at the White Pass and in Colorado. Some of my US photos come from photo charters arranged by Pete Lerro, who is a considerate and skilled operator. Pepe Fabregat was very hospitable at Cuautla and Steve Cossey arranged numerous introductions and gave up a great deal of his time in Bogotá. My visits to railways in Brazil would not have been possible without the great assistance of Bruno Sanches, Leandro Guidini, Julio Moraes, Rafael Bordini and José Warmuth.

Roar Stenersen assisted with information about the Tertitten railway in Norway and Rune Bergstedt, Stig Gustavsson, Robert Herpai, Karl-Gunnar Karlsson, Lars Olof Karlsson, Kurt Möller, Anders Nordebring, Frank Stenvall, Lotta Sjöberg, Staffan Sjöberg and Håkan Zaar have all been most helpful in Sweden. Vadim Anokhin provided indispensable assistance at Rostov-on-Don as did Wolfram Wendelin, Dimitri Babarika and Sergei Trouchelle at Haivoron.

In the UK, Graham Farr at the Welsh Highland Heritage Railway, Julie Stirland and Paul Lewin at the Ffestiniog, Laurence and Jane Garvey at Tywyn, Will Smith at Aberystwyth, Simon Bowden and Andrew Charman at the Welshpool & Llanfair, David Coleman at Corris, Tony Nicholson at Woody Bay, the late Bill Best at Bredgar and Jeremy Martin at the Richmond Light Railway have all offered unstinting assistance and Nigel and Kay Bowman and Jonathan Mann at Launceston were exceptionally hospitable. I've also benefitted from photo charters arranged by Martin Creese, Bob Branch and David Williams. They are all experts in their field and work tirelessly in the interests of their customers, always at prices much lower than those charged elsewhere and sometimes for no financial reward at all.

David also operates further afield, and he and Geoffrey Nickson arranged the highly successful trip which produced my Vivarais photos, a pioneering venture which must have involved an immense amount of preparation. Geoffrey and also Julien Rebillard have been very helpful at the Baie de Somme and Nicolas Moser was exceptionally kind and welcoming at Abreschviller.

Juanjo Olaizola Elordi and Javier Fenández López, the directors of the Azpeitia and Gijón museums in northern Spain, both work far beyond the call of duty in conserving steam operation and have been very helpful, as has Nuria Vila Álvarez at Gijón. My trips to Portugal would not have been possible without the advice and assistance of Ad van Sten and José Silva. Marcus Dettenberg has arranged visits to some of Germany's lesser-known lines and Rüdiger Fach and Rafael Wunderwald helped me during two memorable trips to the Frankfurter Feldbahnmuseum, as did Walter Gekeler at the Härtsfeldbahn. Hans Hufnagel has given good friendship and help in his native Austria and many other parts of the world. August Zopf was almost singlehandedly responsible for setting up the SKGLB museum at Mondsee and very kindly opened it up for me.

Marek Skalka was very helpful at Mladějov as was Svatopluk Šlechta at Tanečník. Zoran Veresic has provided much of the information about his native Serbia and Dževad Hodžić, the transport manager at Banovići, deserves the thanks of many enthusiasts for keeping steam alive there. Keith Chester is an acknowledged expert on the little railways of eastern Europe and Sergei Dorozhkov is immensely knowledgeable about the narrow gauge in the old Soviet Union. Both have always responded enthusiastically and unstintingly to my requests for help. My visits to the Greek narrow gauge would not have been possible without the kindness and help of Nikos Kantiris and his friends at the Athens Railway Club.

Tedros Kebbede and the late Amanuel Ghebreselassie were overwhelmingly hospitable in Eritrea as were Julian Pereira at Ixopo, Hawkin Hansen, Henry Anderson, Les Reed and Anthony Stanton at the Sappi factory at Umkomaas and Maurice Barasa, John Ashworth, Kevin Patience and Geoff Warren in Nairobi. There would probably have been no recent steam trains in Kenya were it not for the untiring efforts of the late Francis Waweru at the Mawenzi Gardens Hotel in Nairobi, who underwrote the financial risk, carried out much behind-the-scenes work – and provided great catering!

Ashok Sharma from Real India Journeys has been a superb guide and friend during both my visits to his ever-fascinating country and Peter Jordan of Darjeeling Tours and Marie Cook of Ffestiniog Travel have also been very helpful. Manfred and Kyi-Kyi Schoeler were of great assistance in Burma and Michael Whitehouse has assisted with information about the Burma Mines Railway. Ray Schofield and the late Chris Yapp were welcoming hosts in Cambodia and Paul Molyneux-Berry has shared his extensive knowledge of the C2s in China. Nothing was too much trouble for the gentleman I know only as Director Chang at the Alishan Forest Railway. Takahide Yamamoto provided an invaluable introduction to the railways of Japan as well as giving me much detailed information and has been a congenial travelling companion in many countries. Toki Sasaki runs a valuable English-language Japanese steam website and has given me much follow-up information. In Australia, Jeremy Browne was most hospitable at the Pichi Richi as were Jean Clowes at the Puffing Billy and Nigel Day and Tristan McMahon in Tasmania.

I've also drawn on many online and written sources for information. With a wide-ranging subject like this, a bibliography would take up far too much room and look little different from the catalogue of any well-stocked railway bookshop! I hope their authors will forgive me for not mentioning their books individually.

I offer my heartfelt thanks to everyone who has offered such generous help and friendship over many years.

Windsor, UK
August 2020

British builders supplied many early locos for service overseas, but mostly failed to embrace later developments in technology and production methods, and lost market share as their designs became overpriced and outmoded. By about 1910 most of their sales were to British-owned railways. One such was the Manila Railway in the Philippines, whose line between Manila and Dagupan City was completed in 1892. 0-6-0T CABANATUAN (KS 777/1905) was one of two similar locos and is now preserved outside Tutuban station in downtown Manila, proudly carrying the old railway's elaborate monogram. Three MR locos have survived, all built by KS. 3 February 2007.

LOCOMOTIVE BUILDERS

Addington	NZR, Addington Works, Christchurch, New Zealand	BR	Ateliers T Robatel, J Buffaud et Cie, Lyon, France
AEG	Allgemeine Elektrizitäts-Gesellschaft, Friedensbrücke, Frankfurt am Main, Germany (previously Hennigsdorf, Germany)	Budapest	Magyar Királyi Államvasutak Gépgyára (later MÁVAG), Budapest, Hungary
		Cail	SA des Anciens Établissements Cail, Paris, France
AK	Alan Keef Ltd, Lea, Ross-on-Wye, Hereford & Worcester, England	ČKD	Českomoravská Kolben-Daněk, Prague, Czech Republic
Alco	American Locomotive Company, Schenectady, New York, USA	Couillet	SA Marcinelle et Couillet, Hainaut, Belgium
		Chrzanów	Pierwsza Fabryka Lokomotyw w Polsce Sp. Akc., Chrzanów, Poland
AFB	Société Anglo-Franco-Belge, La Croyère, Hainaut, Belgium		
Ansaldo	Ansaldo SA, Sampierdarena, Genoa, Italy	CL	Corpet, Louvet et Cie, La Corneuve, France
Ashbury	Ashbury Carriage & Iron Co, Manchester, England	Davenport	Davenport Locomotive Works, Davenport, Iowa, USA
Atlas	AB Atlas, Stockholm, Sweden	ĐĐ	Đuro Đaković Đuro Industrija, Slavonski Brod, Croatia
Avonside	Avonside Engine Co Ltd, Bristol, England	Davidson	G&D Davidson, Hokitika, South Island, New Zealand
Bagnall	WG Bagnall Ltd, Stafford, England	Decauville	La Société Nouvelle des Établissements Decauville Aine, Corbeil, France
Baldwin	The Baldwin Locomotive Company, Philadelphia, Pennsylvania, USA		
		Dickson	Dickson Manufacturing Company, Scranton, Pennsylvania, USA
BL	Ffestiniog Railway, Boston Lodge Works, Porthmadog, Wales		
		Dübs	Dübs & Co Ltd, Glasgow, Scotland
BM	SA Ateliers de Construction du Nord de la France, Blanc-Misseron, France	DW	De Winton & Co, Caernarfon, Wales
		DY	David Young, Beamish, Northumbria, England
Borsig	Borsig AG, Tegel, Berlin, Germany (later Hennigsdorf, Germany)	Esslingen	Maschinenfabrik Esslingen, Esslingen am Neckar, Baden-Württemberg, Germany
BP	Beyer Peacock & Co Ltd, Gorton, Manchester, England		

FJ	Fletcher, Jennings & Co (later Lowca Engineering Co), Lowca, Cumberland, England	KM	Locomotivfabrik Krauss & Co (later Krauss-Maffei), Munich, Germany
FL	Compagnie de Fives-Lille pour Constructions Mécaniques et Entreprises, Lille, France	KS	Kerr, Stuart & Co Ltd, Stoke-on-Trent, Staffordshire, England
Floridsdorf	Wiener Lokomotivfabrik AG, Floridsdorf, Vienna, Austria	LEW	Lokomotivbau-Elektrotechnische Werke, Hennigsdorf, Germany (the old Borsig and AEG factory)
GE	George England & Co, New Cross, Surrey (now London), England		
Hanomag	Hannoversche Maschinenbau AG, Hannover, Germany	LHW	Linke-Hofmann-Werke, Breslau, Germany (now Wrocław, Poland)
Hartmann	Richard Hartmann, later Sächsische Maschinenfabrik, Chemnitz, Germany	Lima	Lima Locomotive Works Inc, Lima, Ohio, USA
HC	Hudswell, Clarke & Co Ltd, Leeds, England	LKM	Lokomotivbau Karl Marx, Babelsberg, Potsdam, Germany (the old OK factory)
Heilbronn	Maschinenbau-Gesselschaft Heilbronn, Heilbronn, Germany	Lundvik	Wallberg & Lundvik Mekaniska Verkstad, Vänersborg, Sweden
Heisler	Heisler Locomotive Works, Erie, Ohio, USA	Manchester	Manchester Locomotive Works, Manchester, New Hampshire, USA
Henschel	Henschel & Sohn, Kassel, Germany	Metropolitan	Metropolitan Carriage & Wagon Co., Birmingham, England
Hitachi	Hitachi Ltd, Chiyoda, Tokyo, Japan		
Horwich	British Railways, Horwich Works, Lancashire, England	Milner	Milner Engineering Chester Ltd, Higher Kinnerton, Chester, England
HSP	SA Forges Usines et Fonderies Haine-Saint-Pierre, Haine-Saint-Pierre, Belgium	Mitsubishi	Mitsubishi Heavy Industries Ltd, Hiroshima, Japan
Humboldt	Maschinenbau-AG Humboldt, Kalk bei Deutz am Rhein, Cologne, Germany	Motala	Motala Verkstad, Motala, Sweden
		MR	The Motor Rail & Tramcar Co Ltd., Bedford, England
Hunslet	Hunslet Engine Co Ltd, Leeds, England	NB	North British Locomotive Co Ltd, Glasgow, Scotland (a 1903 merger of Dübs, SS and NR)
Jung	Arnold Jung Lokomotivfabrik GmbH, Jungenthal, Germany		
Kawasaki	Kawasaki Heavy Industries, Kobe, Japan	NR	Neilson Reid & Co, Glasgow, Scotland
Kisha	Kisha Seizo Co Ltd, Osaka, Japan	Newport	Victorian Railways, Newport Works, Victoria, Australia
KL	Locomotivfabrik Krauss & Co, Linz, Austria	Nippon	Nippon Sharyo Ltd, Nagoya, Japan

Nohab	Nydqvist & Holm AB, Trollhättan, Sweden	Shijiazhuang	Shijiazhuang Motive Power Machinery Works, Shijiazhuang, Hebei, China
NW	Nasmyth, Wilson & Co Ltd, Patricroft, Manchester, England	SLM	Schweizerische Lokomotiv und Maschinenfabrik, Winterthur, Switzerland
OK	Orenstein & Koppel AG, Drewitz, Berlin, (previously Markische Locomotivfabrik, Berlin-Schlachtensee), later at Babelsberg, Potsdam, Germany	Škoda	Škodovy Závody, Plzeň, Czech Republic
		SL	Stephen Lewin, Poole, Dorset, England
Porter	HK Porter Inc, Pittsburgh, Pennsylvania, USA	SS	Sharp Stewart & Co Ltd, Manchester, England (later Glasgow, Scotland)
Portland	The Portland Co, Portland, Maine, USA	Swindon	Great Western Railway, Swindon Works, Wiltshire, England
Precirail	Precirail Sprl, Morlanwelz, Belgium		
Reghin	Atelier Caile Ferate Forestiere, Reghin, Romania	Takatori	Imperial Government Railway, Takatori factory, Takatori, Japan
Reșița	Uzinele de Fier și Domeniile Reșița SA, Reșița, Romania	Telco	Tata Engineering and Locomotive Co, Jamshedpur, Bihar (now Jharkhand), India
RS	Robert Stephenson and Co, Newcastle-upon-Tyne, England	Thompson	Thompson & Co (Castlemaine) Pty Ltd, Castlemaine, Victoria, Australia
SACM	Société Alsacienne de Constructions Mécaniques, Graffenstaden (Elsässische Maschinenbau-Gesellschaft Grafenstaden between 1871 and 1918) and Mulhouse, France	TS	Thomas Smith & Sons (Rodley) Ltd, Rodley, Leeds, England
		Tubize	SA La Métallurgique, Nivelles, Tubize & Le Sambre, Belgium
		VF	The Vulcan Foundry Ltd, Newton-le-Willows, Lancashire, England
Schwartzkopff	L Schwartzkopff, later Berliner Maschinenbau AG, Wildau, Berlin, Germany	Weidknecht	Weidknecht Frères et Cie, Paris, France
Schmoschewer	Schmoschewer & Co, Breslau-Schmiedefeld, Germany (now Wrocław, Poland)	Winson	Winson Engineering Ltd, Daventry, Northamptonshire, England

CANADA AND THE USA

The 3ft gauge Tanana Valley Railway was an impoverished concern which operated out of Fairbanks, in central Alaska. It was probably on the verge of closure when the US government bought it in 1917, as they wanted part of its route for the standard gauge Alaska RR. They continued to run narrow gauge trains until 1930. The old railway only ever owned a few locos. The government added two more, a second-hand 2-8-0 and this smart 4-6-0 no 152 (Baldwin 53296/1920) which was built new for the line. After the closure, she went into store until serving the US army during the Second World War on the White Pass & Yukon Railway, when they were setting up defences against a feared Japanese invasion. After peace returned, she was sent for scrap at Seattle, but was rescued and eventually found a home at the Huckleberry RR in Michigan. Here she leaves its loco yard on the very cold morning of 15 January 2019, carrying an approximation of her original green colour scheme.

The Huckleberry line was built by the local authority at Flint to provide a recreational facility for its citizens. It runs along the formation of an old standard gauge line and opened in 1976. Flint was enjoying a period of considerable prosperity as one of the centres of Michigan's automotive industry, but the good times were coming to an end. Now the car factories have closed and it has become an extreme example of a rustbelt town, and the railway and its associated open-air museum are, if anything, even more appreciated. Here no 152 crosses over a creek off the frozen CS Mott Lake, a reservoir serving the town, on the very cold morning of 15 January 2019. Michigan is far enough north for silhouette views to be feasible even at midday in winter. The leading coach, no 40 of the Ferrocarriles Unidos de Yucatán in south eastern México, was probably built in the 1880s. It is one of many historic vehicles in the Huckleberry's collection.

Above: The 3ft gauge White Pass & Yukon's 2-8-2 no 73 (Baldwin 73352/1947) has completed the twenty-mile climb from the coast at Skagway and has crossed into British Columbia at an altitude of 874m. She is dwarfed by the mountains at the White Pass on 13 June 2011 as she runs beside the frozen Summit Lake, a part of the headwaters of the Yukon River.

Opposite above: No 73 has left her train at Fraser loop and takes water at the station on 13 June 2011. The first train on a short section of the line out of Skagway, Alaska, ran in 1898 and the railway was completed through to Whitehorse, now the capital of the Yukon, in 1900. Four of these 2-8-2s were supplied between 1938 and 1947; they were the railway's last steam locos, not counting the many brought in by the army during the Second World War. No 73 had become the last one in service by the time she was withdrawn in 1964 and was restored for heritage train operation in 1982.

Opposite below: 2-8-0 no 69 (Baldwin 32962/1908), the other working steam loco on the WP&YR in recent years, runs through the Skagway River gorge on 11 June 2011 near the end of her journey from Fraser. Until the 2-8-2s arrived, she was the railway's youngest steam loco. The WP&YR was promoted to tap into the goldmining boom around a tributary of the Klondike River. Production there reached a peak in 1903, but by then the vast numbers of people in search of instant wealth had moved on to pastures new in central and western Alaska. Traffic on the line fell away and it was left with surplus locos. No 69 was withdrawn in 1954 and sold two years later to a tourist railway in the Lower 48, as Alaskans like to call the continental US. She was bought back in 2001 and re-entered service in 2008, but hasn't worked since 2013. Like many of the railway's coaches these four predate the railway and were built for lines in the Lower 48 between 1883 and 1887.

16 • NARROW GAUGE PANORAMA

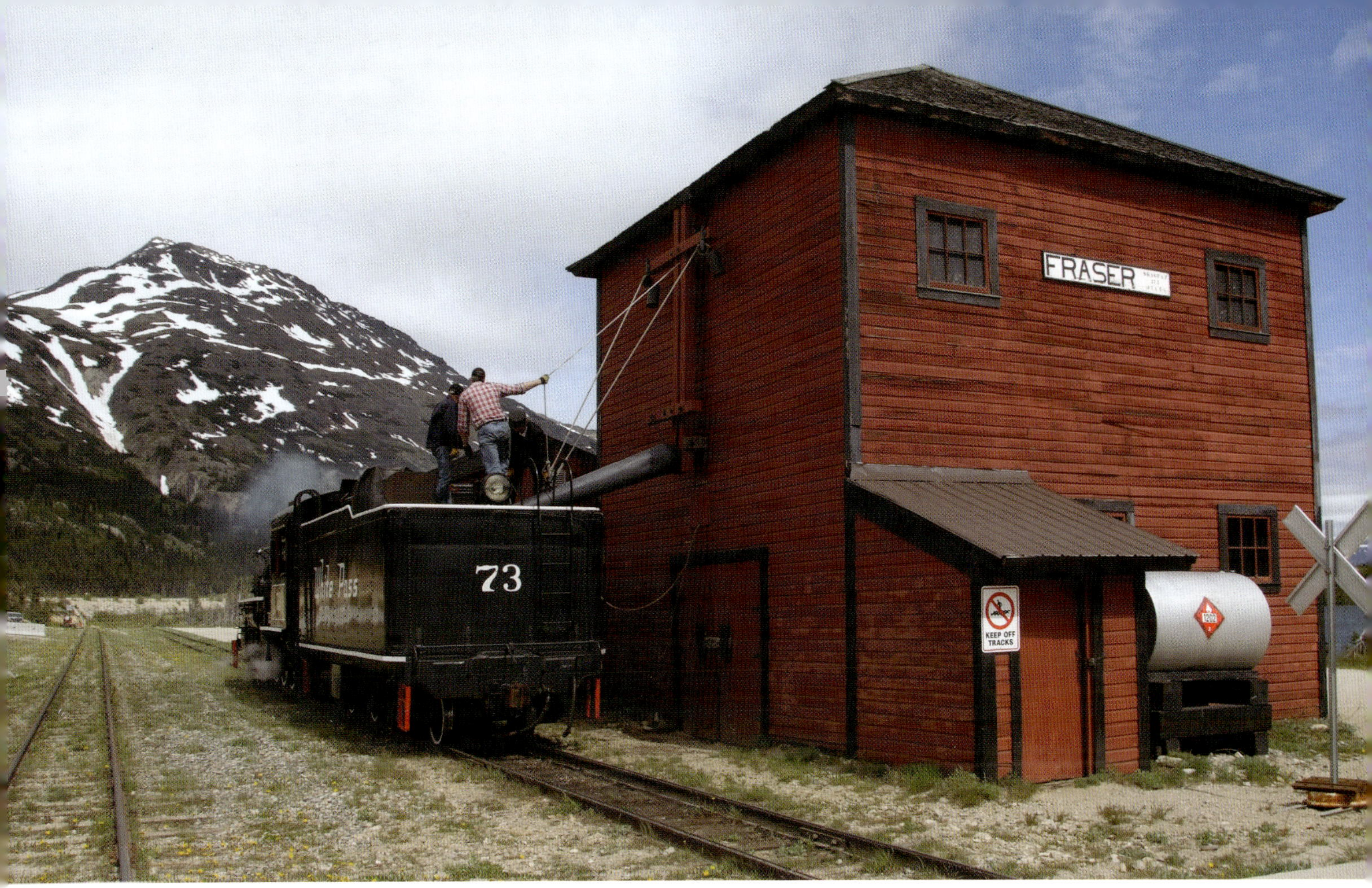
FRASER
KEEP OFF TRACKS
1202
73
White Pass

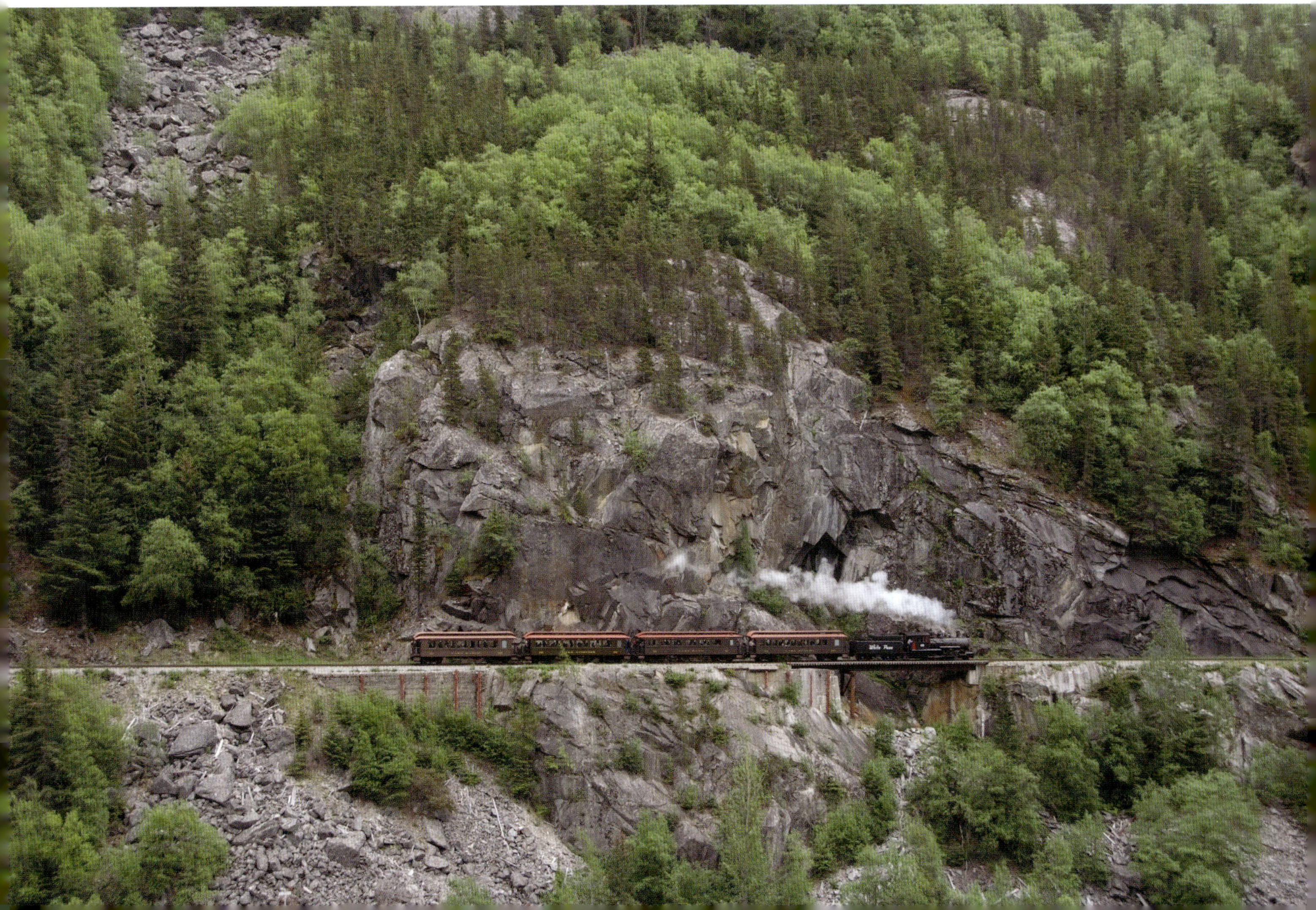

Above: No 69 crosses the Thompson's or Tutshi River bridge with a short freight train on 12 June 2011. The boxcar was one of five built for the Colorado & Southern Railway in 1910 which were sold to the US Army in 1943 for use on the White Pass, and the caboose was immediately converted from another of them. After the opening of a road through from Canada to Skagway in 1982, the railway closed to regular traffic. Its southern section reopened six years later as a tourist line, mainly to serve the burgeoning cruise ship traffic along Alaska's Pacific coast for which Skagway had become a major port of call.

Opposite: Midway between White Pass and Skagway, the railway enters the Laughton glacier gorge, though the glacier now finishes at a much higher altitude. Here no 69 leaves a tunnel on 12 June 2011 and passes over a wooden trestle bridge, one of the most spectacular spots on the entire line.

CANADA AND THE USA • 19

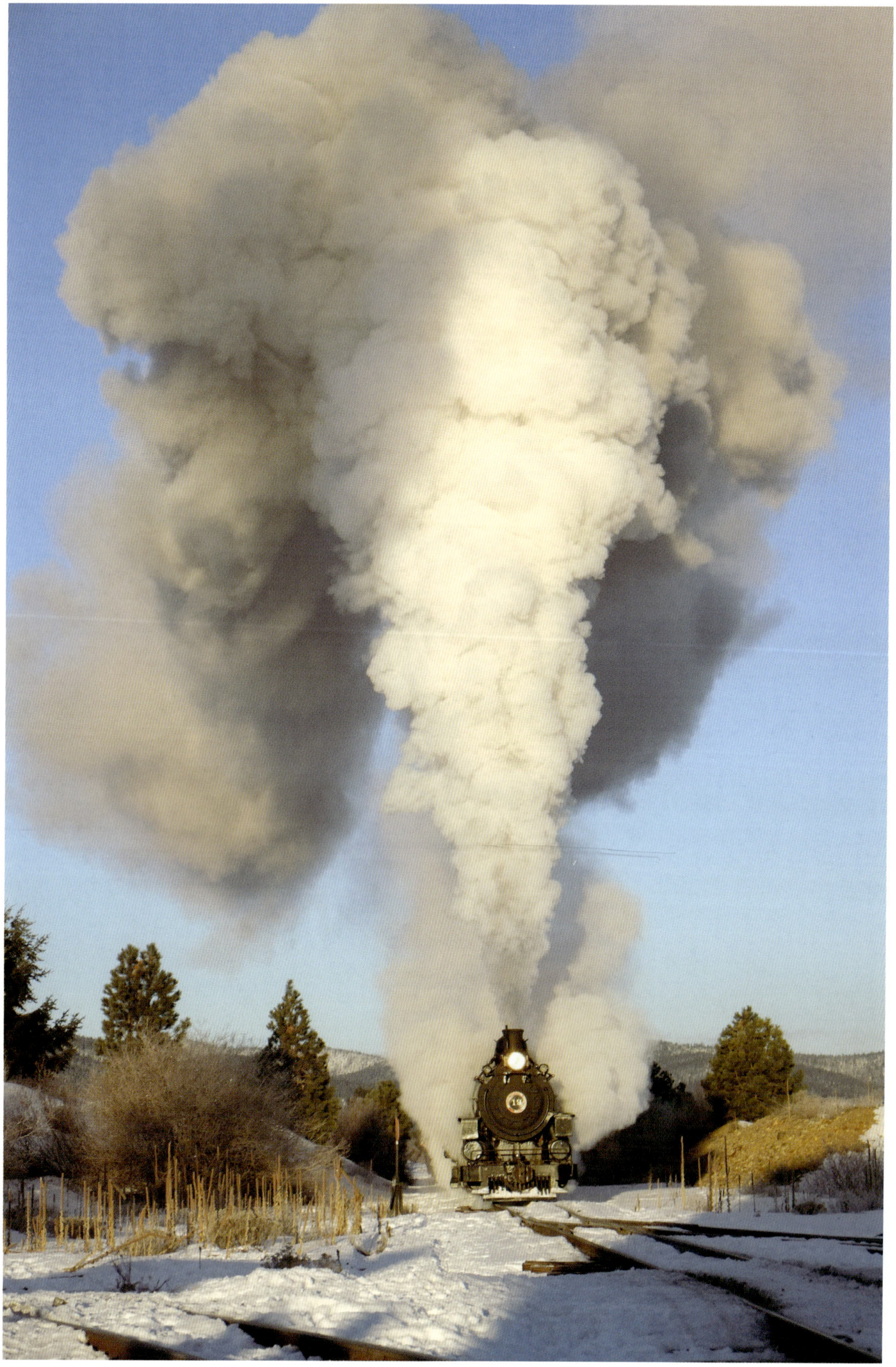

Above: The 3ft gauge Sumpter Valley Railway was built to serve the logging industry in north eastern Oregon, though it enjoyed a brief period of exceptional prosperity at the start of the twentieth century when gold was discovered in the Powder River valley. It was comprehensively dredged and has been almost barren ever since. On 2 February 2014, no 19 heads towards McEwen past one of the many troughs left over from the dredging, with the Elkhorn Mountains as a backdrop.

Opposite: The preserved section of the 3ft gauge Sumpter Valley Railway runs for about five miles through the broad Powder River valley between Sumpter and McEwen in eastern Oregon. No 19 (Alco 61980/1920) makes an all-out effort as she heads towards McEwen at sunrise on 2 February 2014. She is one of two similar locos on the railway. In 1940 they were replaced by two second-hand Mallet tank locos which were stripped of their tanks and ran with the tenders of the 2-8-2s, while the locos themselves were sold to the White Pass line. After the Sumpter Valley closed the Mallets and the tenders went to work in Guatemala. The Mallets were eventually scrapped but the tenders survived. The preservation society bought the 2-8-2s and the tenders and reunited them.

WH Eccles no 3 (Heisler 1306/1915) and SVR 2-8-2 no 19 stand at McEwen on the evening of 1 February 2014. The Eccles concern ran one of the many logging branches off the SVR's mainline, and their locos frequently operated over its metals. The SVR was built in stages westwards from its junction with the Union Pacific at Baker City. It opened to McEwen, twenty-two miles away, in 1891 and services were extended to Sumpter five years later.

The SVR was mostly owned by the Oregon Lumber Co, and the railway's primary purpose was always to haul logs to their lumberyard in South Baker City, home to their huge three-truck Shay no 7 (Lima 3349/1929). She was the very last narrow gauge version of these geared locos to be built. Nearly all the SVR mainline closed in 1947 and no 7 hauled most of the wrecking trains. All that remained was a very short section which continued to serve the lumberyard until it closed in 1961 and no 7 was out of a job. Later that year, she was sold to Elliott Donnelley, an enthusiast and a supporter of the Hesston Steam Museum, in northern Indiana, where she found a new home in 1970. I saw her there on 14 January 2019. She dwarfs the United Fruit Company's little 2-6-0 no 2 (Porter 4514/1909), one of at least fifteen similar locos which worked in its banana plantations in Guatemala. The gentleman working in her cab is Ted Rita, the museum's enthusiastic director, and he was putting the finishing touches to her restoration. Both locos are now in working order and run on the museum's short railway during the summer.

Above: Eastern California's Sierra Nevada mountains have already received a dusting of snow on 23 September 2017 as Southern Pacific 4-6-0 no 18 (Baldwin 37395/1918) stands near Laws station. For many years it was the northern terminus of the old 3ft gauge Owens Valley line, originally part of the Carson & Colorado Railway. Its first section south from Mound House, near Carson City, opened in 1880 and it reached Keeler, 300 miles away, three years later. It was taken over by SP in 1900, after which some parts were converted to standard gauge and others closed. Passenger traffic ended as long ago as 1938, and the last freight train ran between Laws and Keeler in 1960. Three of these locos were acquired by SP when it took over the Nevada-California-Oregon Railway in 1927. The distinctive round-topped tender shows that she's an oil-burner.

Opposite above: No 18 heads away from Laws with her short train on 22 September 2017. Alas, she doesn't have far to run as only 600 yards of track remain at what is now a museum devoted to the old line. To the right are water and fuel oil tanks and a turntable. The tall cream-coloured building is a water pumphouse. The nearest vehicle began life in 1882 as a clerestory-roofed coach. It was used as a caboose after 1938 and was subsequently downgraded, being fitted with a boxcar-shaped roof in the late 1940s and freight bogies in 1952.

Opposite below: The 3ft gauge Eureka & Palisade RR's no 4 *Eureka* (Baldwin 3763/1875) was supplied shortly before the opening of this 85-mile line in north eastern Nevada on 22 October 1875. In 1896 she moved to a logging railway at Hobart Mills in California, and stayed there until it closed in December 1937. She was sold for scrap, but was rescued by Warner Bros in 1939 and became a Hollywood star. Her last movie was *The Shootist* in 1976, co-starring John Wayne who was also making his farewell appearance. On 15 December 2018, she begins a short journey while visiting the Boulder City branch of the Nevada State Railroad Museum, not far from Las Vegas.

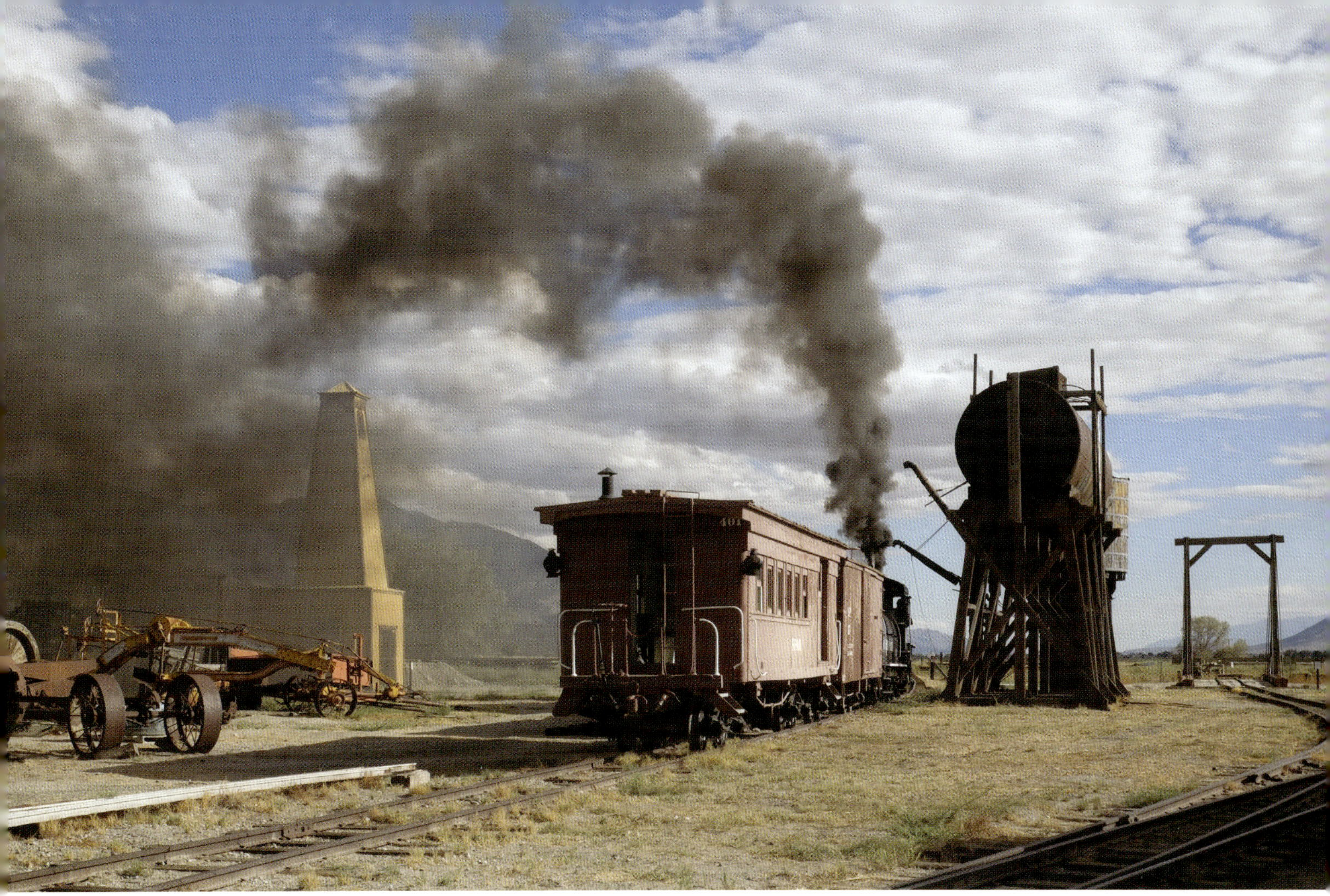
401

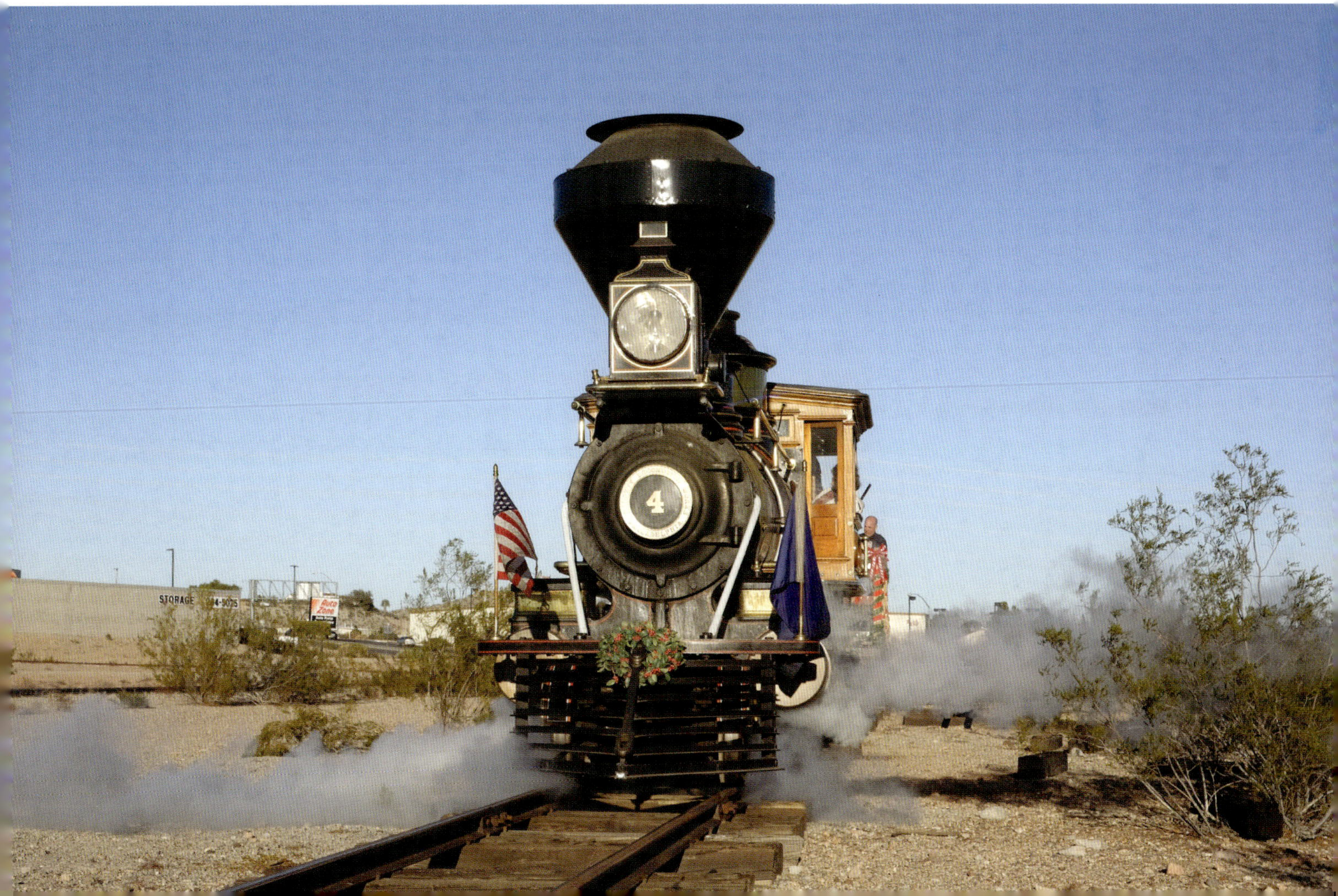
4
STORAGE

In the 1870s, many US locos were finished in highly elaborate paint schemes, and *Eureka* was no exception. Now restored to her original condition, she shows off her magnificent livery at Boulder City, just before sunset on 15 December 2018. Between 1976 and 1978, the California State Railroad Museum at Sacramento was in the process of restoring a similar loco, and obtained permission to strip off the newer paint from *Eureka* to record and copy the original. What was left was then sandblasted and the loco was repainted in plain black shortly before moving from Hollywood to an amusement park near Las Vegas. *Eureka* was badly damaged by fire in 1986 and might well have been scrapped were it not for Dan Markoff, a Las Vegas railfan. Well aware of her historical importance, he bought her, took her home and set about restoring her to working order. Thanks to the Californian museum's work he was able to recreate her original livery.

In the early 1870s, General William Jackson Palmer, the founder of the 3ft gauge Denver & Rio Grande RR, which later became the Denver & Rio Grande Western, was thwarted in his attempts to build south from Alamosa to the Rio Grande and onwards to México City. Instead, he set his sights on the mineral riches of the San Juan mountains, and the new railway swung abruptly to the west at Antonito. On 21 September 2011, Rio Grande K-36 class 2-8-2 no 489 (Baldwin 58590/1925), temporarily renumbered 485, climbs towards Cumbres summit on what is now the Cumbres & Toltec Scenic RR. Ten K-36s were built in 1925, and all have survived apart from no 485 which was scrapped after falling into a turntable pit in 1955. Five are on the C&TSRR and normally work all trains. The renumbering wasn't as fanciful as one might think, as many of no 485's parts were reused during an overhaul of no 489 at the Rio Grande's Salida shops. They were very much in situ when the C&TSRR first overhauled the loco and some are probably still there now.

Above: Heading east from Cumbres, the line drops sharply down towards Cumbres Creek, and on into the Los Pinos valley. Here K-36 no 487 (Baldwin 58588/1925) takes her train along the lower level of Tanglefoot Curve on 21 September 2011. The black wagons are stockcars in US parlance, or cattle wagons to us British enthusiasts. In 1939 the Rio Grande adopted the so-called flying herald, with its sloping letters, to replace the older lettering as seen on no 478 in the following photos. It was the winning entry submitted by a lady secretary in a staff competition. The original standards instruction from the Chief Mechanical Officer required that the letters should lean towards the back of the tenders on each side. However the draftsman who prepared the drawing to illustrate the new herald mistakenly showed the letters leaning forwards, and this is how they were usually applied.

Opposite above: No 487 crosses Cascade Trestle on the afternoon of 22 September 2011. The present bridge dates from 1889 and is one of two on the line built to a German design which avoided the need for cross-bracing between the piers.

Opposite below: C-18 class 2-8-0 no 315 (Baldwin 14352/1895) and K-27 class 2-8-2 no 463 (Baldwin 21788/1903) stand at Antonito engine shed on 23 May 2014. No 315, originally no 3 *Elkton* of the Florence & Cripple Creek RR, arrived on the Rio Grande in 1917 after its old line closed. She was restored by volunteers after many years on static display. The fifteen K-27s were the Rio Grande's first 2-8-2s and were originally Vauclain compounds. No 463 is one of two survivors.

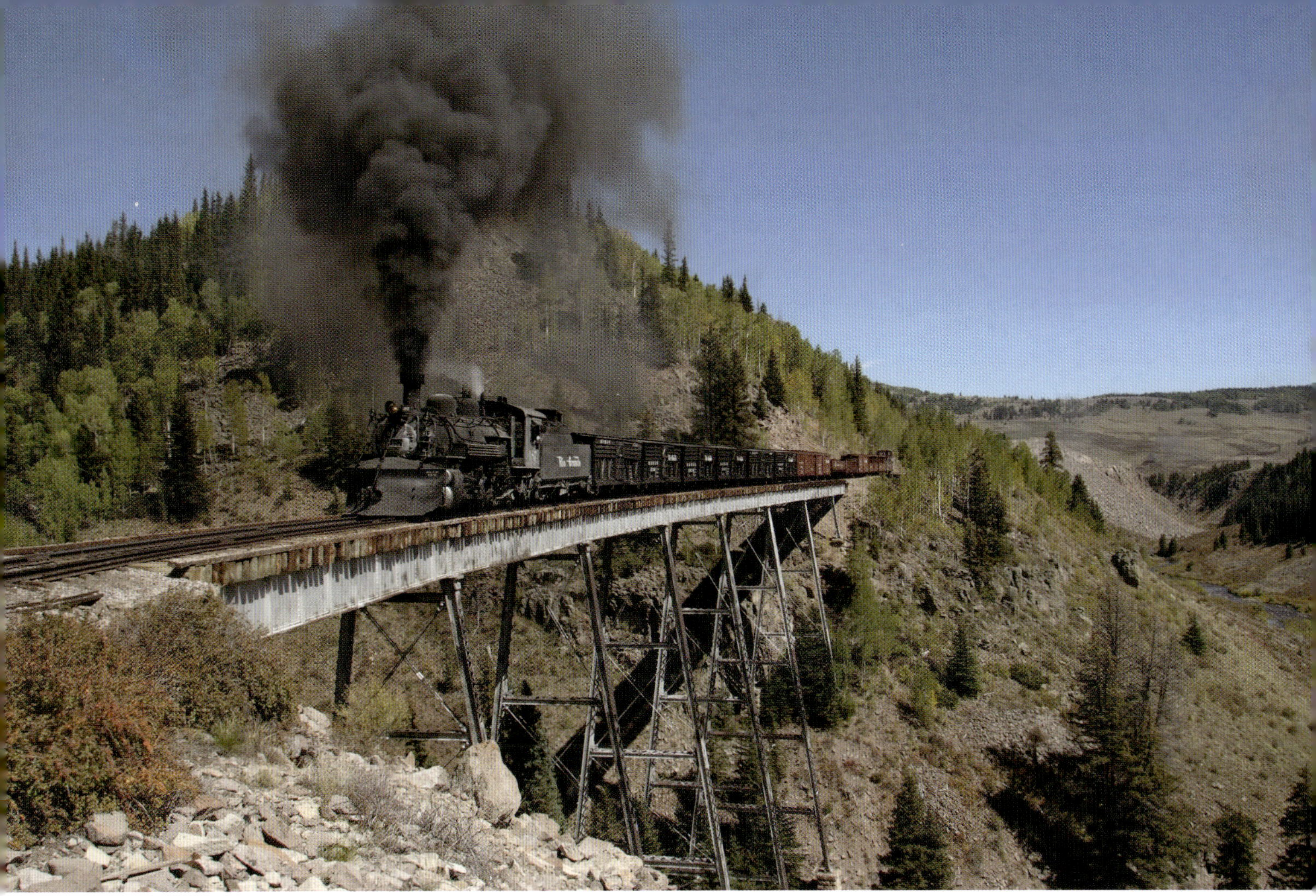

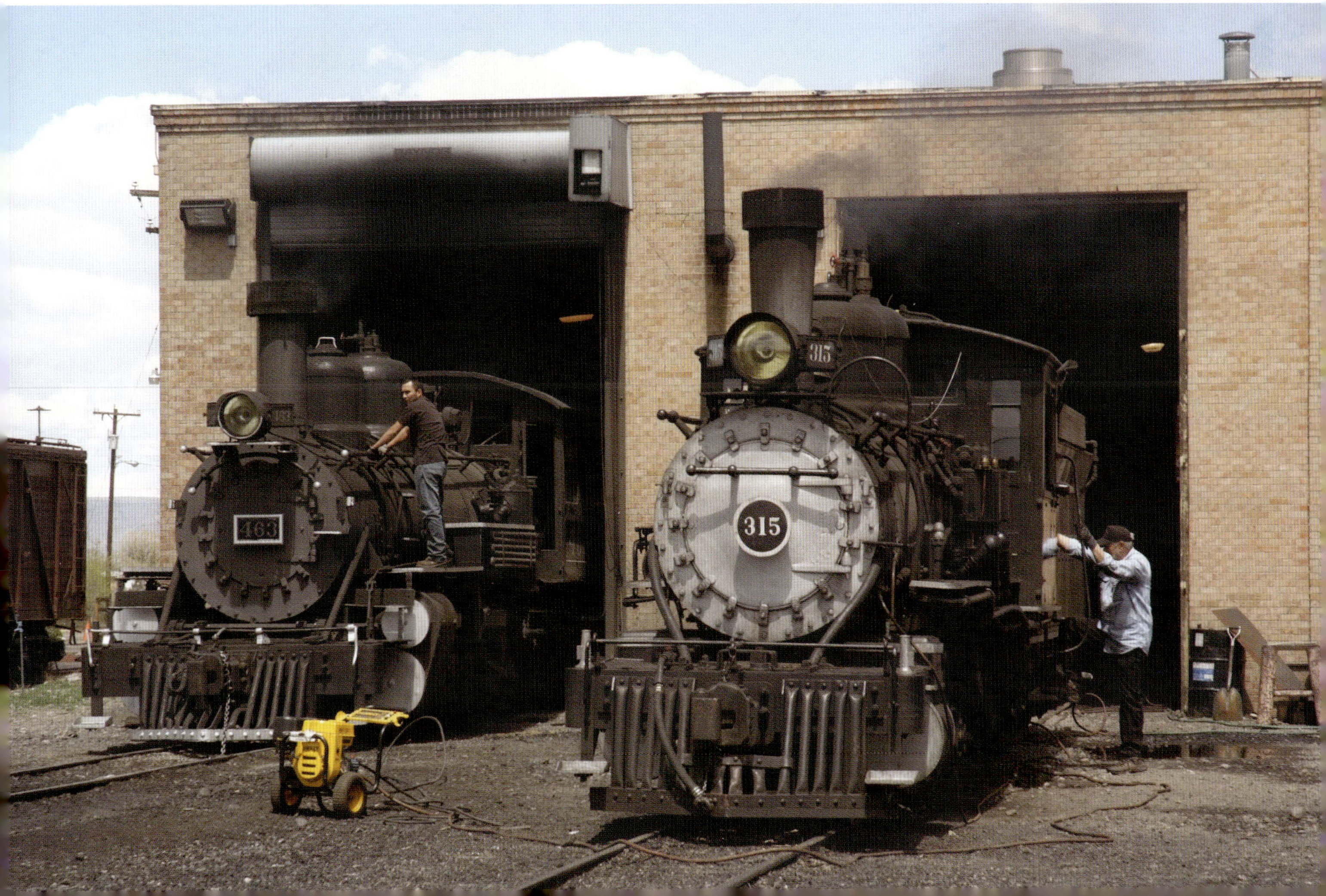
463
315

No 464 (Baldwin 21796/1903), the other surviving K-27, lives far away on the Huckleberry line. The icicles hanging from the watertank at Crossways station on the evening of 15 January 2019 tell their own tale!

The Durango & Silverton RR, which now operates the Rio Grande's old Silverton branch, is one of the world's great scenic railways and this spot, high above the Animas River near Rockwood station, is perhaps its most spectacular location. On the afternoon of 23 September 2011, a friend and I had it to ourselves, apart from a few feathered friends for occasional company, notably a bald eagle, one of the country's most emblematic birds. K-28 class 2-8-2 no 478 (Alco 64989/1923), which had piloted a train to Silverton, was running light back to Durango.

32 • NARROW GAUGE PANORAMA

Above: The same train a little further north. The last two coaches are luxurious ones, painted in the Rio Grande's pre-1917 red, and are very smart indeed.

Opposite: It is sunrise on 24 September 2011 at the High Bridge north of Rockwood. The first three coaches of no 478's train are painted in the dark green which the Rio Grande used between 1917 and the early 1950s. Ten K-28s were built in 1923. They were regarded as fine, fast locos and were entrusted with the Rio Grande's principal narrow gauge passenger trains. Seven were requisitioned by the US army during the Second World War for the White Pass line and were scrapped in 1945. The army wanted all ten but fortunately the Rio Grande managed to hold onto the three which are now at the D&S.

Above: No 478 stands on the turntable at Durango on 23 September 2011. Four oil-fired locos similar to the K-28s were built for the Oahu Railway in Hawaii in 1925 and 1926. Locos on the D&S have always burned coal, but the line has obtained drawings for the Hawaiian oil-firing equipment and intends to convert at least one K-28 after a recent devastating bushfire was blamed on cinders from a loco.

Opposite above: No 15 (Baldwin 41196/1914) is one of six 2-8-2s which served the 3ft gauge East Broad Top RR in Pennsylvania for about forty years until it closed in 1956. The company which built the line was chartered in 1856, but construction was delayed by the US Civil War and it didn't open until 1871. Its raison d'être was to carry coal from mines on the eastern side of Broad Top Mountain and it kept a large fleet of steel hopper wagons, mostly built in its own workshops. Some have moved to other heritage railways where they are useful for transporting ballast and other permanent way materials, but more than 150 are still at the EBT. Sadly, most are derelict and stripped of fittings, but a few are in running order. Here no 15 hauls some of them across Aughwick Creek Road on 7 October 2011.

Opposite below: No 15 pauses with her coal train north of Orbisonia in the evening of 7 October 2011. In 1960, five miles of the line reopened as a heritage railway and operated until 2011 when services were suspended. In February 2020, the excellent news arrived that almost the whole of the old railway and its locos and rolling stock have been bought by a charitable company. It plans to rebuild and reopen first the five miles and eventually much more.

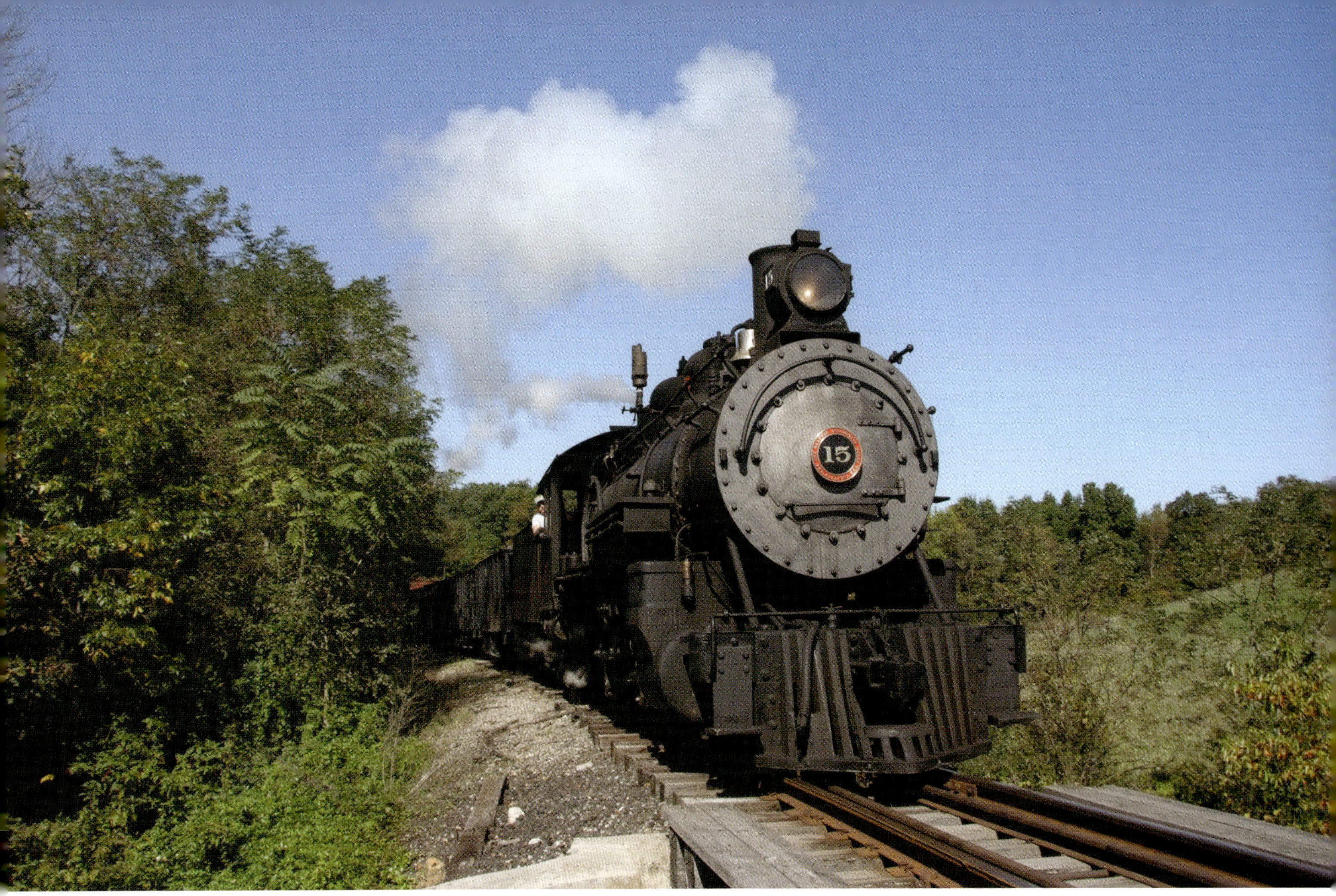
15

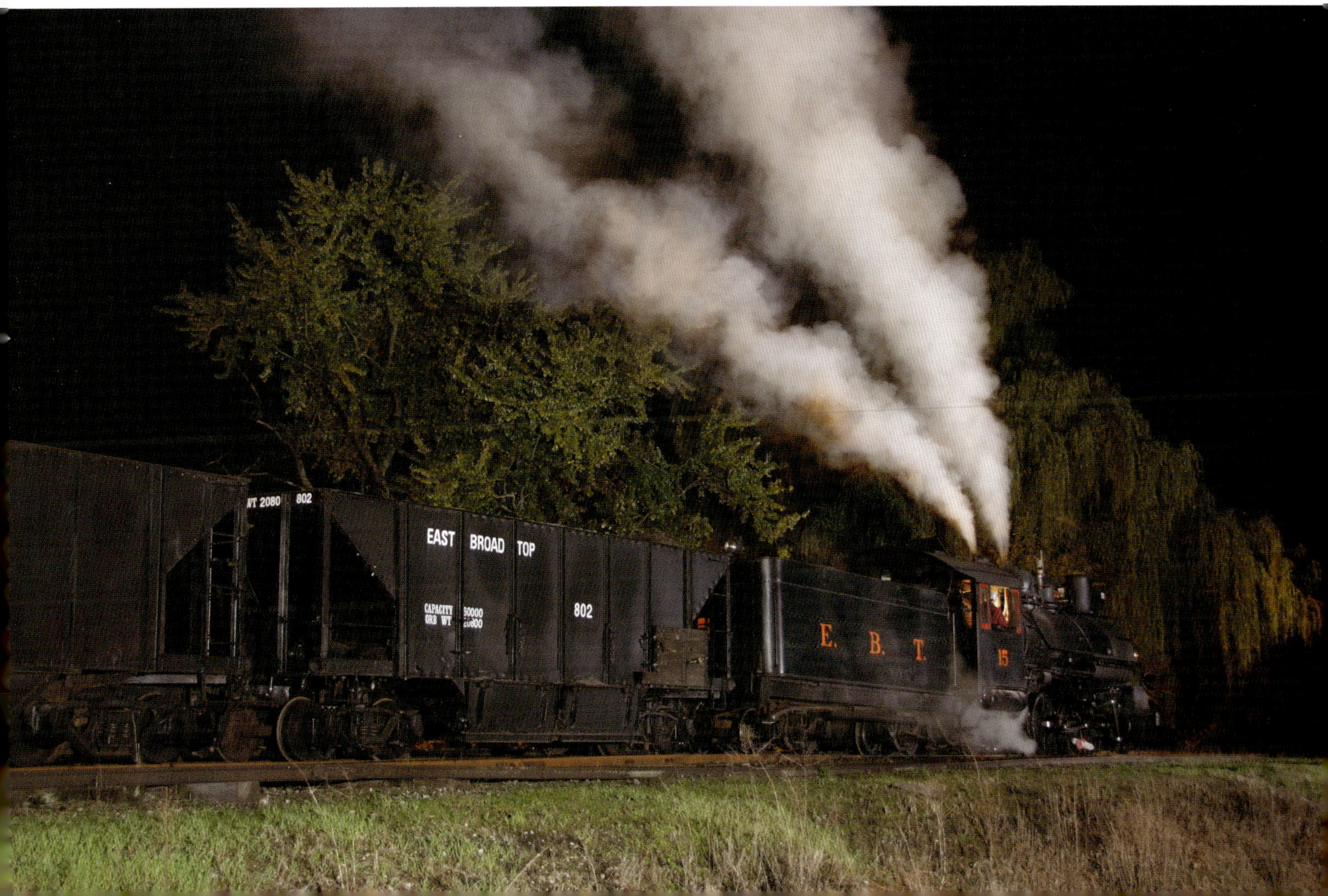
EAST BROAD TOP
802
E. B. T.
15

Christmas train! The East Tennessee and Western North Carolina RR was a very long name for a railway, especially a little 3ft gauge one! People began to call it Tweetsie after the sound of its locos' whistles, and the name stuck. Its first section, from a junction with the Southern Railway at Johnson City, opened in 1881 and eventually it reached Boone, high in the Blue Ridge Mountains. The district suffered badly during the 1930s depression. To cheer things up, Tweetsie repainted its locos green with gold lining, copied from the Southern which in turn had reportedly copied the colour from the UK's Southern Railway, and added embellishments including red chimney caps and numberplates. Here 4-6-0 no 12 (Baldwin 45069/1917) stands at the Tweetsie theme park's station near Boone at dusk on 14 December 2018.

Two of Tweetsie's 4-6-0s served the US army on the White Pass line during the Second World War, and only three remained to see out its final years. This was a friendly railway and there was much genuine sadness when the last train ran in 1950. Enthusiasts from Virginia saved no 12, helped by Tweetsie's management who sold her for much less than her scrap value. Their venture wasn't successful and in 1957 local businessman Grover Robbins stepped in. He bought the loco and amid much local rejoicing set up the present theme park in the outskirts of Blowing Rock, a town which straddles the Eastern Continental Divide a few miles south of Boone. Its railway is nearly three miles long, and no 12 has to work hard on its steep gradients. The coaches are copied from one which ran on the old Tweetsie and which was probably converted from a freight car. The loco is still green; she carries non-authentic lettering, but in the dark this wasn't prominent as she crossed a road at the entrance to the station on 14 December 2018.

Above: I visited a few days after blizzards had swept through the Blue Ridge Mountains. These had turned to heavy rain, but this didn't deter the large numbers of people who turned up for a ride on Tweetsie that evening. The entire route was lit up. The good people of North Carolina certainly know how to celebrate Christmas in style! Here the event is over, and only no 12's headlight is still turned on as she backs towards her shed. It was the last act in an unusually enjoyable evening.

Opposite above: About a dozen of us gathered at the 4ft 8ins gauge Mount Washington Cog Railway's base station on the damp morning of 23 October 2011. As we bought our tickets, the cheerful booking office lady assured us that it was sunny at the summit – though she didn't mention that snow had fallen overnight, and that the scene there was truly magical! 0-2-2-0 no 9 *Waumbek* (Manchester, 1908) has stopped outside the summit station while the staff hack ice out of the points. She is the younger of two locos still in service. The line was the world's first cog railway when a part opened to passengers in August 1868, and it reached the summit in July 1869; it has a maximum gradient of 37.41 per cent, exceeded only by the 48 per cent on the Pilatusbahn in Switzerland.

Opposite below: Conditions at the summit are not always so delightful. On 31 August 2014, 0-2-2-0 no 2 *Ammonoosuc* (Manchester, 1875) was almost invisible in the thick fog! This was an all-steam railway until 2008, but it now has seven diesels which are in charge of almost all services, and steam is generally only used on the first round-trip of the day.

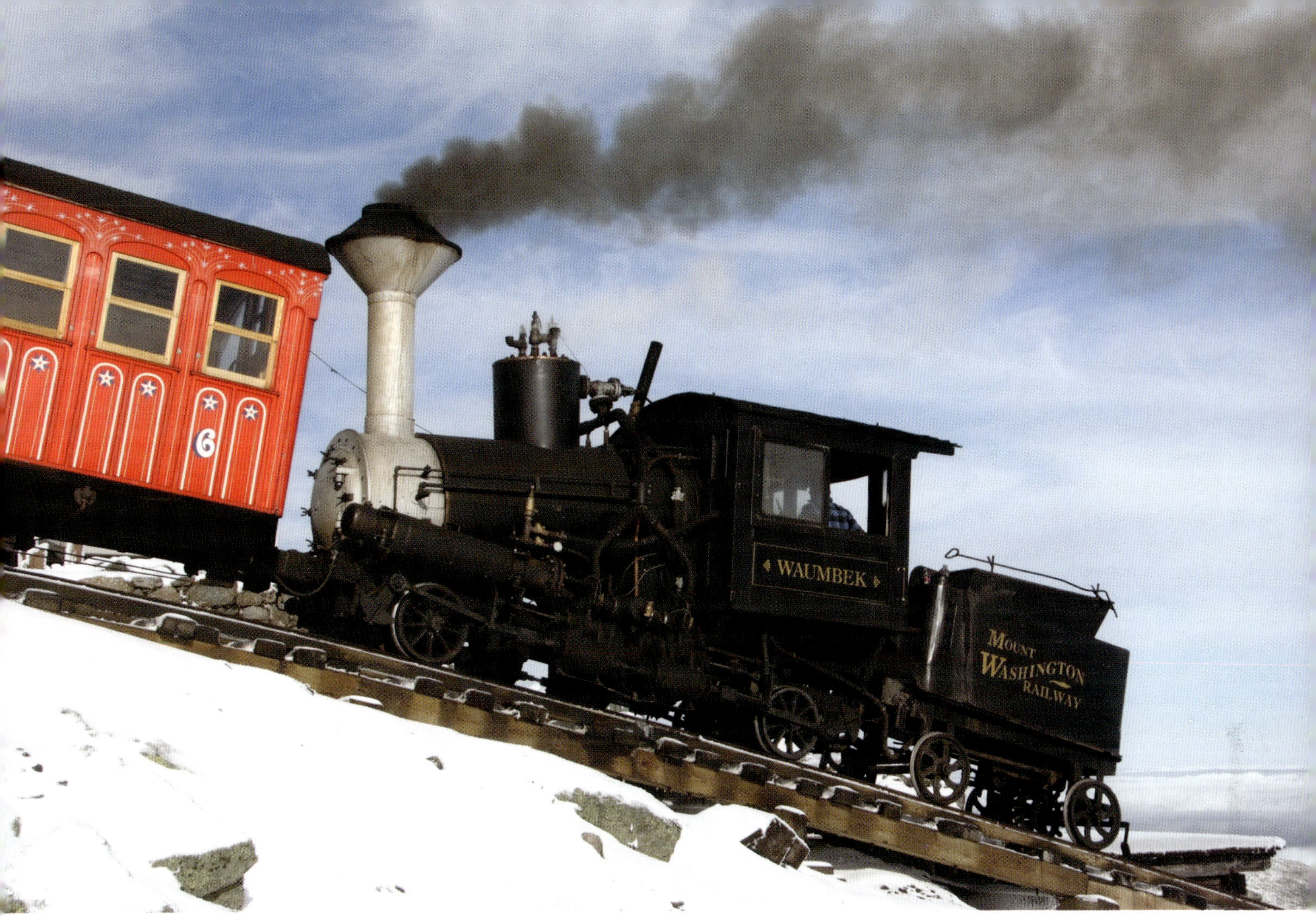
6
WAUMBEK
MOUNT WASHINGTON RAILWAY

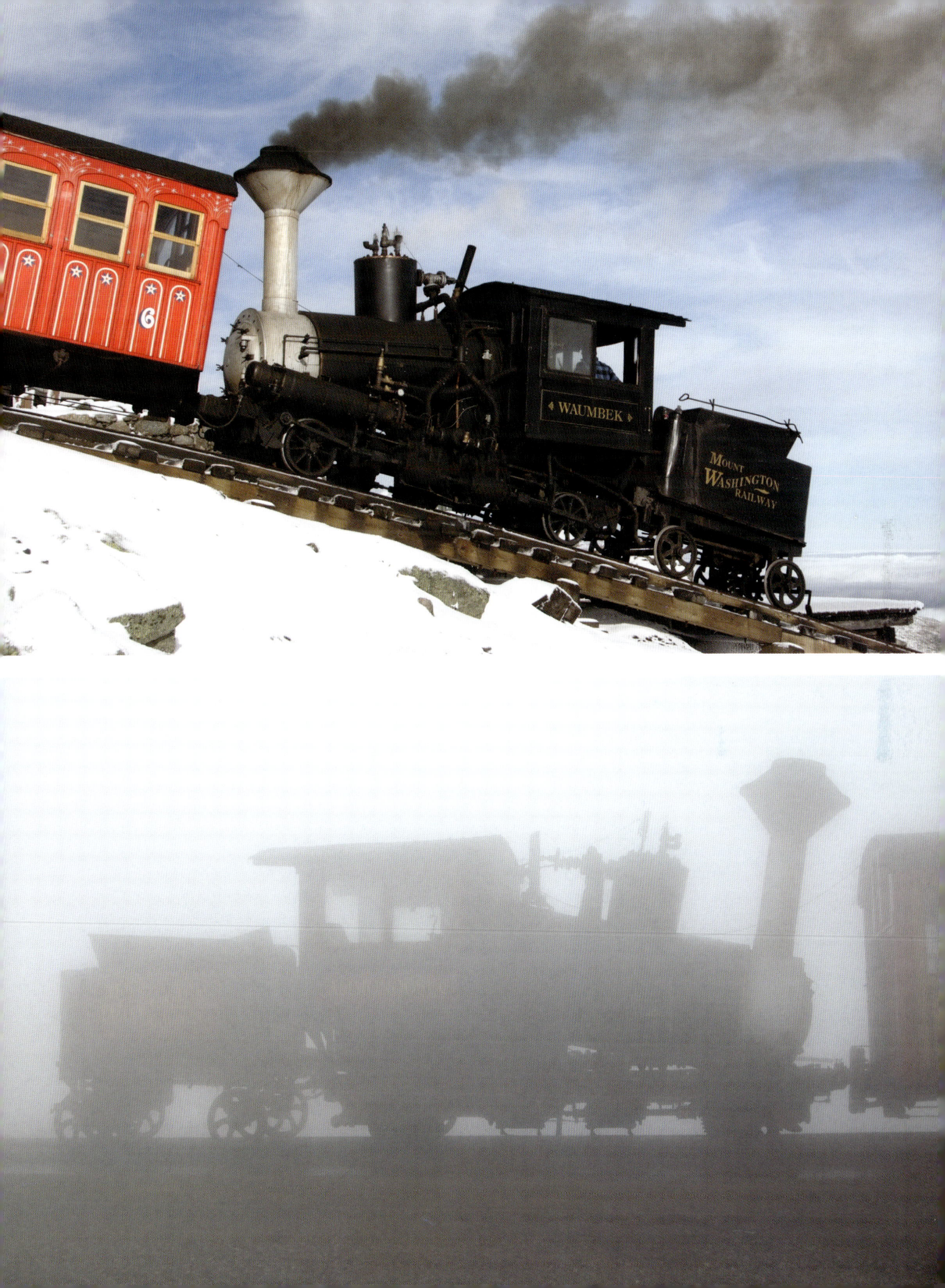

0-4-4 Forney tank no 9 (Portland 624/1891) sets off from Top of the Mountain on the 2ft gauge Wiscasset, Waterville & Farmington Railway on 14 January 2017. The railway opened in 1895 as the grandly-named Wiscasset & Quebec, but its mainline never reached further than twenty eight miles beyond Wiscasset, a small port on the estuary of the Sheepscot River in Maine. Financial reconstructions brought the less ambitious name by which it has been known ever since; one of them involved a takeover by no less a person than the vice-president of the FW Woolworth company. The railway closed in 1933, and preservationists began to reconstruct a short section in 1989. No 9 was built for the Sandy River RR in northern Maine, moved to the Kennebec Central RR in 1924 and then to Wiscasset in 1933 just a few months before the closure. In 1937, she was rescued by enthusiasts led by one Frank Ramsdell and moved to his farm in Connecticut. She was later looked after by his daughter Alice, and on her death in 1994 passed to her nephew Dale King, who generously allowed her to return to the railway the following year.

MÉXICO

Cuautla, on the Ferrocarriles Nacionales de México's 3ft gauge line south of México City, was a major division point where locos were usually changed. With this machinery, its engine shed was fully equipped to keep its occupants in good shape. Many Mexican locos were destroyed during a devastating civil war between 1910 and 1920. To make good the losses on the narrow gauge, twenty of these G-030 class 2-8-0s were built in 1921, and a further eight in 1924. A section of the railway north from Cuautla was kept on as a heritage line after it closed to regular traffic, but by the time I visited on 18 November 2012 it had been cut back to just a few hundred metres at the station. No 279 (Baldwin 55110/1921) was still serviceable, but sadly parts were stolen after her boiler certificate expired in 2013 and there are currently no plans to restore her.

GUATEMALA

Guatemala's first railway opened in 1880 and reached Guatemala City in 1884. The fine central station there became the hub of the 3ft gauge International Railways of Central America, formed by the merger of several local lines in 1912. Trains left for Guatemala's Atlantic and Pacific coasts and for its Mexican border where they connected with a NdeM standard gauge branch, as well as for El Salvador which was also served by IRCA. All this has gone, but the station houses an attractive museum of the old railway. No 205 (Baldwin 74135/1948) was one of the last of a series of generally similar 2-8-2s which had been built since 1930. 2-8-0 no 34 (Baldwin 15337/1897) started life as the FC de Central Salvador's no 2, and later moved to the FFCC de Guatemala; both lines were IRCA constituents. 14 April 2012.

Utter dereliction surrounded 2-8-2 no 199 (Baldwin 74129/1948) on 15 April 2012 at what was once Zacapa engine shed, and two more woebegone 2-8-2s stood outside. Services in Guatemala became erratic after IRCA's lines there were nationalised in 1968 and came to a complete standstill in 1996. Things looked up in 1997 when a company run by Henry Posner III, a US railroad entrepreneur and enthusiast, took over, but in 2007 continued political interference brought operations to a halt once more, and Mr Posner's company was ejected. With large-scale theft of rail since then, and also of steel from the many viaducts, any rapid resumption of services seems unlikely. Mr Posner is one of several professional railwaymen who are now involved in the charitable company which has rescued the East Broad Top.

EL SALVADOR

An altogether happier scene awaited me at San Salvador engine shed on 13 April 2012 when I arrived to find the staff steaming this 2-8-0 for my benefit, even though she was supposed to be unserviceable. What kind people! IRCA's Salvadorean operation was nationalised in 1975; the country's other railway was already in public ownership and the combined undertaking became known as Fenadesal. Here their no 12 (Baldwin 58224/1925), formerly IRCA no 102, has steam up and is ready to venture outside. Just visible to the left is the cab of sister loco no 101 (Baldwin 58441/1925). IRCA's formation was masterminded by Minor Keith, a US railway entrepreneur and also the vice-president of the United Fruit Company which needed better transport to serve its banana plantations. For much of its existence, the railway was effectively a United Fruit subsidiary.

COSTA RICA

In 1884, gold was discovered near Las Juntas de Abangares in northern Costa Rica. Minor Keith ran a mine there and named this tiny 18-inch gauge 0-4-0 (Alco 30196/1904) *Cristina* after his wife. The loco now has this stylish home in the town. There are the skeletal remains of a second loco at the old mine which now houses a museum. 16 April 2012.

The FC al Pacifico was one of the country's principal 3ft 6ins gauge railways. For four years, 2-4-0 no 1 *Maria Cecilia* (Dickson 1020/1898) was its only loco and was used for construction work until its first section opened in 1902. She was withdrawn in 1933 after the line was electrified and was set aside for preservation. Here she stands outside the Pacifico's works at San José on 17 April 2012.

Mystery surrounds the origins of the Pacifico's unusual 0-4-2ST no 14 *Gandoca*, though she may have started life in Panama and been captured by the Costa Ricans after straying across what was then a disputed border. She was withdrawn in 1970 after many years as the San José works shunter and now resides next to *Maria Cecilia*. Her builder is unknown. 17 April 2012.

COLOMBIA

Above: The 3ft gauge FC Nacionales de Colombia's 4-8-0 no 76 (Baldwin 73095/1947) started out life as no 10 of the FC Ambalema-Imbagué, a line which was only 65km long and was run by the Department of Tolima, one of the country's principal coffee-growing regions, until being taken over by the state railway in 1953. Here she heads through Simón Bolívar Park in Bogotá early in the morning of 10 December 2011, soon after beginning her journey to La Caro with a Christmas train.

Opposite: No 76 has to work hard as she climbs towards La Caro on 10 December 2011. These 4-8-0s were designed back in 1924 by PC Dewhurst, the state railway's talented chief engineer. The leading axle is flangeless and the rear one incorporates Cartazzi slides. These features, and their high adhesive factor of 85 per cent, made them especially suitable for the country's twisty mountain railways and they were nicknamed *las serpientes*, or *the snakes*, by Colombia's enginemen. Mr Dewhurst moved away in 1929 and orders for his 4-8-0s ceased. The Ambalema line had few sharp curves and wasn't very hilly but had used the 4-8-0 design since 1928 and when they needed new locos in 1947 ordered two more, nos 9 and 10. Altogether, no fewer than 108 served Colombia's railways.

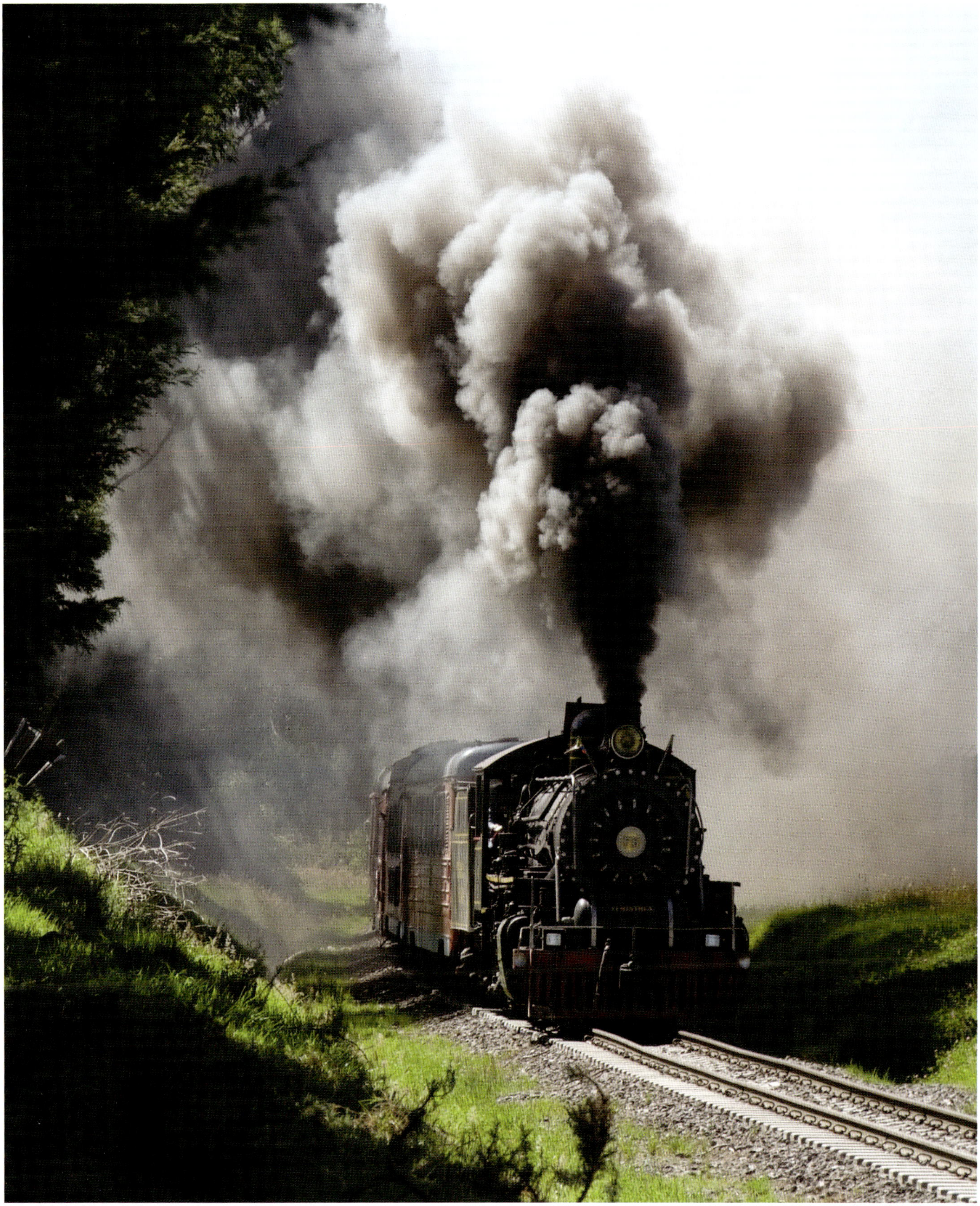

Above: A happy family scene with no 76 at La Caro on 10 December 2011, though the furry member in the pipe, and the young lady on top of it, are more interested in me than the train! Regular steam working in Colombia finished in the 1970s. It returned in 1982 when Dr Eduardo Rodriguez, its assistant general manager, oversaw the repair of several locos for a weekend tourist operation. It used luxury coaches built in the 1950s for a service over a newly-completed railway between Bogotá and Santa Marta on the Caribbean coast, which laid over in the city at weekends.

Opposite above: Public tourist trains operate from Bogotá every Sunday throughout the year, mostly to Zipaquirá, an attractive old Spanish colonial town. They became a much-loved institution within the city but stopped running when the state railway closed down in 1992. Dr Rodriguez and colleagues purchased the locos and coaches and the service, now called *Turistren*, resumed on 31 May 1993. Dr Rodriguez travelled on the train on 11 December 2011 when friends and I were visiting and treated us to footplate rides – a really hospitable person. Note the size of the crew's lunch and how they're keeping it warm. Food is a serious matter in Colombia! The Zipaquirá line was built to metre gauge, and only converted to 3ft in 1953.

Opposite below: Colombia is also a land of music and no fewer than three bands travelled on the train. This was a really fun ride and audience participation was compulsory!

COLOMBIA • 51

BRAZIL

Above: The 2ft 6ins gauge railway at São João del Rei, a Portuguese colonial city in Brazil's Minas Gerais state, was built by the Estrada de Ferro Oeste de Minas, and at its greatest extent was no less than 602km long, though this had shrunk to 202km by the time commercial operation finished in 1982. Happily, heritage trains still run on the 12.8km section between São João del Rei and Tiradentes and, like Turistren, this is a year-round operation. 4-6-0 no 41 (Baldwin 38011/1912) peeps out from under the splendid overall roof at São João del Rei station before setting off on 24 August 2012.

Opposite: No 41 passes a Volkswagen Beetle in the outskirts of São João del Rei on 24 August 2012. Production of these cars continued in Brazil until 1996, eighteen years after it finished in Germany, and they are still a familiar sight there.

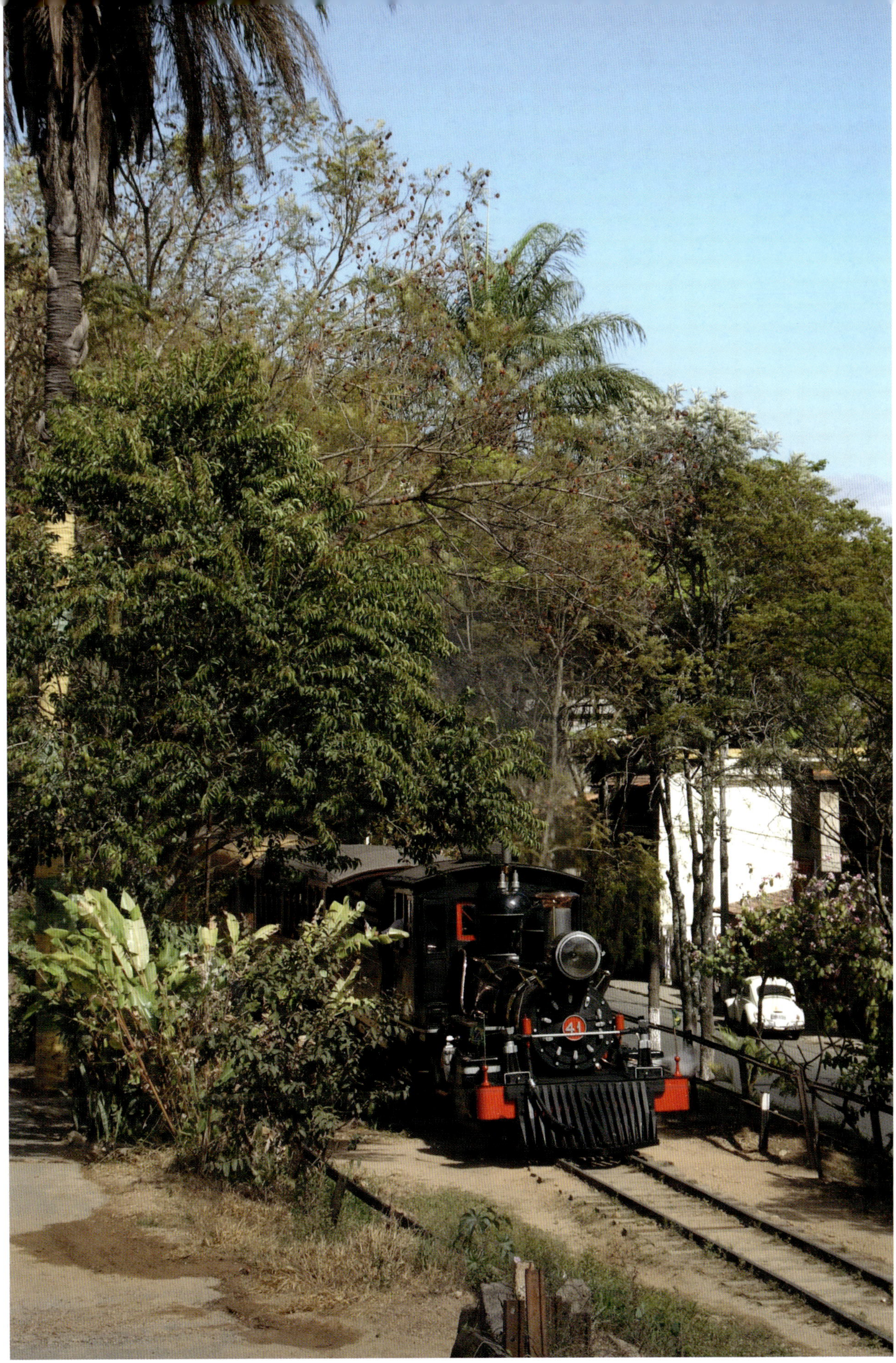

54 • NARROW GAUGE PANORAMA

Above: The ABPF's other section is based at São Lourenço where EF Central do Brasil 2-8-2 no 1424 (Alco 59712/1927) waits to set off for Soledade de Minas on 26 August 2012.

Opposite: The Oeste de Minas also ran a large metre gauge system and in 1931 became part of the Rede Mineira de Viação, another constituent of which was the Rio & Minas Railway which had originally been British-owned. Its line north from Cruzeiro closed in the early 1990s. The Sul de Minas chapter of the ABPF, Brazil's main preservation society, looks after 90km of it and operates trains over two sections, each about 10km long. On the more southerly one RMV Pacific no 332 (Baldwin 58552/1925) attracts admirers at Coronel Fulgêncio on 20 August 2012 after she has completed her journey from Passa Quatro.

BRAZIL • 55

For many years, EFDTC relied on its 300 class 2-10-4s to work most of its traffic. They were fast, powerful machines and are still remembered with affection at Tubarão. Her working days are over, but 2-10-4 no 300 (Baldwin 62355/1940) still looks impressive in the steam depot and museum there on 7 July 2013. She was originally EF Central do Brasil no 1652 and later EF Noroeste do Brasil no 817 before moving to Tubarão. These locos' smokebox doors look as though they came straight from the SNCF, France's state railway. They may well have originated on a large, but unsuccessful, series of French-built locos supplied to Brazil in the early 1950's. Behind her is no 53 (Baldwin 53830/1920), previously no 408 of the EF Noroeste do Brasil, one of four Pacifics to have run on EFDTC. They worked its passenger trains for many years until they ended in 1968. I saw one of them acting as the yard shunter at Tubarão engine shed in 1977 and these were perhaps their final duties. Just peeping into the left foreground in 2-8-0 no 100 (Alco 60512/1919), one of three similar locos on the system. She ended her days working at Imbituba docks, from where the region's coal was shipped out.

To help out the 300s, EFDTC bought fourteen of these 200 class 2-10-2s second-hand from Argentina in 1980. No 205 (Škoda 1982/1949) stands in Tubarão yard just after sunrise on 6 July 2013. She was formerly Ferrocarriles Argentinos' no 1352, and later EFDTC no 407. She was modified at Tubarão by L.D. Porta, the innovative Argentine engineer, to include his advanced exhaust system – easily recognised by the forward-sloping chimney needed for the blastpipe to clear the superheater header. They left their previous home by rail in a single long cavalcade and passed through Bolivia on their way to Brazil before completing their journey to Tubarão by road.

Just across the Rio Tubarão lies the huge coal-fired Capivari power station, the largest of its kind anywhere in South America. It was home to two 2-8-2s which are believed to have been the last steam locos built for mainline service anywhere in South America. In the 1980s they were taken over by EFDTC, but kept their former numbers. At dusk on 7 July 2013, no 5 (Jung 11944/1954) crosses the river on a new bridge built after catastrophic floods destroyed its predecessor in 1974. The cloudy weather combined with the power station's appalling pollution made for an almost monochrome photo, relieved only by the loco's headlight and the glow in the cab from her firebox.

ARGENTINA

The sun had just risen over the mountains on 22 October 2014 as 2-8-2 no 4 (Baldwin 55432/1922) crossed the inhospitable terrain south of El Maitén on Ferrocarriles Argentinos' 750mm gauge Esquel branch. Construction of the railway began in the early 1920s and most of the rolling stock dates from then, though the restaurant car which formed an essential part of the train on this all-day journey was built only in 1955. Travelling conditions before then must have been bleak indeed!

No 4 approaches Leleque, the first significant settlement south of El Maitén. The foothills of the Andes accompany the railway for almost its entire distance between El Maitén and Esquel. Some of the Patagonian Welsh settled in the district in the late 1800s and maybe the mountains reminded them of home!

No 4 crosses one of the many mountain streams which flow into the Rio Chubut and on towards the distant Atlantic Ocean. The cow doesn't give the train a second glance and maybe has seen it all before!

ARGENTINA • 63

FRANCE

On 22 April 2006, 2-6-0T no 15 (HSP 1316/1920) enters Lanchères-Pendé station, between Noyelles-sur-Mer and Cayeux-sur-Mer on the CF de la Baie de Somme. This metre gauge system, in the north of the Département de la Somme, closed to regular traffic between 1969 and 1972 and was rescued by enthusiasts almost immediately. It is now a hugely successful heritage operation and makes a major contribution to the local economy. Steam working on the old railway ended in 1957 and the locos were scrapped, but no 15 is similar to some built to make good losses during the First World War. She worked on the line between St-Just-en-Chaussée and Froissy in the Département de l'Oise, the last remaining section of the old Voies Ferrées d'Intérêt Local. It closed in 1961 and kept going latterly because of its important sugar beet traffic. Northern France's large sugar beet industry dates from the Napoleonic War, when imports from the Caribbean were difficult, but only really became economically viable when the cost of imported sugar rose after France abolished slavery in its colonies in 1848. The leading coach was built by Decauville in 1906 for the PLM railway for service on its line between Orange, in the Rhone valley, and Buis-les-Baronnies.

4-6-0T no E.332 (FL 3587/1909) worked on the Réseau Breton until it closed in 1969. The RB was state-owned, though operation was conceded to a private company. After preservation in Switzerland, she moved to the Baie de Somme in 2006, and on 24 April 2009 was making her first public journey after restoration. Here she climbs the bank out of St Valery on the Cayeux line.

Above: 0-6-2T no 3714 *Beton-Bazoches* (BR, 1909) was built for the CF Départemental de Seine et Marne. She was designed to run cab-first in view of the railway's numerous roadside sections; to quote the départemental instruction, '*La longeur de la chaudière peut géner la visibilité du mécanicien aux passages à niveau*', or the long boiler limits what the driver can see at level crossings. After most of the system closed, she was kept on until 1965 to work sugar beet trains between Nangis and Jouy-le-Chatel and arrived at the Baie de Somme in 1971. The CF du Nord built the line between Noyelles and St-Valery-sur-Somme as a standard gauge branch. It opened back in 1858, and when the metre gauge arrived in the district in 1887 rails for it were laid between the existing ones. Here *Beton-Bazoches* is midway along the mixed gauge section beside the saltmarsh on 28 April 2013. The coaches were built for the Somme lines in 1921 by Manage in Belgium to make good First World War losses.

Opposite above: This 2-6-0T (Cail 2296/1889) is typical of many of France's late nineteenth century metre gauge locos, though she was built for Ferdinand de Lesseps's ill-fated Panama Canal venture. This had failed by the time she was delivered, and she moved on to become the FFCC de Puerto Rico's no 2. She spent many years in retirement in Michigan, and first steamed again in 2003. Here she crosses the old bridge over the River Somme at St-Valery on 9 September 2004.

Opposite below: This very pretty 0-6-0T is the CF des Côtes-du-Nord's no 36 (CL 1675/1925). On 22 April 2006, she passes Morlay on the line between Noyelles and Le Crotoy while visiting the Baie de Somme. The CdN closed in 1957. The leading coach is the PLM one.

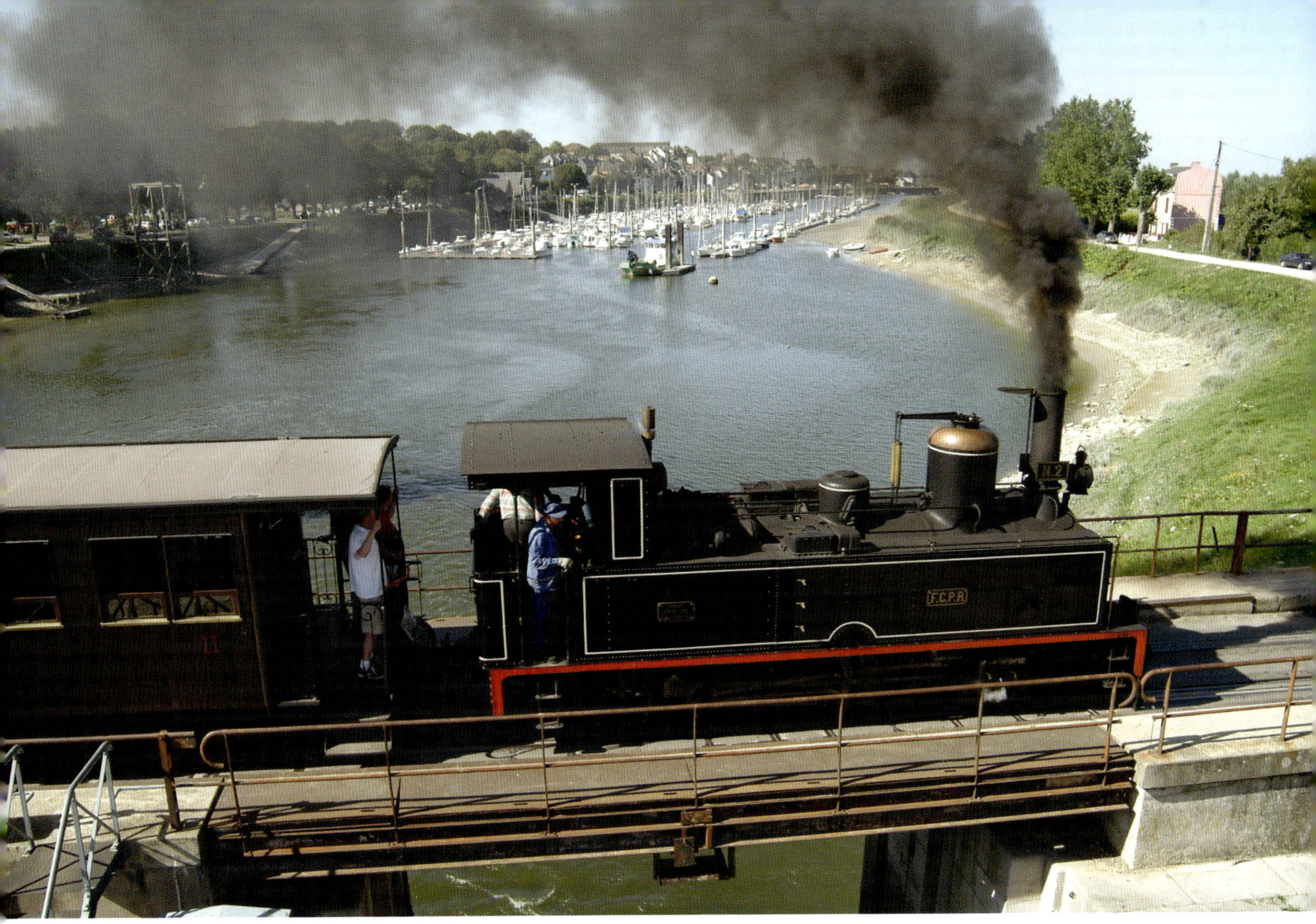
F.C.P.R

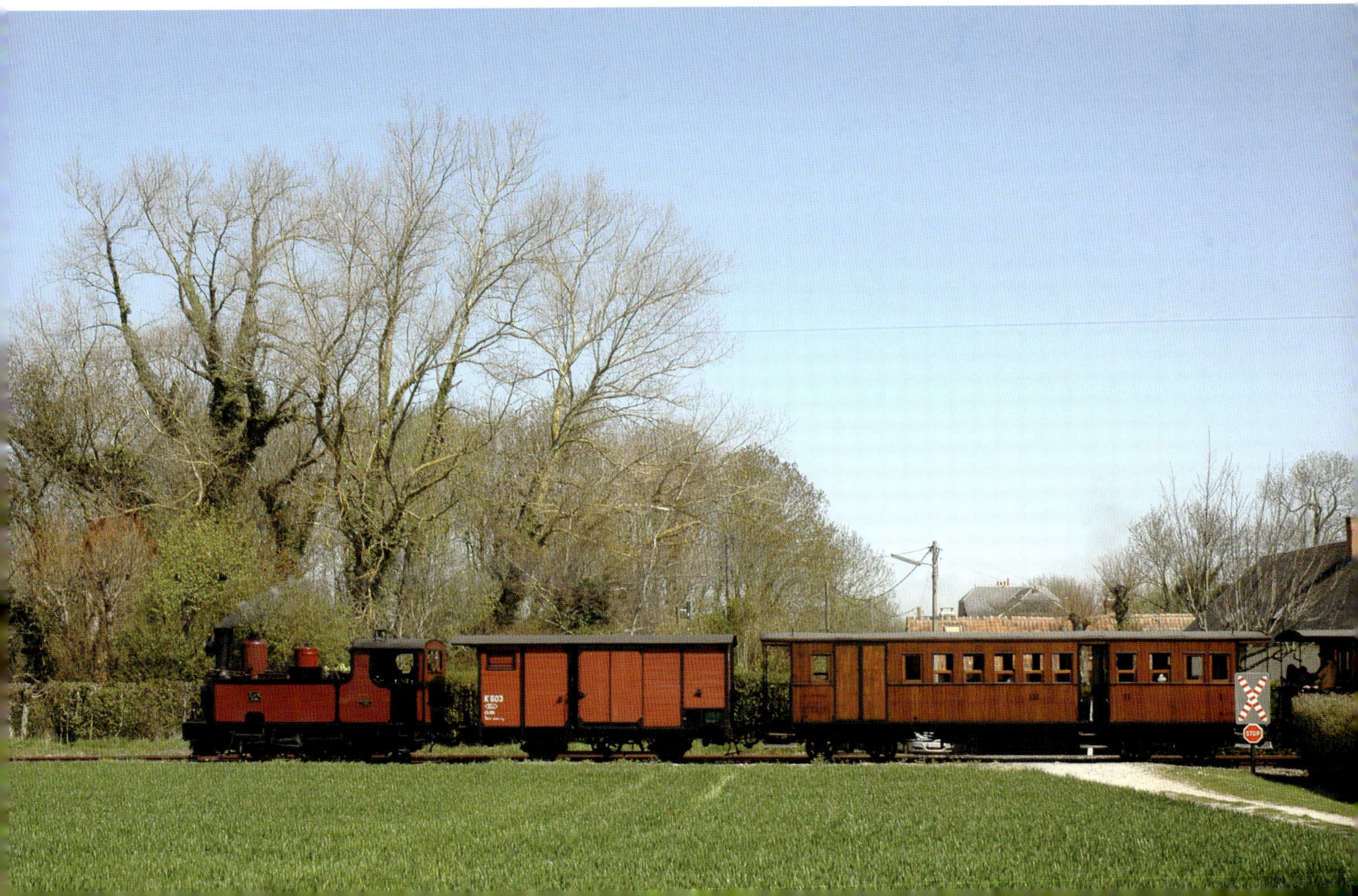

Like the RB and the CdN, the Tramways à Vapeur d'Ille-et-Vilaine operated in Brittany. Their 0-6-0T no 75 (CL 1234/1909) makes use of the small turntable at Cayeux, typical of the French narrow gauge, during a visit on 27 April 2013. She was rescued after the TIV closed in 1950, and both she and CdN no 36 now live at a preservation centre at Crèvecœur-le-Grand, on the route of an old line which once formed part of which was once served by the Voies Ferrées d'Intérêt Local. Most of the metre gauge locos still surviving in northern France in the 1960s have been preserved either there or at the Baie de Somme.

The little Lartigue monorail line built in the 1890's between Feurs and Panissières, in the Département de la Loire, was the only public railway of its kind apart from the Listowel and Ballybunion in County Kerry. It was equipped with two four-coupled tank locos built by Biétrix et Cie of St Etienne, altogether larger and heavier than the Listowel line's three-coupled tender locos. The initial test runs with no 1, *Feurs*, between 1895 and 1898 didn't go well. The line wasn't allowed to open, though this seems to have been due more to local political and commercial interference than to any insuperable technical difficulties. No 2 *Panissières* was only delivered in 1898 and seems hardly to have run at all. Its promoters eventually gave up and in 1902 everything was scrapped. The railway is still fondly remembered in the district and much of its route now forms a public footpath with signs pointing out some of its features. This replica of *Panissières* was built by nine students of boilermaking at the Lycée Claude Lebois in St-Chamond between 1999 and 2001, and I saw her at Panissières on 15 April 2019.

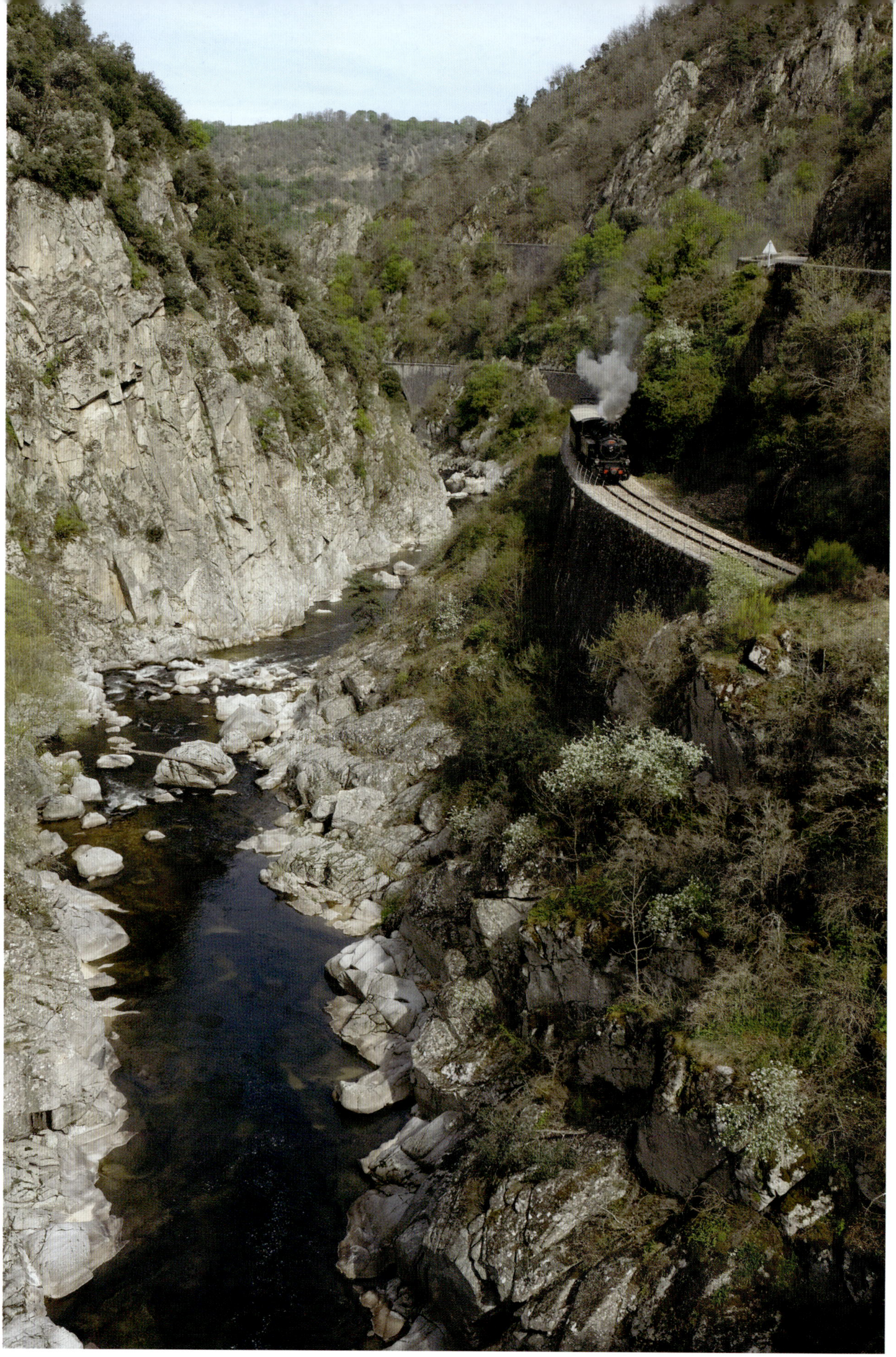

Above: Nearer Lamastre the countryside becomes more open. No 203 (SLM 1492/1903) was one of the railway's original series of Mallets constructed in Switzerland because French builders didn't then have the required expertise. She's crossing the picturesque Arlebosc viaduct on 17 April 2019. Eight of the Swiss locos were built between 1901 and 1905. I was told they were preferred to the later French machines because of their lower centre of gravity.

Opposite: The Vivarais railway climbed up from the Rhône valley into the Massif Central and was built between 1898 and 1903. It has always been one of the country's most celebrated metre gauge systems, both for its magnificent scenery and for the series of huge 0-6-6-0 Mallet tanks which were built for it between 1902 and 1932. The section between Tournon-sur-Rhône and Lamastre, in the Département de l'Ardèche, was rescued by enthusiasts in 1968. Here no 414 (SACM 7629/1932) works a mixed train through the spectacular Doux gorge west of Tournon on 15 April 2019. The four-wheeled yellow and black coach dates from the railway's early years. These vehicles were universally nicknamed the *cages à poule* or *chicken coops*.

Above: No 414 waits with timber wagons at Colombier-le-Vieux–St Barthelemy-le-Plain (what a long name!) before setting off for Tournon on 15 April 2019. She was one of four of the railway's last type of Mallets, all built in 1932. There were also two of an intermediate design which haven't survived.

Opposite above: The line closed in 2008 after a short-lived partnership with the départemental government collapsed, and it was handed to a commercial organisation. It used to share the SNCF's station at Tournon and left the town over a mixed-gauge section, but this was denied the new operators. They did much to redress matters by building a fine new station beyond the SNCF junction in traditional style, including this typically French engine shed. Here are nos 403 and 414 on 15 April 2019.

Opposite below: Up in the hills enthusiasts have preserved another section of the old Vivarais system between St-Agrève and Raucoulles-Brosettes in the Départements de l'Ardèche and la Haute-Loire. They have 0-4-4-0 Mallet tank no 101 (BM 336/1906), one of four which once worked on the PO-Corrèze system on the western side of the Massif Central. Like the RB this line and its locos were owned by the SNCF. On 14 April 2019, no 101 works a mixed train north of Le Chambon-sur-Lignon. The townspeople there are mostly Huguenots and have a long history of rebelliousness against authority. During the Second World War, they openly assisted Jewish people fleeing the Nazis and the collaborationist Vichy regime. It is believed that thousands were saved, something for which the town has received international recognition.

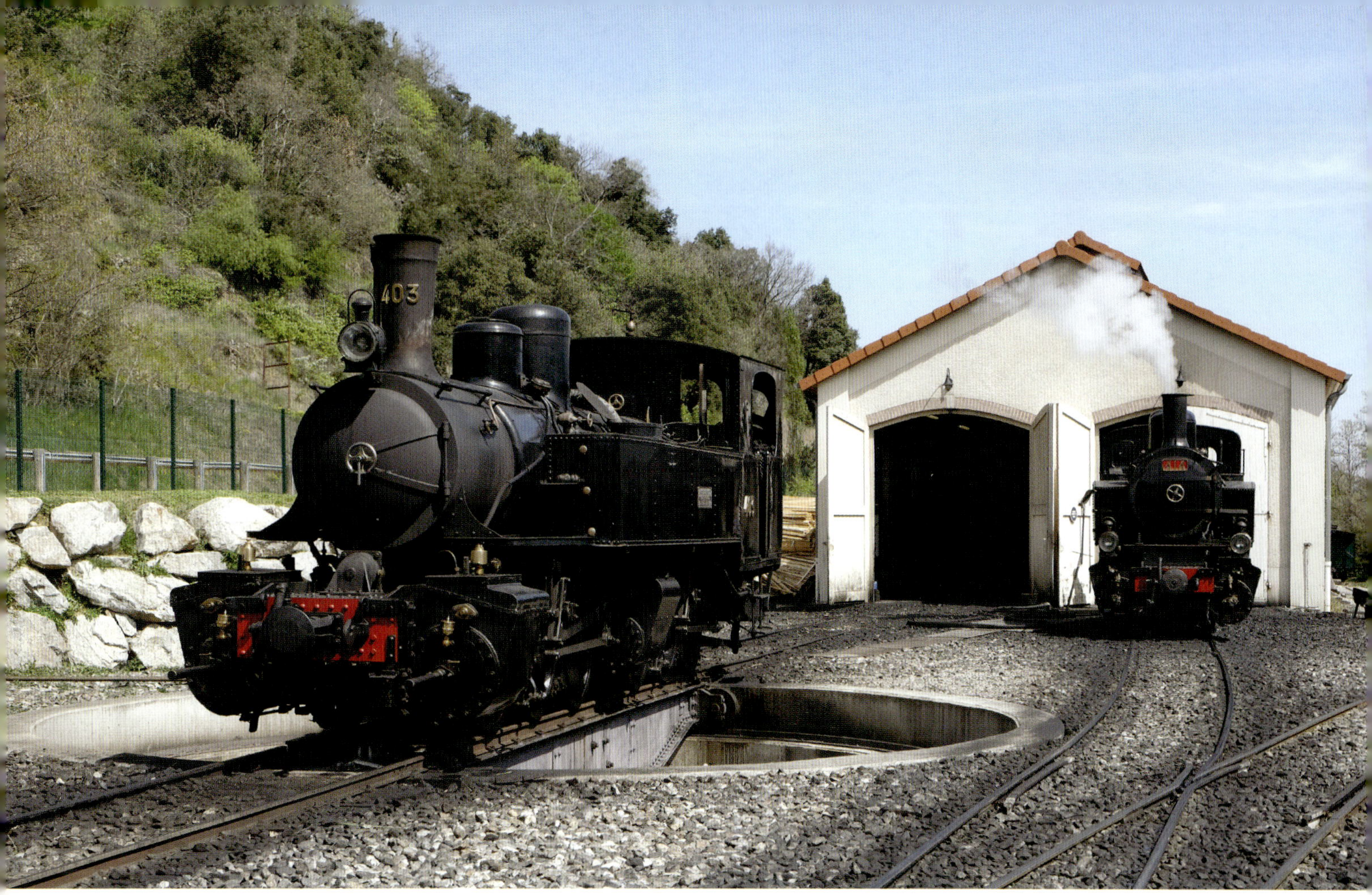
403

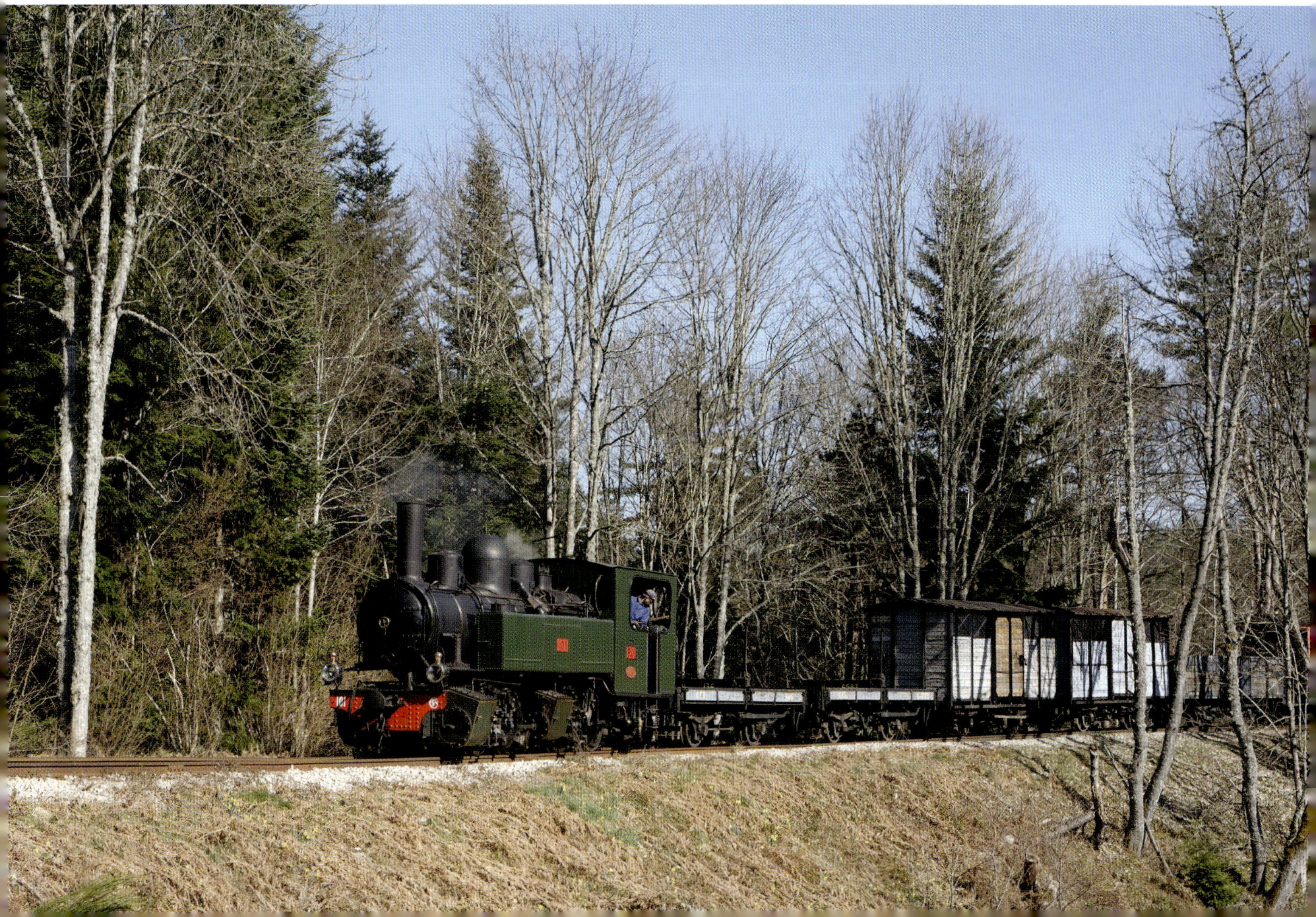

The Alsatian engineer Frederic Weidknecht set up a base in Paris in 1876 and started to deal in small locos. At first, he imported them, mostly from Krauss and Heilbronn, but in 1880 his firm built a small 0-4-0T, their works no 104. The building date of this little 600mm gauge Weidknecht loco isn't known, but her antiquated appearance suggests she may not be much younger. She worked at a tile factory at Chagny, in Burgundy, which was founded in 1881, and now lives in the garden of the Henri Malartre motor museum at Rochetaillée-sur-Saône where I saw her on 14 July 2011.

Abreschviller, in the Vosges mountains, lies in the part of Lorraine which, along with Alsace, became German territory in 1871. The region is heavily forested and the first section of an extensive 700mm gauge forestry railway was built in 1884, known to the Germans as the Waldbahn Alberschweiler. By the time the region was returned to France in 1918, it had become a 50km-long system, and it later grew to a maximum extent of 73km. The first locos were two 0-4-0Ts built by Heilbronn. Neither has survived but there's a similar one at the excellent Frankfurter Feldbahnmuseum (see page 152). They were supplemented by this 0-4-4-0 Mallet tank (Heilbronn 476/1907) which shares some of their distinctive looks. She was the only Mallet which Heilbronn ever built and has spent all her life on the railway. After the old line closed in 1964, the section between Abreschviller and Grand-Soldat was saved by enthusiasts. Here the Mallet runs round her train at Grand-Soldat on 11 July 2018.

Above: The French army adopted 0-4-4-0 Péchot-Bourdons for its 600mm gauge field railways as early as 1888 after they were advocated by Colonel Prosper Péchot, though by 1914 only sixty-two had been built. The type was essentially a Double Fairlie but had only one centrally mounted dome. 280 were ordered from Baldwin on 1 February 2015, and another fourteen came from North British. Some served the Germans after 1940, possibly moved from France's Maginot line where many had been based. No 215 (Baldwin 43367/1916) was found in a shed at Chemnitz and is believed to have been used to carry away rubble from bombed-out buildings in Magdeburg. She spent nearly seventy years in a Dresden museum, but is now at the excellent Frankfurter Feldbahnmuseum where I saw her on 7 December 2019. In 1920, one final Péchot-Bourdon was built by Baldwin for the Imperial Army in Japan, but her charms don't seem to have been appreciated there.

Opposite: In 1910, Decauville entered into a know-how sharing agreement with OK, after which they introduced their Progrès class 5-tonne 0-4-0Ts and 8-tonne 0-6-0Ts, technically a considerable advance on their previous models. The French military bought large numbers of the Progrès 0-6-0Ts during the First World War, and many were sold after peace returned. Decauville 1652/1916 was one of three which went on to work on a public railway, the 600mm gauge CF du Nord-Est, and carried this attractive livery. When it closed in 1935, they were sold to the Toury sugar factory where they worked until the 1960s. She is now at the CF de la Haute Somme which originated as another First World War line, was later adapted to serve a sugar factory at Dompierre and is now run by enthusiasts. This train is running beside the Somme Canal near Froissy on 23 May 2010; the leading wagon once carried sugar beet on the Tramway de Pithiviers à Toury, a public 600mm gauge line which served the sugar factories at both the towns in its title.

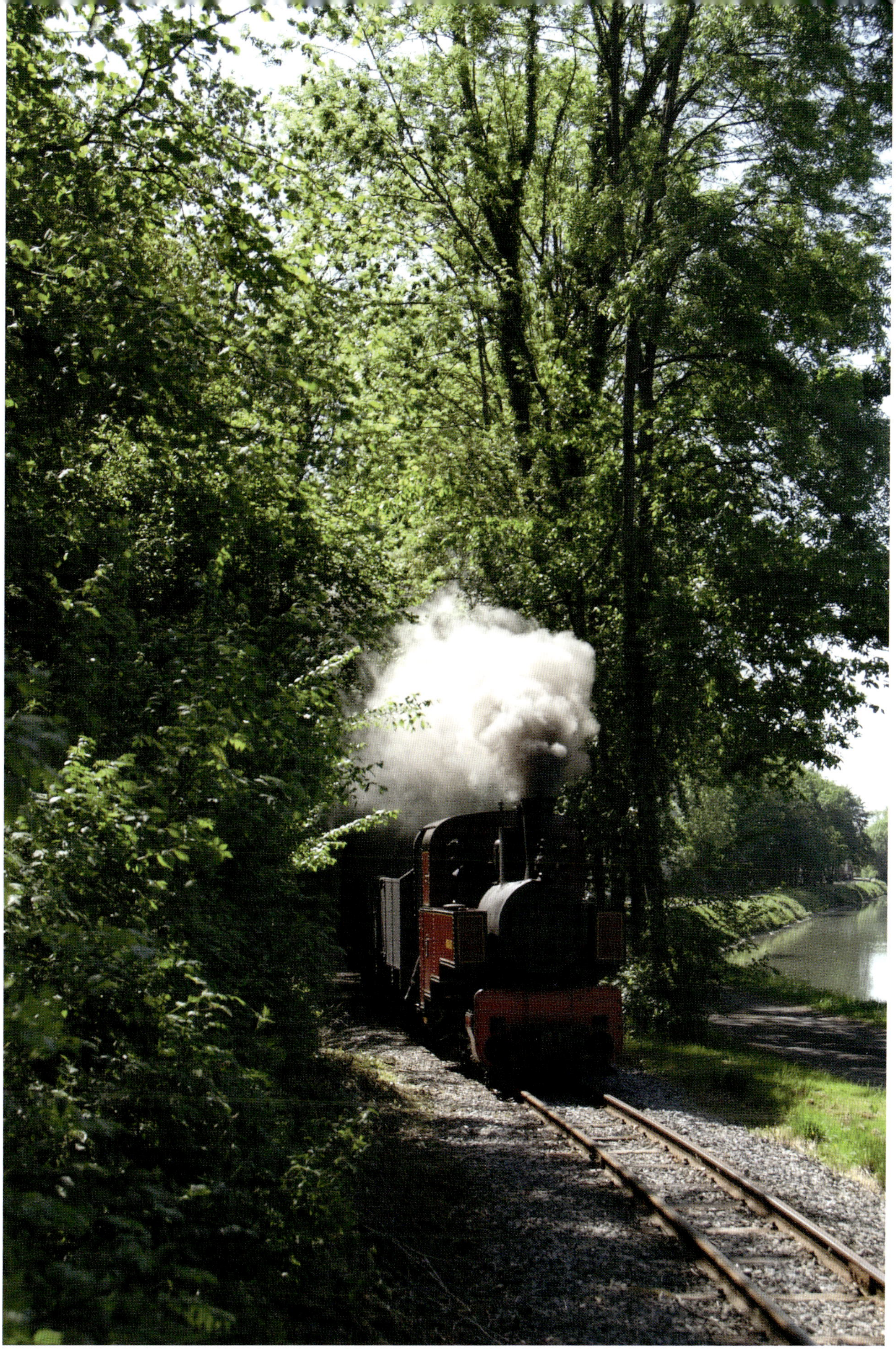

The British army only came to understand the usefulness of field railways some eighteen months or so after the start of the First World War, when delays in the transport of soldiers and munitions through the mud of the Western Front threatened their entire war effort. At much the same time, they took over a section of the front from the French and could see for themselves the effectiveness of their 600mm gauge lines. By the middle of 1916, they were building hundreds of miles which were soon organised as the War Department Light Railways. Their first steam loco type was Hudswell Clarke's Ganges class 0-6-0T. They bought sixty-six between 1916 and 1919, along with another ten 2ft gauge ones for military installations in Britain and Ireland. Many of their Ganges locos went on to lead second lives in industry. The only ex-WDLR survivor is *Pejao* (HC 1375/1919) which I visited at the old Santarem railway museum in Portugal on 13 January 2010. She became one of six locos to work on the 600mm gauge railway which connected Pejao colliery, in the north of Aveiro District, with Pedorido, a port on the River Douro about 40km upstream from Porto. She still carries her Pejao khaki paint. The army also painted its first few locos khaki but soon changed to black. The splendid coach to the right is a part of the old Portuguese royal train. The museum has since closed and most of the exhibits, including *Pejao*, are now at the Museu Nacional Ferroviário at Entroncamento.

The Ganges loco which became WDLR's no 104 was one of two which had been ordered back in 1914 by the Ashanti gold mining concern, in what is now Ghana, but was diverted for war service. Her replacement there, HC 1238/1916, returned to the UK for preservation, and on 16 November 2019 was visiting the Leighton Buzzard Railway in the guise of no 104. Here she stands at the head of a train of skip wagons as dusk was falling. On the left fellow Ganges loco no GP39 (HC 1643/1930), one of two bought by Surrey County Council for road construction work and the last to be built, makes a cameo appearance and helps to create the illusion that this was a busy loco depot on the Western Front. The Ashanti loco only survived because she suffered a major derailment and spent many years buried and completely out of view. The lining applied to WDLR's early locos was a luxury which they soon abandoned! The first two Ganges locos were 2ft 6ins gauge and were exported to India which perhaps explains the class name. All the others went to WDLR apart from the two Ashanti locos, the two in Surrey and seven built for the Thai railways in 1921. No GP39 later became *Bronllwyd* at the Penrhyn Quarry Railway and is now preserved at the Statfold Barn Railway in Staffordshire. Two of the Thai locos are believed to be the only other survivors.

WDLR soon needed larger locos and a neat 4-6-0T design was produced by Hunslet, though they couldn't supply in anything like the numbers required. Other British loco-builders were fully committed, in the case of Kerr Stuart because the French army had got in first with a large order for copies of Decauville's Progrès 0-6-0Ts. WDLR turned to Baldwin, which modified a 4-6-0T design previously supplied to the French army in Morocco and built no fewer than 495 within just seven months. On 3 May 2019 nos 303 (Hunslet 1215/1916) and 778 (Baldwin 44656/1917) stand at the corrugated iron engine shed at Leighton Buzzard, which looks remarkably like some of the sheds on the Western Front. After the war no 303 worked in the Queensland sugar industry, while no 778 was one of fifty sent to India and ended up at the Upper India Sugar Mills in Uttar Pradesh.

Even Baldwin couldn't keep up with the demand for ever more locos and WDLR bought 100 of these 2-6-2Ts from Alco. They were better than the 4-6-0Ts as they ran equally well in either direction. Four were sold to the Pithiviers line, three of which became the only survivors. No 1257 (Alco 57148/1916) is now one of several locos with First World War connections at the excellent Tacot des Lacs at Grez-sur-Loing, near Fontainebleau. Patrick Mourot, who runs the railway, kindly moved her out into the sunshine for me on 26 August 2019. Another is at the excellent museum at the Pithiviers heritage line, and the third is at the Ffestiniog Railway, though it has been cut down to suit their restricted loading gauge and looks rather different.

Patrick is at the controls of ex-US Army 2-6-2T no 5104 (Baldwin 46828/1918), later *Felin Hen* at the Panrhyn Quarry Railway, as she runs on the Tacot des Lacs beside the River Loing on 10 September 2013. The US entered the war on 6 April 1917, and Baldwin built 195 of these 2-6-2Ts between September and December. *Felin Hen* is the only survivor and ended up in Queensland, where she was rebuilt as a 0-6-2T. Patrick and his friends faced a major task to restore her to her original condition, though they managed to slip in the post-war *Felin Hen* name in a subtle way! Davenport built a further eighty similar locos from October 1918, three of which are preserved in the US, and Vulcan another thirty in 1919, but the war ended before most of them were completed, and none reached Europe.

NORWAY

The first section of the 750mm gauge Urskog-Hølandsbanen railway south from Bingsfoss opened in 1896. On 12 December 2010 2-6-2T no 7 *Prydz* (Henschel 28463/1950) runs down the hill from Fossum and approaches Bingsfoss on what's now the Tertitten heritage line. She was the youngest loco on UHB and the last steam loco of any gauge to be added to the stock of NSB, the Norwegian state railway. UHB led a hand-to-mouth existence for many years before NSB took over in 1945, and probably only survived thanks to the resourcefulness of Eigil Prydz, its long-serving manager. NSB didn't usually name its locos but made a well-deserved exception with no 7.

Dusk at Fossum on 11 December 2010 and *Prydz* has just arrived with her train. Looking at these photos brings back just how cold it was. Even the sea had frozen!

SWEDEN

The 891mm gauge Dala-Ockelbo-Norrsundet Järnväg ran for 86km between Linghed and Norrsundet and opened in 1876. Its motive power included three of these 0-6-6-0 Mallets. When it closed in October 1970, the Jädraås-Tallås Järnväg heritage group took over a short section along with much of the rolling stock and has operated it ever since. The DONJ's operating base was at Jädraås, and the large range of buildings there has survived intact. It is the end of the day on 22 July 2006 and no 12 (Atlas 113/1910) is backing into Jädraås engine shed. Space there is so tight that her rear coupling needs to overhang the windowsill for her to fit in!

Above: The DONJ's steam railcar *Majorn* (Atlas 18/1888) sets off from Pallanite for Jädraås on 22 July 2006.

Opposite above: The DONJ was not the only Swedish narrow gauge line to operate steam railcars. This streamlined model (Lundvig, 1900) was no 1 of the 891mm gauge Nordmark–Klarälvens Järnvägar, which served the district to the north of Lake Vänern and was one of two on the line. She was withdrawn in 1937. Today she lives, appropriately, in the old railcar shed at the NKlJ's Hagfors depot which houses its museum and is home to a comprehensive collection of its stock. It's a shame she's lost the tip of her nose! Just visible to the left are 0-6-2Ts nos 5 *Lovisa Tranæa* (Avonside 1114/1875) and 7 *Hagfors* (Nohab 175/1883). The line's first section opened in 1877. It was sufficiently busy to be electrified in stages from 1921; a new generation of electric locos arrived in the 1960s, but its fortunes went downhill and the last section closed in 1990. 22 September 2015.

Opposite below: Slite-Roma Järnväg 2-8-0T no 3 *Dalhem* (Henschel 18152/1920) stands at Hesselby station on the 891mm gauge Gotlands Hesselby Järnväg on 26 July 2017. Island railways often have a distinctive character and those on Gotland, out in the Baltic Sea between the Swedish mainland and Latvia, were no exception. The SlRJ was one of several independent lines there and opened in 1902. They were all nationalised in 1947 and the following year became part of SJ, but the SlRJ did not fare well. Only occasional services ran after 1953 and it was abandoned two years later. The island's last railway closed in 1962 and the GHJ began operations on part of the SlRJ's route ten years later.

SWEDEN • 87

Above: *Dalhem* and her train approach Roma, where several lines converged, on 26 July 2017. SJ had an issue with Roma's name; in 1954 they renamed the station *Roma Kloster* after a ruined Cistercian monastery in the outskirts of the town in case it became confused with the capital of Italy!

Opposite above: The 891mm gauge Västergötland-Göteborgs Järnvägar ran a secondary mainline out of Gothenburg along with several branches and served a large district to its northeast. The mainline opened in 1900; the section nearest Gothenburg closed in 1967 and much of the rest followed in 1970. In the same year passenger traffic ceased throughout the system, and the last freight trains ran in 1986. The 12km-long section beside Lake Anten, included in the 1970 closure, was one of the prettiest parts of the railway, and in 1971 it was taken over by Anten-Gräfsnäs Järnväg, a heritage group. They have assembled an impressive collection of 891mm gauge stock from both VGJ and further afield. VGJ 4-6-0 no 24 (Nohab 982/1911) runs close to the lake near Humlebo on 17 July 2008.

Opposite below: 2-6-0 no 3147 (Nohab 848/1907) of SJ, the Swedish state railway, enters Ankarsrum on the 891mm gauge Hultsfred-Västervik Järnväg on 11 July 2015. The line is 68km long and opened in 1879. It went on to become part of a much longer railway which was taken over by SJ in 1949 and continued to serve a substantial part of southeastern Sweden until 1984. Now the HVJ is a heritage line. It is mostly diesel-worked but steam trains sometimes run when there's a loco in working order. No 3147 has spent her entire lifetime there.

SWEDEN • 89

Above: A period scene at Ankarsrum station on 11 July 2015 complete with no 3147, just visible behind the building, and a Volvo 121 on the forecourt. Still often seen in Sweden, these cars were built for ten years from 1957.

Opposite above: When the 600mm gauge Nättraby-Alnaroyd-Elmeboda Järnväg closed in 1945, its 2-6-2T no 4 *KM Nelsson* (Motala 520/1914) was sold to the Aspa pulp mill at the northern tip of Lake Vättern. The mill was a major buyer of equipment from Sweden's public 600mm gauge railways as they closed from the 1930s and was the source of much of the stock at the Östra Södermanlands Järnväg's museum line. On 26 September 2009, *KM Nelsson* and the Jonkoping-Gripenbergs-Järnväg's no 9 (Motala 568/1915), the only other loco of the type, leave Mariefred station, ÖSlJ's operating centre.

Opposite below: This pretty little 600mm gauge 2-4-2T started life as the Stavsjö Järnväg's no 2 *Virå* (Motala 272/1901) but was sold as early as 1918 to Ballangen iron ore mine in Norway. She was acquired by ÖSlJ in 1965 and here stands at Mariefred engine shed on 26 September 2009. One of ÖSlJ's volunteers described her to me as 'a gem, yes; everybody´s darling engine here. Steams beautifully and runs like an angel – better than any of our coaches do. Our max permitted speed on the ÖSlJ is 15mph – VIRÅ does 35 easily.' What can I add?!

SWEDEN • 91

Long before the First World War, the German army followed the French lead and began to build 600mm gauge light railway equipment. At first, they used 0-6-0Ts semi-permanently coupled back to back, considered less vulnerable to enemy action than the Péchot-Bourdons. Later they changed to 0-8-0Ts with Klien-Lindner axles, often called *Brigadeloks*, 2,573 of which were constructed by fifteen builders in the years up to 1919. When the war was over, several found their way into industrial service in Sweden. This one, Hartmann 4290/1919, worked at Emfors Bruk, near Västervik. Here she sets off from Mariefred harbour with a freight train during a gala on 26 September 2009.

IRELAND

Most of the 3ft gauge County Donegal Railway closed on 31 December 1959, though freight services on the section west of Strabane as far as Stranorlar lingered on until 6 February 1960. It was the largest narrow gauge system in the British Isles, one of the longest-lived and, with its pretty red steam locos, one of the most popular with enthusiasts. Four of the steam locos have survived, but none has run since its demolition was completed later in 1960. Class 5A 2-6-4T no 2 *Blanche* (NW 956/1912) stands at the head of a CDR train at the Ulster Folk and Transport Museum at Cultra on 13 September 2019. She received a heavy overhaul in 1957, and still carries the paint applied then. The loco on the left is 4-4-0T no 2 Kathleen (RS 2613/1887) of the 3ft gauge Cavan & Leitrim Railway.

Above: Most passengers bound for Donegal changed to the narrow gauge at Strabane. This imaginative display at the Cultra museum shows the nameboard that greeted them. The places named in the third line were served by the 3ft gauge Londonderry & Lough Swilly Railway with which the CDR connected at Letterkenny. The others were all CDR destinations. Beyond it, *Blanche* looks as though she's eager to leave on 13 September 2019. The section west from Strabane as far as Stranorlar was the oldest part of the CDR. It opened in 1864 as a broad gauge line and was converted to 3ft in 1894.

Opposite above: 2-6-4T No 4 *Meenglas* (NW 828/1907) is a class 5, an earlier type with shorter tanks. She had recently been repainted in her 1950s livery and stood outside the Foyle Valley Railway Museum at Derry on 13 September 2019. After a period of closure for several years the museum has now been taken over by Destined, a charity which helps young people with learning difficulties to integrate into society. It was heart-warming to experience the fulfilment they gained from their involvement in the new project.

Opposite below: 0-6-2T no 5 *Slieve Callan* (Dübs 2890/1892) waits to leave Moyasta Junction on the 3ft gauge West Clare Railway on 2 August 2010. The old West Clare line had become the last public narrow gauge railway anywhere in Ireland when it closed in 1961. This short section at Moyasta has been revived, thanks to the hard work and commitment of Jackie Whelan, a local businessman, and he has ambitious plans to extend it.

IRELAND • 95

The 3ft gauge Tralee & Dingle Light Railway, in Ireland's far southwest, opened in 1891 and the last train ran in 1953. Its no 5 (Hunslet 555/1892) was the first inside-framed 2-6-2T to run anywhere in the British Isles and also the largest loco on the railway, its others all being 2-6-0Ts. She didn't witness the closure, as she moved to the Cavan & Leitrim Railway in 1951, and worked there until it, too, closed in 1959 and she was withdrawn. She has survived thanks to the generosity of Edgar T Mead, a US enthusiast who rescued her, took her across the Atlantic to a museum in Vermont, and in 1988 sold her on to enthusiasts in Tralee for a nominal sum. A 3km long section of the old line between the outskirts of Tralee and Blennerville was rebuilt as a heritage railway and reopened in 1993. The T&D became a part of the Great Southern Railways in 1925, and they added the *T* to its locos' numbers to indicate that they came from Tralee. Here she raises steam at Blennerville engine shed on 7 August 2004. Sadly, she has been out of use since 2006, but there is talk of restoring her to working order. It would be wonderful if she can run over this short but attractive line once again. It is a really valuable addition to the historic railways of this beautiful country which now form some of its most distinctive heritage attractions.

WALES

Very early in the morning of 16 September 2016 600mm gauge 0-4-0T *Marchlyn* (Avonside 2067/1933) is the nearest of several locos inside the Penrhyn quarry's old Coed-y-parc workshop. I wonder how many generations of enginemen have warmed themselves on that splendid cast iron stove!

Above: No fewer than three old Penrhyn locos are in the yard at Coed-y-parc on 16 September 2016. From left to right they are 0-4-0ST *Winifred* (Hunslet 364/1885), 0-4-2ST *Stanhope* (KS 2395/1917) and *Marchlyn*. The short section of the old line which had been revived there was full of Welsh slate railway character but, sadly, the venture failed, and it was dismantled a few months later.

Opposite above: Many Penrhyn locos have been preserved away from Wales. Nigel Bowman bought 0-4-0ST *Lilian* (Hunslet 317/1883) from the quarry in 1965, and he and his wife Kay have run her at the Launceston Steam Railway in Cornwall since they opened it in 1983. Nigel is at the controls as *Lilian* runs round her train at New Mills on 19 September 2019. This delightful setting is reminiscent of some of the more bucolic corners of the old Penrhyn quarry system, which was also the source of the distinctive bullhead rail. *Lilian* and *Winifred* are two of the three members of Penrhyn's Port class.

Opposite below: The 600mm gauge railway at Pen-yr-Orsedd quarry at Nantlle was home to about ten De Winton vertical-boilered 0-4-0T's. The Caernarfon firm's products worked at many North Wales quarries before being displaced by the newer and more powerful Quarry Hunslet 0-4-0STs. *Chaloner* (DW, 1877) went new to Pen-y-Bryn quarry, also at Nantlle, before moving to Pen-yr-Orsedd in 1888 and was probably the last in service anywhere in North Wales when she was withdrawn in 1952. In 1960 she was bought by Alf Fisher, and on 22 June 2019 was visiting the Ffestiniog Railway. Here she stands with her train of engineering wagons on their mainline at Boston Lodge. The tracks in the foreground have probably been unchanged for more than 100 years and form the northern extremity of the works yard. Until recently they were connected with the mainline here.

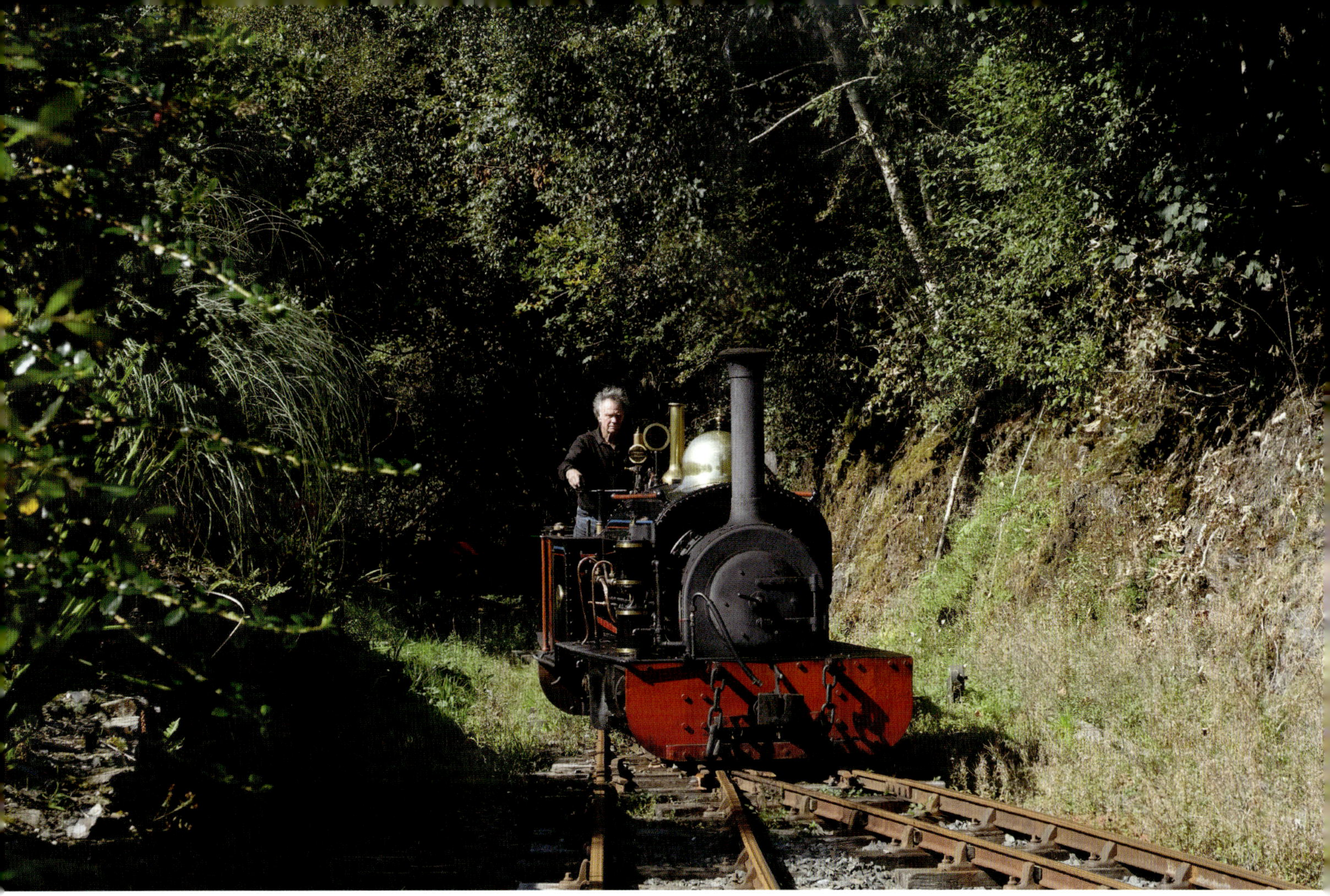

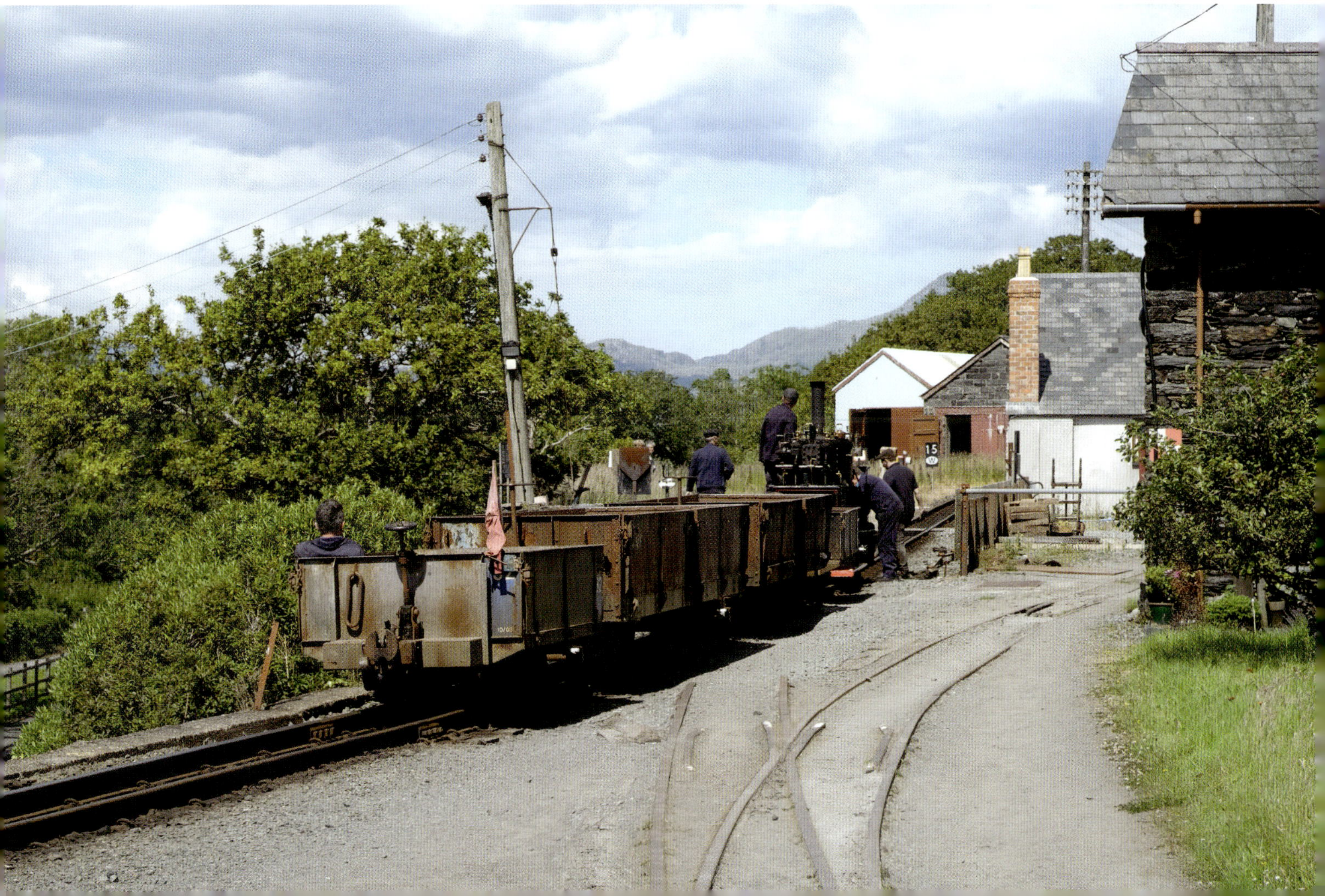

Above: *Chaloner* looks thoroughly at home at Boston Lodge engine shed on 22 June 2019 with the mountains as a backdrop, though at Nantlle the message about the lights would surely have been in Welsh! The gentleman wearing glasses is Dave Fisher, Alf's son. De Winton's factory was opposite the Welsh Highland station in Caernarfon, and their impressive drawing office building still stands.

Opposite above: Pen-yr-Orsedd operated three Hunslets which were delivered in what was described as Midland Railway red. Here's *Sybil* (Hunslet 827/1903) at the Brecon Mountain Railway's engine shed at Pant on 25 September 2003. Behind her is the cylinder block for a replica of 2-4-4 Forney tank no 10 of the Sandy River & Rangeley Lakes RR in Maine, which the railway is building as a very long-term project.

Opposite below: Dorothea quarry lay a little further down the Nantlle valley from Pen-yr-Orsedd. Its steam locos only hauled spoil trains, horses being used on its galleries. 600mm gauge 0-4-0ST *Dorothea* (Hunslet 763/1901) had become derelict by 1942 and was truly skeletal by 1970 when she moved away for restoration. Kay Bowman later took her on and has completed the work magnificently, backed up by meticulous research to ensure that the loco is now in her original condition in all respects. Kay told me that conservation was a high priority and about 90% of her original parts were reused, the main exceptions being the bottom parts of her tank which had rusted away and her chimney cap, the original of which disappeared many years ago. Kay and Nigel kindly moved her out into the sunshine for me at Launceston on 19 September 2019.

WALES • 101

Other than some early De Wintons, the only other steam loco at Dorothea was *Wendy* (Bagnall 2091/1919), one of her builder's standard 6x9ins cylinder 0-4-0STs. She arrived in 1930, second-hand from the Oakeley slate quarries at Blaenau Ffestiniog. Here she is visiting Amberley Museum on 6 July 2009. Dorothea and Pen-yr-Orsedd were both served by the 3ft 6ins gauge Nantlle Railway and had mixed-gauge track which must have looked a little like that at Amberley. They were considerate enough to provide the enginemen in their quarries with cabs, unlike the much larger concerns at Dinorwic and Penrhyn! For many years the loco was looked after by a preservation group based in Hampshire, but she has now become one of the many residents at the Statfold Barn Railway.

The 600mm gauge Ffestiniog Railway's first four locos were built as 0-4-0 side tanks with tenders and were delivered between July 1863 and March 1864. Their works numbers are not known, but some surviving old parts have the numbers 199 and 200 stamped on them. No 3 *Mountaineer*, the first to be delivered, was withdrawn as long ago as 1880. The other three were rebuilt into the 0-4-0ST+Ts familiar today, and here they stand at Porthmadog Harbour station early in the morning of 12 October 2013. On the right, no 1 *Princess* (GE, 1863) is at the head of the Ffestiniog's train of superbly restored nineteenth century 4-wheeled coaches, the oldest of which also dates back to 1863. She was the last loco to run on the old railway before it closed in 1946 but has never been used since. To the left is no 4 *Palmerston* (GE, 1864) and between them no 2 *Prince* (GE, 1863) which, with *Princess*, had recently been repainted in what is believed to be their 1890s livery. 0-4-4-0 Double Fairlie no 10 *Merddin Emrys* (BL 1/1879) makes a cameo appearance on the far left.

0-4-4 Single Fairlie no 9 *Taliesin* (VF 791/1876) was the only one of her type on the Ffestiniog. She was a popular and much-used loco and had become completely worn out by the early 1920s. Sadly she was scrapped but now there is a reincarnation, BL 5/1999. She is somewhat larger than the original, and in particular her dome is higher to comply with modern boiler regulations, but she retains much of the original loco's appeal, and also relives her reputation as a fast, free-steaming machine. On 4 November 2019, she crosses one of the railway's typical slate embankments between Minffordd and Penrhyn. The two first three coaches were built by Brown Marshalls in Birmingham, the four-wheelers in 1863-4 and the bogie one in 1876. The fourth is one of two built by the Gloucester Railway Carriage and Wagon Co in 1879. The brake van, with its unusually-shaped curvy roof, is a replica of an original which came from Brown Marshalls in 1873.

A glimpse of the modern Ffestiniog and the superb scenery through which it runs, seen from below the footpath over the hill from Portmeirion. 0-4-4-0 Double Fairlie no 12 *David Lloyd George* (BL 4/1992) has crossed the Cob and runs around the curve past Boston Lodge works on 12 April 2007. The works was set up in 1842 and its historic buildings are off to the right. They occupy the site of a quarry from which stone used in the construction of the Cob between 1807 and 1811 was taken, and the earliest buildings, a row of prominent white-painted cottages next to the running line, date from then. They were originally used to house the workers building it. The Cob's main purpose has always been to reclaim land from what had been the estuary of the Afon Glaslyn. The locos partially on view in the foreground include *Taliesin* and *Merddin Emrys*. Out at the entrance to the yard, the Ffestiniog's Simplex 4w i/c loco (MR 507/1917) is shunting one of the 4-wheeled carriages. She was one of many which WDLR bought for service just behind the front line where the smoke from steam locos would have been a give-away to the enemy. She is believed to have been their no LR2228 and was acquired by the Ffestiniog in 1923.

It's dusk on 5 November 2019 and high tide at the Cob as *Merddin Emrys* crosses with a long freight train. Near the front are two historic bolster wagons once used for carrying rails. Further back are numerous slate wagons. *Merddin Emrys* was the first of no fewer than five Fairlie locos to have been constructed at Boston Lodge, and a sixth is currently under way.

2-6-2T *Russell* (Hunslet 901/1906) is the only survivor of the old Welsh Highland Railway's locos, and many of us have waited all our lives to see her run again on her old line. Here she crosses the Afon Glaslyn at Pont Croesor on 21 June 2019, her first day of working public trains to Beddgelert – a real midsummer delight! The leading coach is a most interesting vehicle; it has a glazed central section and open compartments at each end – suitable for all Wales's changeable weather! It was built in 1891 by Metropolitan for the North Wales Narrow Gauge Railways, which operated the central section of today's WHR, and is known as the Gladstone car after the Liberal prime minister who once travelled in it. The coach's body was rescued in 1988 from a garden in Llanbedr. The green coach is an original 1893 Ashbury one which survived, complete with its original bogies, in a field at Waunfawr. It was cut down in height in 1923 to fit the Ffestiniog's loading gauge, as was *Russell* eighteen months later, and in 1931 became the UK's first narrow gauge licensed buffet car. The dark red coach is a replica of a NWNGR Ashbury vehicle, the original of which was built in 1893. There is also a little bit of the GWR here as the 4-wheeled brake van, no 136, is one of three it built for the Vale of Rheidol in 1938. Happily, its early British Railways' red colour matches that of two of the WHR coaches.

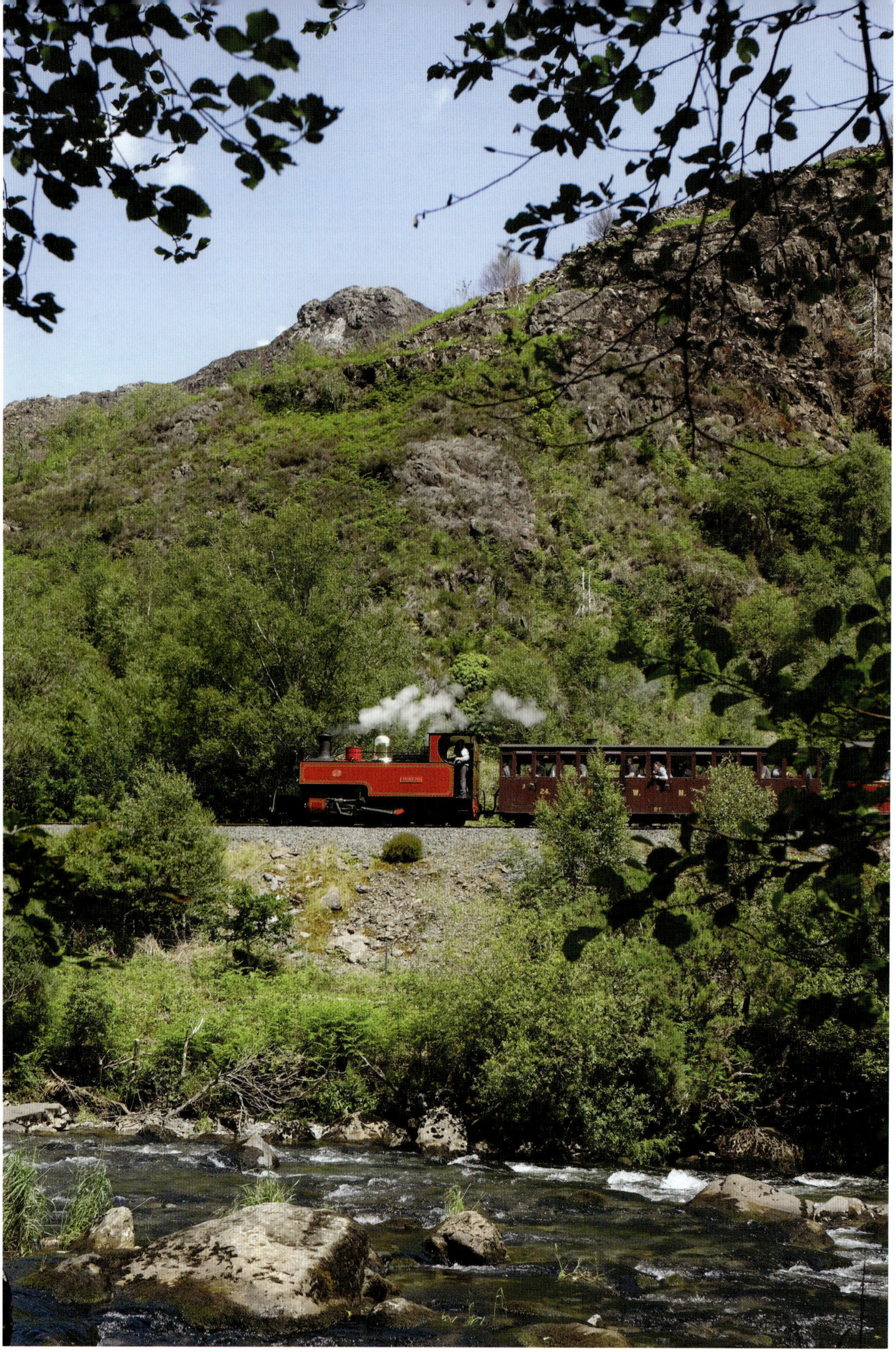

Above: This view of Cnicht to the left and the Moelwyn mountains on the right is one of the classic sights on the southern part of the Welsh Highland Railway. The Ffestiniog's England 0-4-0ST+Ts were occasional visitors to the old line in the 1920's and 1930's as it was chronically short of serviceable locos. On 22 June 2019 *Prince* passes Ty-newydd Morfa on her way south from Croesor Junction, where the 1922-built line from Aberglaslyn joined the old horse-worked Croesor Tramway, whose route the WHR followed to Porthmadog. The tramway opened in 1864 to transport slate from quarries up in the hills between Cnicht and the Moelwyns. There were several cable inclines. After the standard gauge Cambrian Railways reached Porthmadog in 1867 they shared an interchange with the tramway at what became known as Beddgelert Siding, nowadays the home of the Welsh Highland Heritage Railway. After 1922 the tramway north of the junction continued much as before. It outlived the old WHR and a part remained in occasional use until 1959. The sharp-eyed may notice *Russell* attached to the back of this train.

Opposite: *Russell* runs through the Aberglaslyn Pass on 22 June 2019. The old WHR closed in 1937, and its reconstruction more than sixty years later must be one of the greatest achievements in UK railway preservation. The leading coach, built by the Ffestiniog in 2002, is a replica of another Ashbury vehicle, the original having been supplied to the NWNGR in 1894. *Russell* worked the last train on the old WHR and was then stored until being requisitioned by the government in 1942. She spent the rest of the Second World War at an ironstone quarry near Hook Norton in Oxfordshire, and in 1948 found a new home at Fayle's Tramway, which served claypits in Dorset. She entered preservation in 1954, and a few years ago was magnificently restored to her original condition.

Above: *Russell* was built as plans were progressing for what eventually became the WHR and, until it was completed in 1923, she worked on the NWNGR. Autumn colours abound as she runs through the woods near Nantmor on 3 November 2019. She has carried the air pump on her front ever since she was built. The NWNGR's adoption of airbrakes by the early 1890s was most advanced for its time. They were also used on the WHR, something which distinguished it from the Ffestiniog which still uses the older and less efficient vacuum braking system.

Opposite above: Ex-WDLR 4-6-0T no 590 (Baldwin 45172/1917) arrived on the WHR in 1923 and worked until the 1937 closure. She was scrapped in the 1940s but here no 607 (Baldwin 45190/1917) takes her place as she leaves the long tunnel from Nantmor and enters the Aberglaslyn Pass on 3 November 2019.

Opposite below: The vast area of reclaimed land formed by the construction of the Cob at Porthmadog reaches as far inland as Aberglaslyn. The last rays of sunshine lit up *Russell* on 3 November 2019 as she headed across the flat land towards Croesor Junction. The entire train is a credit to the Welsh Highland Heritage Railway, only a small voluntary group, which has restored it over many years.

WALES • 111

Sherpa (Milner 106/1978) is a half-scale model of a Darjeeling B class 0-4-0ST and runs on the 12¼ inch gauge Fairbourne Railway. Designed by Neil Simkins, she was built for the Réseau Guerlédan in Brittany, and moved to Fairbourne in 1985. The view of the Mawddach estuary from Penrhyn Point must be one of Wales's finest sights, with the long wooden Barmouth Bridge which carries the standard gauge Cambrian coast railway in the foreground and Cadair Idris as a backdrop. For once no-one is paying any attention to *Sherpa* as British Railways 2-6-0 no 76079 (Horwich, 1957) runs onto the bridge with a steam special on 21 August 2005. Sadly, a new signalling system now prevents mainline steam operation there. Other interesting half-scale model locos at Fairbourne include 0-6-4ST *Beddgelert*, the original of which was built (and probably also designed) by Hunslet in 1878 for the NWNGR and withdrawn when *Russell* arrived in 1906.

The 2ft 3ins gauge Talyllyn Railway was owned by Sir Henry Haydn Jones for many years from 1911. When he died in 1950, closure looked inevitable, but his widow very kindly entrusted it to an enthusiast group. It was the first ever rescue of a railway by volunteers and paved the way for the worldwide preservation movement we know today. The line is almost unique in having all its original locos and coaches in service. On 20 March 2018 0-4-2ST *Talyllyn* (FJ 42/1864) and 0-4-0WT *Dolgoch* (FJ 63/1866) take the old coaches and some wagons up the Fathew valley east of Brynglas. The coaches were also built in the 1860s, the first three and the brake van by Brown Marshalls and the fourth by the Lancaster Carriage & Wagon Co. Dolau Gwyn, a magnificent seventeenth century manor house, can be seen to the right on the far side of the valley. Snow lies under the hedges. In 2015 both locos were restored to what's believed to be the livery they carried when they were new.

Above: *Talyllyn* runs into Brynglas station on 20 March 2018. The railway was built to serve a slate quarry at Bryn Eglwys, in the hills above Abergynolwyn, and its fortunes were inextricably linked to it. Sir Haydn, as he was always known, was the local MP. He bought the quarry, along with the railway, to preserve employment when it faced almost certain closure, and continued to run it until it suffered a devastating rockfall in 1946, fortunately at a time when no-one was working there. His wife came from a slate-mining family in Chicago and very probably introduced him to the idea of quarry ownership. Note the fencing slabs, very characteristic of the Welsh slate-mining districts.

Opposite: A silhouette view as *Talyllyn* and *Dolgoch* head up the valley above Brynglas at sunset on 19 March 2018.

WALES • 115

Above: A leafy scene on 4 July 2019 as *Dolgoch* and the railway's original coaches cross Dolgoch viaduct, the most substantial structure on the line.

Opposite above: The 2ft 3ins gauge Corris Railway's large engine shed and workshops building at Maespoeth Junction dates from the introduction of steam locos in 1878. It was always distinctive and it is fortunate that it has survived, thanks to the Forestry Commission which took it over and kept it in good shape after the railway closed in 1948. The preservation society's 0-4-2ST no 7 (Winson 17/2005), a replica of the old line's Tattoo class no 4 (KS 4047/1921), sets off for a day's work on 17 March 2019.

Opposite below: No 7 and her train of replica coaches, with their superbly elaborate livery, pass the shed on 17 March 2019. The revival at Corris by a small group of volunteers has been one of the great success stories in Welsh preservation in recent years, and they have ambitious plans for expansion. The railway served the Aberllefenni Slate Quarry which was acquired in 1935 by Sir Haydn, again to preserve local employment. It closed in 2003 after a working life of more than 500 years.

WALES • 117

Above: No 7 again on 17 March 2019. The railway skirts around Corris churchyard on this stone-walled embankment as it makes its unobtrusive entry into the village. It is a really delightful little railway.

Opposite above: The 2ft 6ins gauge Welshpool & Llanfair Light Railway served the rural community in the Banwy valley and is another line which runs unobtrusively through the woods and fields for much of its route. *The Earl* (BP 3496/1902), running in her final British Railways condition, peeps out through the trees as she climbs away from Welshpool and approaches Cwm Lane on 18 October 2016.

Opposite below: The 600mm gauge Vale of Rheidol Light Railway opened in 1902. It had been promoted in order to carry timber from the forests inland from Aberystwyth for use as pit props in the South Wales collieries and also to serve the lead mines around Devil's Bridge, but the timber traffic never really took off and the mines were in terminal decline. Instead the line became tourist-orientated almost from the start. In 1913 it was bought by the Cambrian Railways, but was starved of investment and was in a poor state by the time the GWR took over in 1922. It clearly didn't match up to their standards, as they soon built new locos, upgraded the track and began to provide better carriages. The railway's final few miles run through the spectacular Rheidol gorge. 2-6-2T no 8 (Swindon, 1923) passes Faen Grach with a mixed train on 10 November 2017. The grey cattle wagon, no 38089, was one of two built by the GWR in 1923 in the hope of attracting new traffic, but by then the few eligible passengers in the valley were travelling by road! The wagons were regauged to 2ft 6ins and sent to Welshpool in 1937. After various adventures no 38089 returned to Aberystwyth in 2015, and this was its first outing after restoration to its original condition.

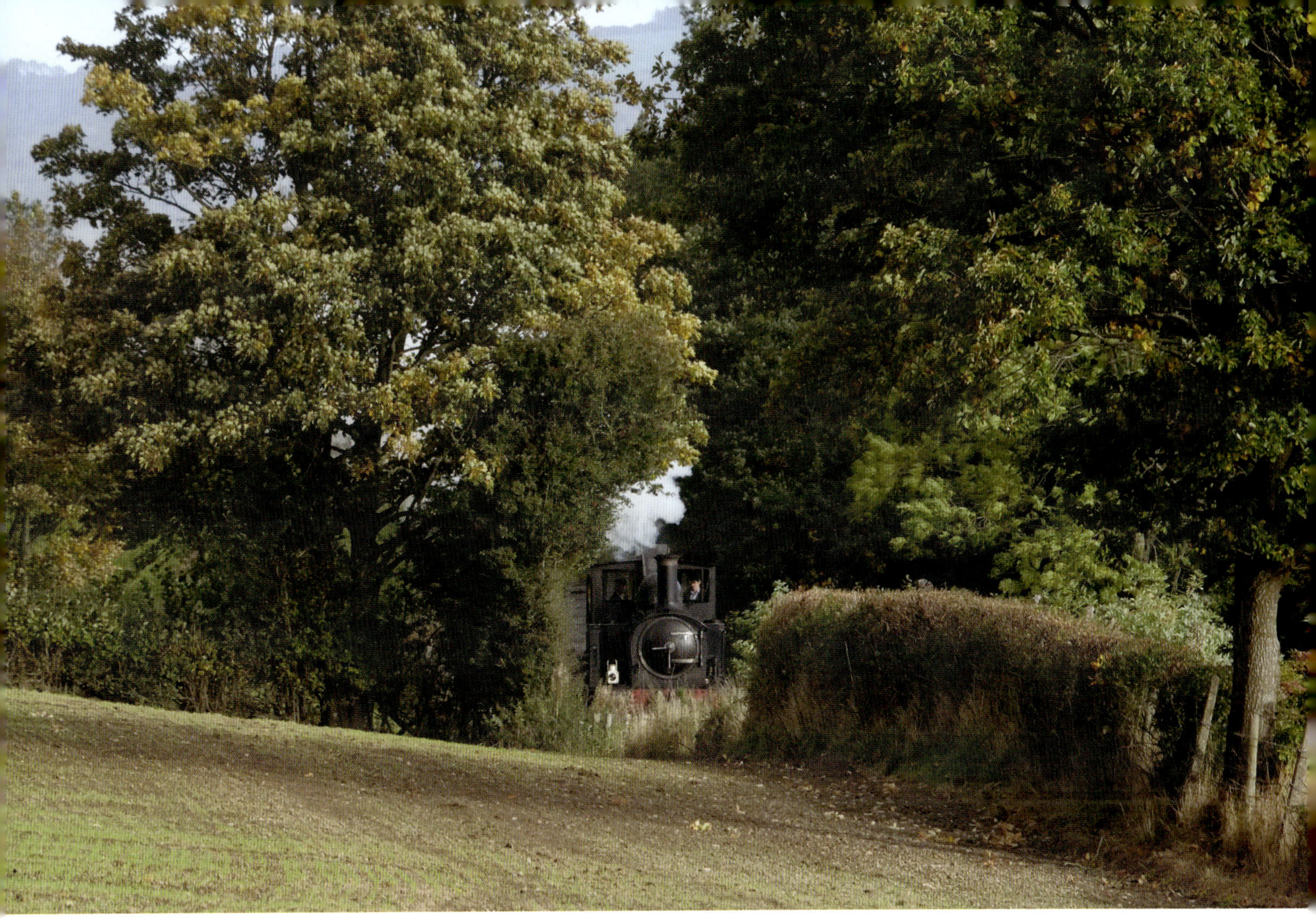

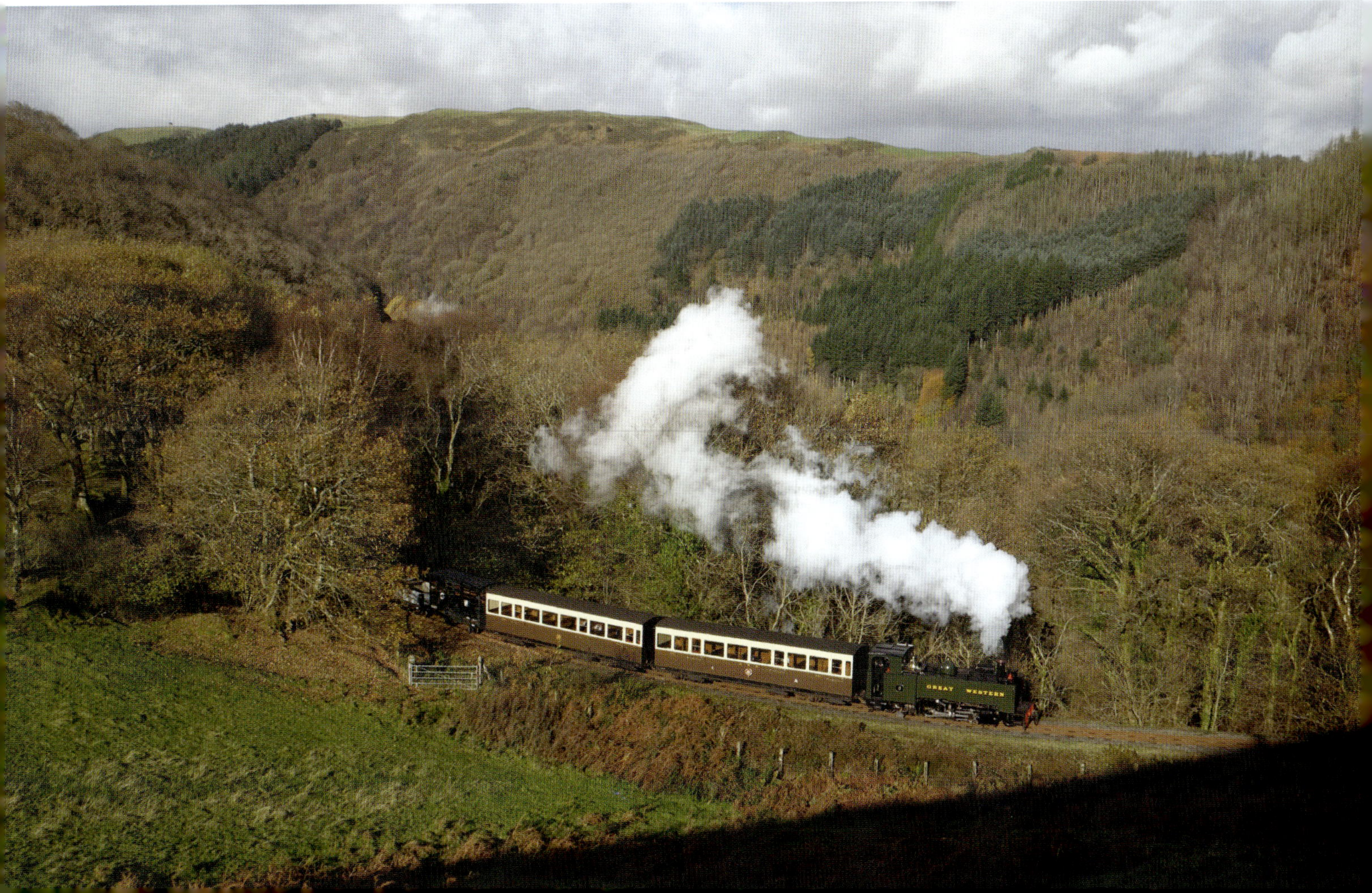
GREAT WESTERN

Above: 2-6-2T no 7 (Swindon, 1923) crosses the wooden Rheidol bridge, near the end of her journey to Aberystwyth on 17 March 2019. The leading vehicle is no 137, one of the three brake vans built by the GWR in 1938 like no 136 at the Welsh Highland. Sadly, the third one, no 135, was scrapped by British Railways in 1968. After nationalisation in 1948 they ran the line until it was sold in 1987.

Opposite above: Shortly before sunset on 17 March 2019 no 7's fire is raked out at the railway's newly-constructed servicing yard, part of a major upgrade of its facilities at Aberystwyth. She is overlooked by the National Library of Wales, and also by large numbers of starlings which are taking off to join the murmuration or starling cloud at Aberystwyth's sea front, before they roost on the girders under the pier. It is often a spectacular feature at dusk between October and March. The use of outside Walschaerts valve gear was unusual on the GWR. The cylinders and motion on these locos was based on those fitted to a series of ninety seven steam railcars built between 1903 and 1909 and they may well have incorporated standard parts which Swindon held in stock, or have come secondhand from earlier railcars which were being withdrawn when these locos were built.

Opposite below: For many years after the line's route into Aberystwyth was altered in 1968, the locos and coaches were housed in the old mainline engine shed built by the GWR in 1938. It is nearly dark as no 8 blows down at its northern entrance on 10 November 2017. The yellow-painted shearlegs replaced the old standard gauge ones which were outside the shed, close to where no 8 is standing.

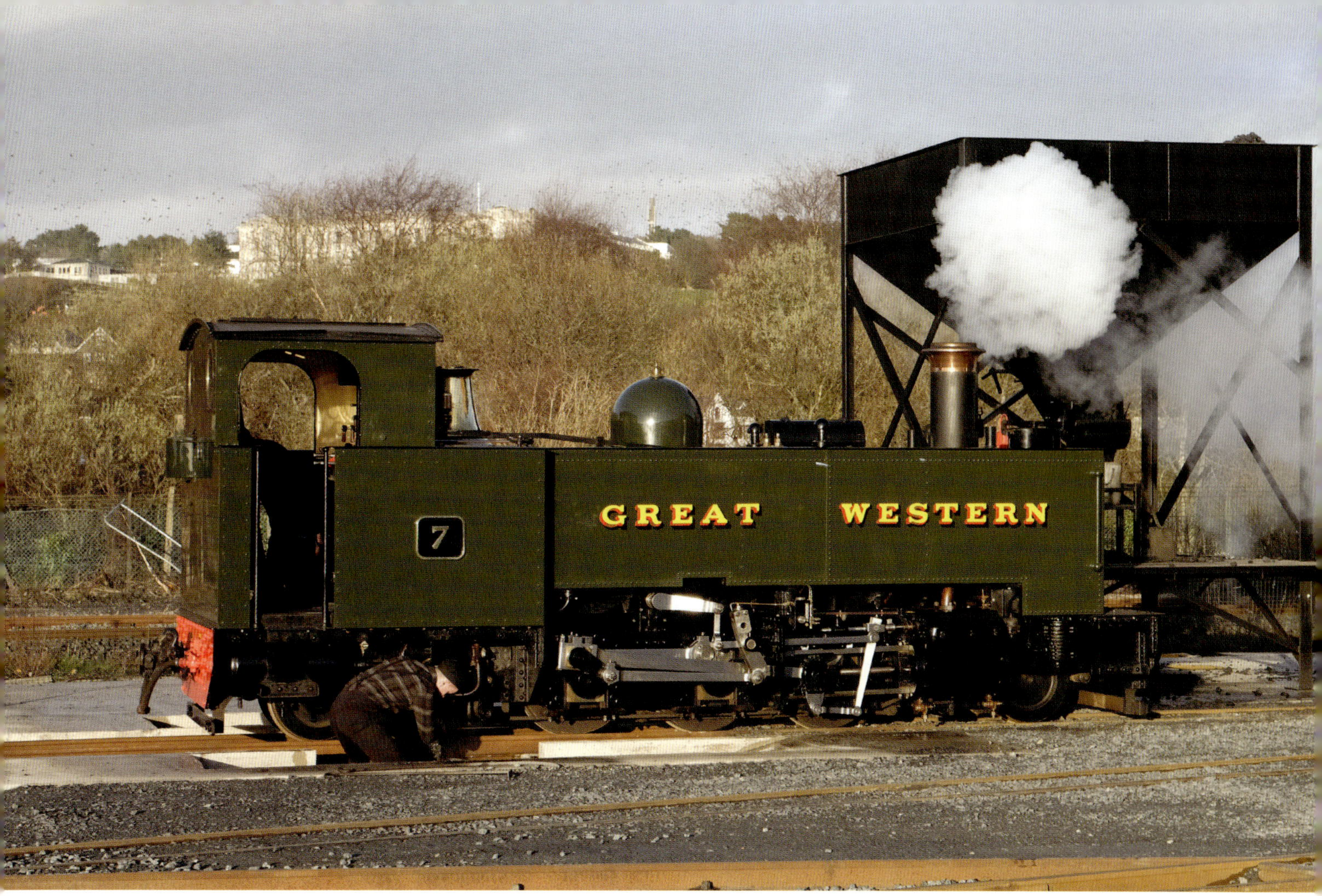
7
GREAT WESTERN

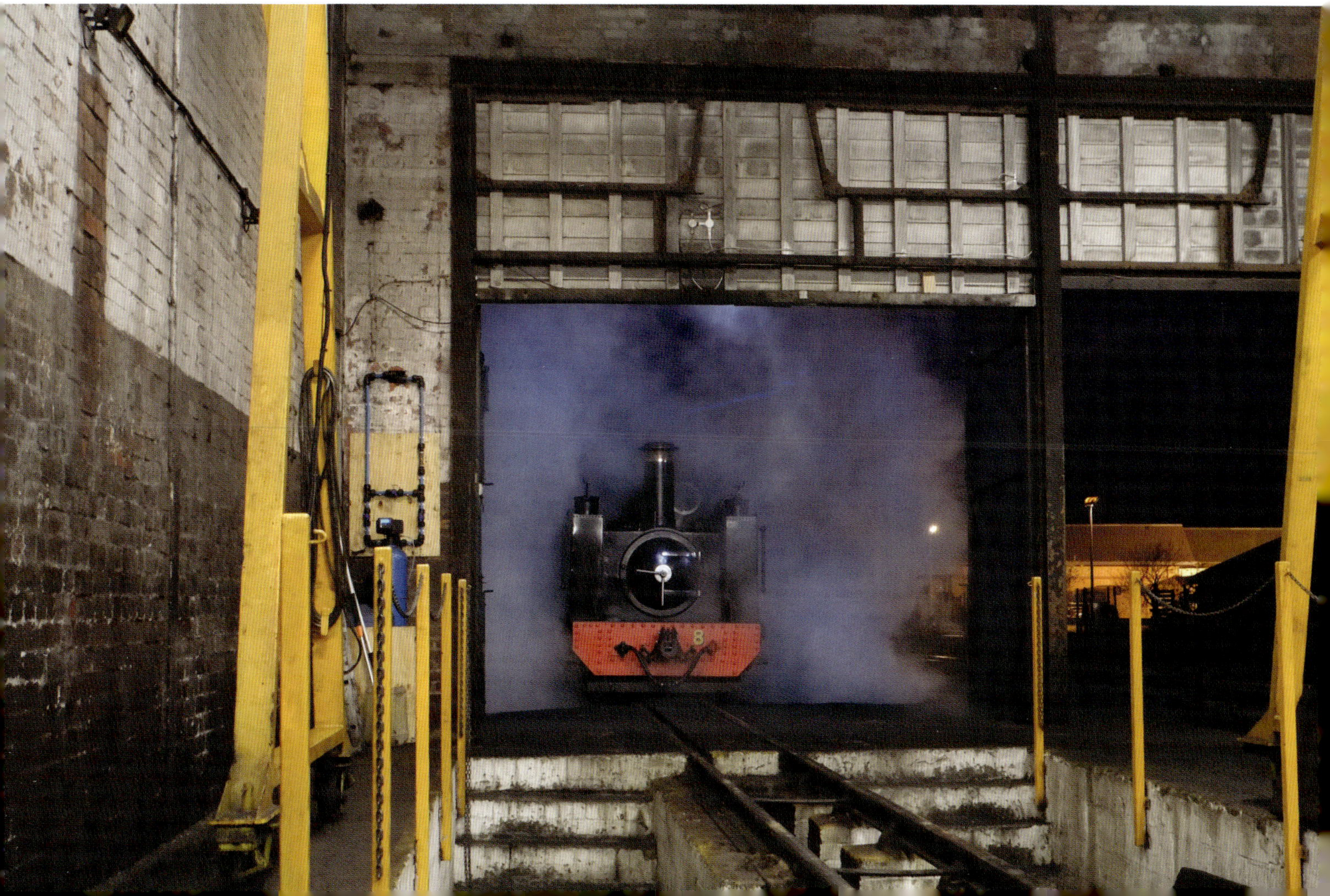
8

In its standard gauge days, the shed was well known throughout the old GWR system for the immaculate condition of its residents, especially the Manor class 4-6-0s which worked the Cambrian Coast Express on the first stage of its journey to Paddington, and also many local trains to Machynlleth and Carmarthen. The new occupants are just as shiny! For accounting purposes 2-6-2T no 1213 (Swindon, 1924) was treated as a renewal of an original VoR loco and carries her number, but in reality she was newly-built and is identical to nos 7 and 8. Under BR she became no 9. All the line's closed coaches, like the ones on the left of this photo, were built in 1938; they matched the GWR's contemporary mainline ones and were far superior to their predecessors. There are two open coaches on the right. Four of these were built in 1923 and three more in 1938. The railway has recently built a new engine shed and workshops as part of its upgrading work and, as I write this, construction of a large new carriage shed is under way. The charity which has owned the railway since 1996 has amassed a collection of historic locos from all over the world, most of which have never been on public view, and the plan is to use the old GWR shed to display them. 10 November 2017.

ENGLAND

The revival of a short section of the 600mm gauge Lynton & Barnstaple Railway in North Devon is another of preservation's great successes in recent years. Hardly any of its coaches survived the closure of the old line in 1935 and none of its locos, with the possible exception of one which was exported to Brazil and has never been heard of again. Nearly everything has had to be built from scratch. The Ffestiniog's Boston Lodge works built new coach underframes, but the bodies include a few original parts. On 29 September 2018 2-6-2T *Lyd* (BL 6/2010) and 2-4-2T *Lyn* (AK 92/2017), both replicas, haul a train up the hill to Woody Bay from Killington Lane, not far from Parracombe. In the old days, the magnificent view down the Heddon Valley towards the Bristol Channel and the Welsh coast opened up as trains bound for Lynton passed Killington Lane. It must have been a highlight for passengers but lasted for less than one mile before disappearing behind hills as the train approached Woody Bay. How fortunate it is that this was the first part to be rebuilt. The sheep at the head of that line clearly possesses outstanding leadership skills!

ENGLAND • 123

Above: Two ladies out walking their dogs greet *Lyn* and *Lyd* near Killington Lane on the sunny evening of 29 September 2018. *Lyd* is a copy of *Lew* (MW 2042/1925), the loco which went to Brazil. Her construction was begun by James Armstrong-Evans, an early supporter of the line's reconstruction, but was more than he could achieve unaided and the Ffestiniog completed the work. She is now a frequent visitor to Woody Bay. The original *Lyn* (Baldwin 15965/1898) was scrapped a few weeks after the closure. This superb replica, the result of a crowdfunding venture, first ran in 2017.

Opposite above: Cloud is starting to blow in off the Bristol Channel a little later that evening as *Lyn* and *Lyd* set off from Killington Lane with the last train of the day. The railway has well-developed plans to extend past Parracombe as far as Blackmoor Gate. The wreath on the smokebox of *Lyn* is a copy of one left on the buffer stop at Barnstaple Town station by a well-wisher from Woody Bay on the day after the closure. Its message read, 'To Barnstaple & Lynton Railway, with regret and sorrow from a constant user and admirer. Perchance it is not dead but sleepeth.' How good it is that this section isn't sleeping any longer!

Opposite below: Killington Lane was also home to Devon County Council's Beacon Hill roadstone quarry which had its own 600mm gauge railway. When the council began to build the Parracombe by-pass in 1925 they laid a temporary line which crossed the Lynton & Barnstaple, though there doesn't seem to have been any junction. To work it they bought at least four second-hand Wren class 0-4-0STs, amongst twenty-seven which had been used on the construction of the A127 Romford–Southend-on-Sea road until it opened in 1924. *Peter Pan* (KS 4256/1922) followed them to Devon from the Southend scheme in 1929, though she didn't reach Beacon Hill until about 1950. She was rescued for preservation in 1959 by the late Max Sinclair, to whom we are indebted for saving several little locos. Here she hauls a typical rural contractors' train at the 600mm gauge Amerton Railway in Staffordshire on 13 June 2004.

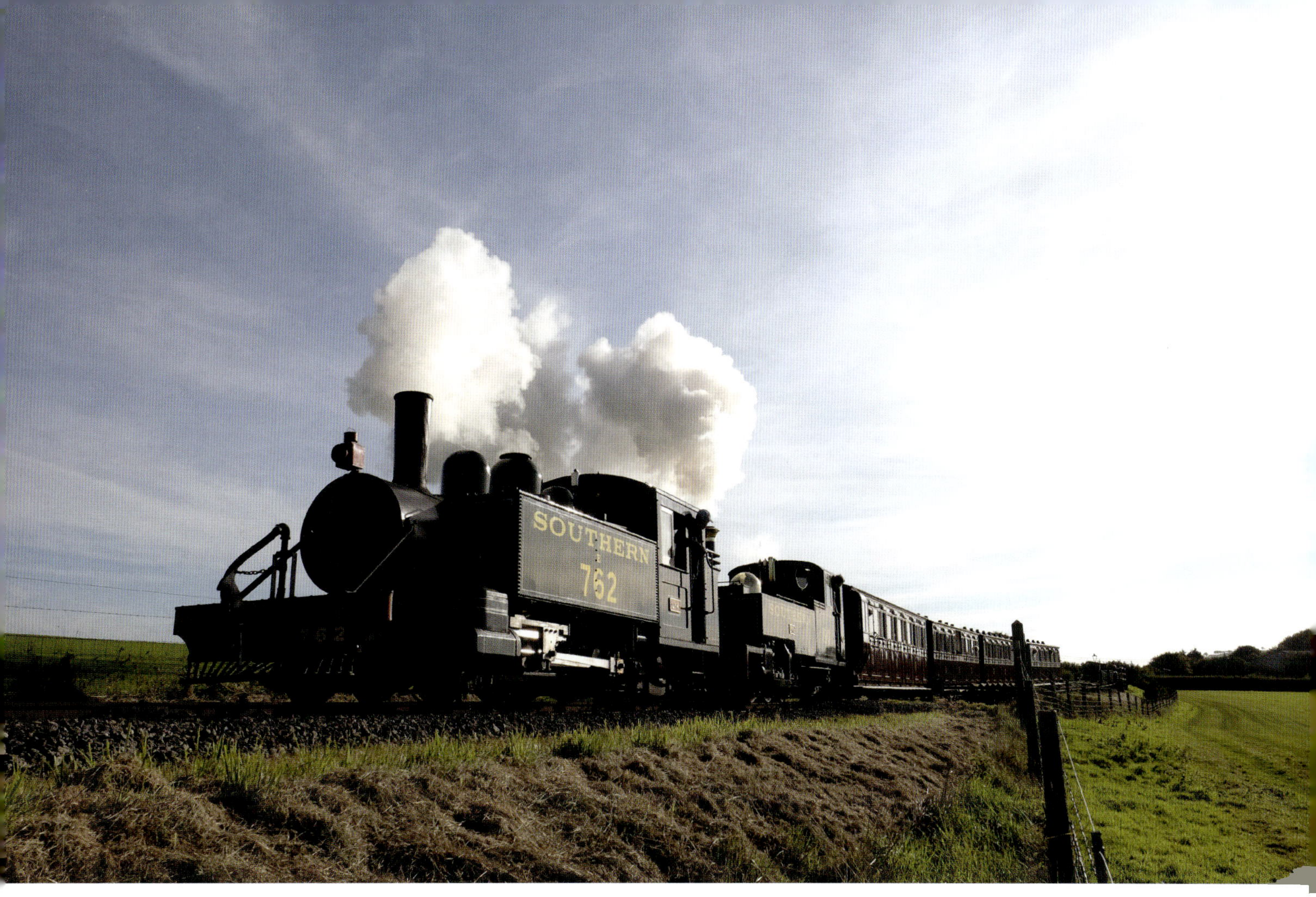
SOUTHERN
762

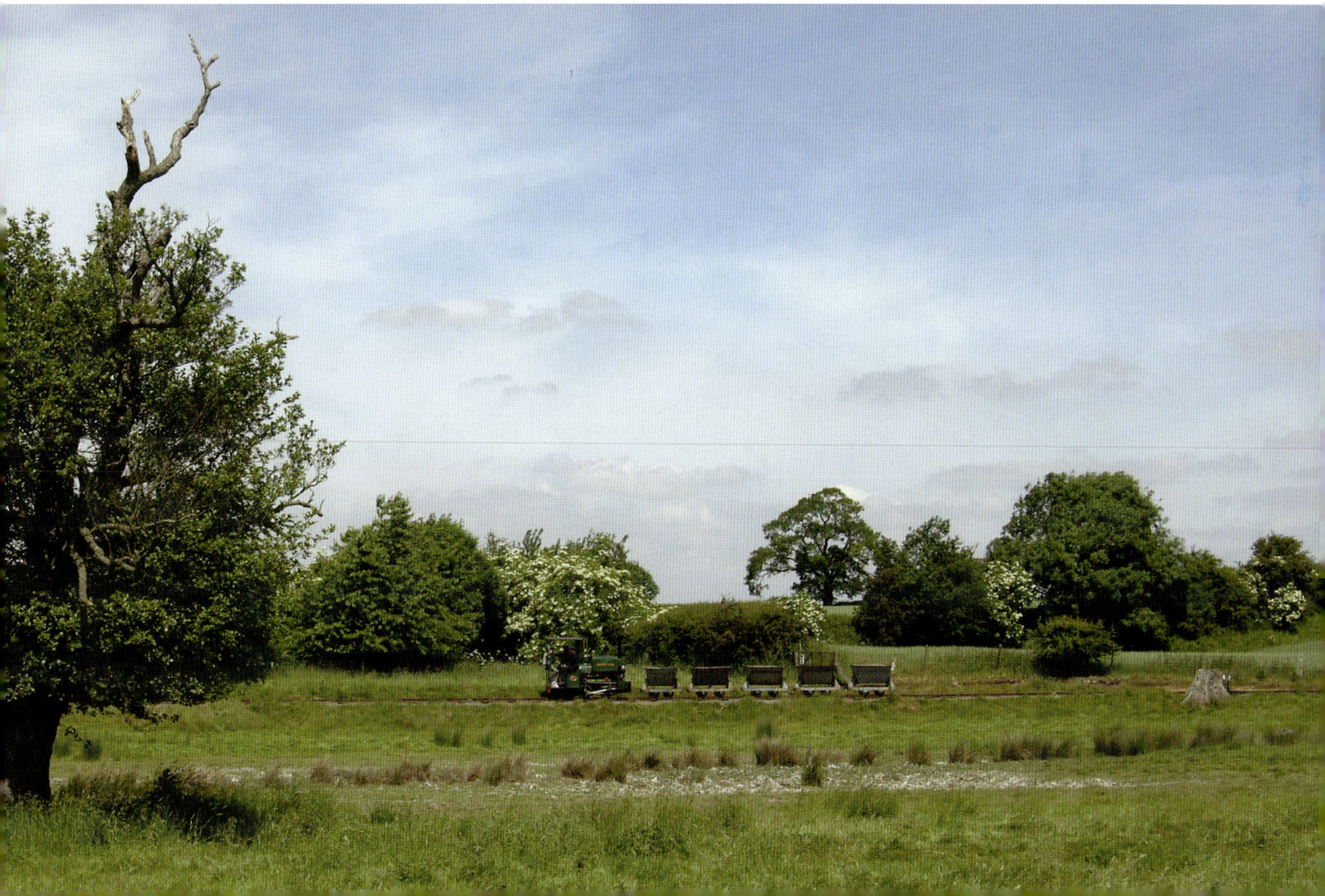

0-4-0T *Samson* (SL, 1874) was possibly the first of her builder's idiosyncratic locos. She spent her working life on a tramway serving the Cornish Hush mine in Weardale until she was scrapped in about 1904. This 600mm gauge replica (DY 2/2016) normally lives at Beamish museum in County Durham, but on 6 September 2019 was visiting the Richmond Light Railway in Kent. She looks very much at home as she raises steam in their woodyard. She has a single cylinder and geared drive and her flywheel seemed to need a degree of coaxing whenever she set off. A delightful loco!

PORTUGAL

Another really heartening event in 2019 was the return of occasional steam operation on the metre gauge in Portugal after an absence of many years. It is about 4.00am on the damp morning of 14 December 2019, the first day of public services. 2-4-6-0 Mallet tank no E214 (Henschel 19877/1923) of CP, the state railway, raises steam in the loco yard at Sernada do Vouga, and shows off her swivelling front engine unit on a sharply curved siding. The diesel standing alongside the station building, CP no 9004, was built by Alsthom in 1964 as the FC del Tajuña's no 1025 (see page 137), and moved to Portugal in 1974.

Above: Just after sunrise on the frosty morning of 4 January 2020, no E214 makes a steamy departure up the steep hill out of Aveiro station with her train of period carriages which were all built between 1913 and 1925. Most of Portugal's metre gauge railways ran to the north of the Douro valley. Many of us enjoyed their spectacular scenery but now they have all been closed and two sections of the old EF Vale do Vouga, fondly called *Vouguinha* locally, are the only ones still in use. They may lack the rugged grandeur of the Douro lines, but their gentler scenery is still very attractive.

Opposite above: This is the only time I have been able to stand at one end of a tunnel and photograph a train entering the other! No E214 sets off from Eirol station on 15 December 2019. The Vale do Vouga was built by a French company and its stations would not look at all out of place on France's metre gauge railways. Its first section was opened by the King of Portugal in 1908. The Aveiro line followed in 1911, but the King could not officiate as he had been deposed the previous year and soon afterwards settled in Twickenham.

Opposite below: Turning up unannounced outside a Portuguese army base clutching a camera had an obvious downside, but I needn't have worried! I was welcomed into the Tancos base and soon introduced to the curator of a museum devoted to its old 500mm gauge training railway. Weighing five tonnes *Tancos* (Decauville 103/1889), the only survivor amongst its locos, was a beefed-up version of her builder's early lightweight 0-4-0Ts. During Portugal's 1974 revolution troops from Tancos were ordered to go to Lisbon and fire on demonstrators but they joined them instead, thus ensuring the overthrow of the country's fascist dictatorship. 13 January 2009.

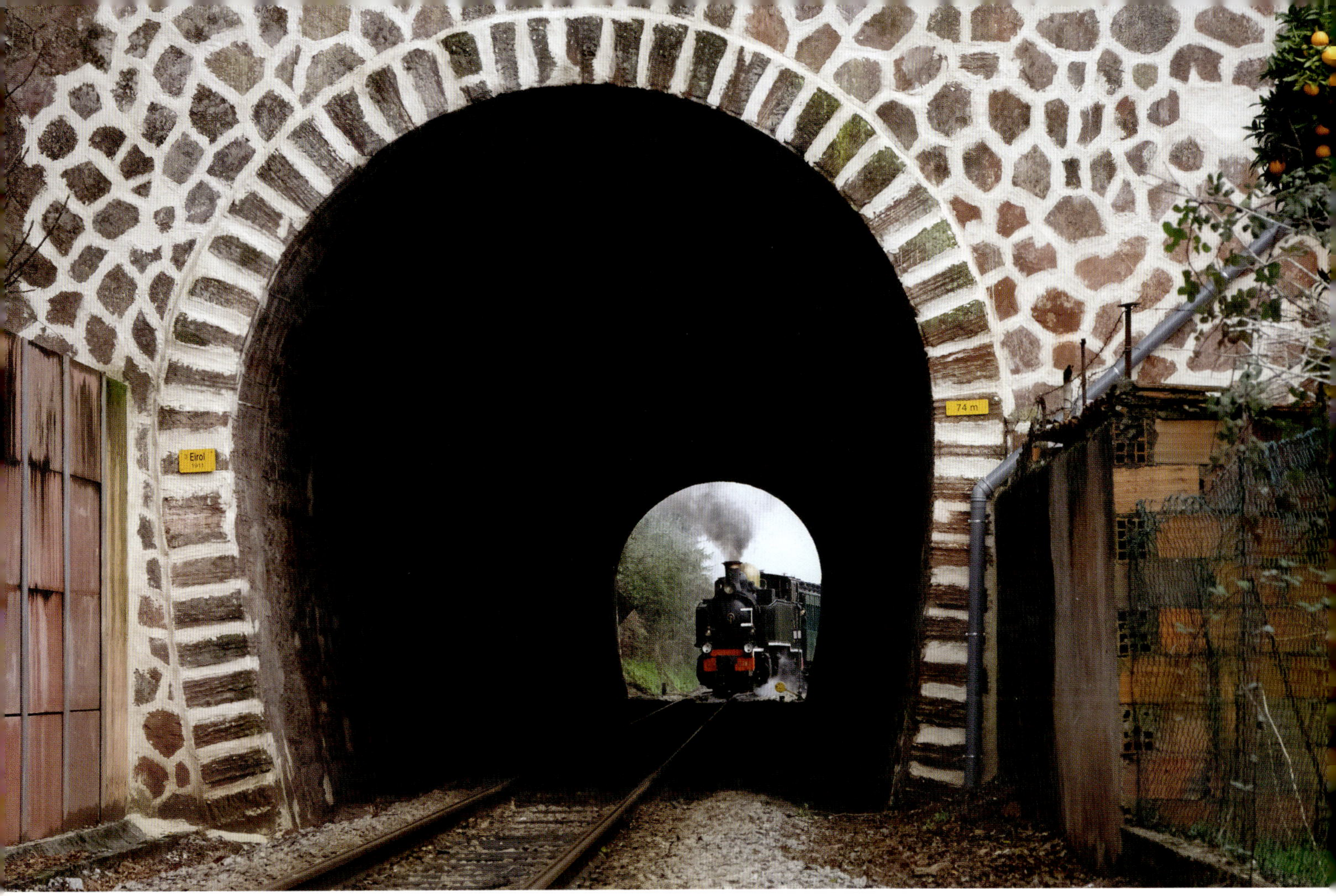

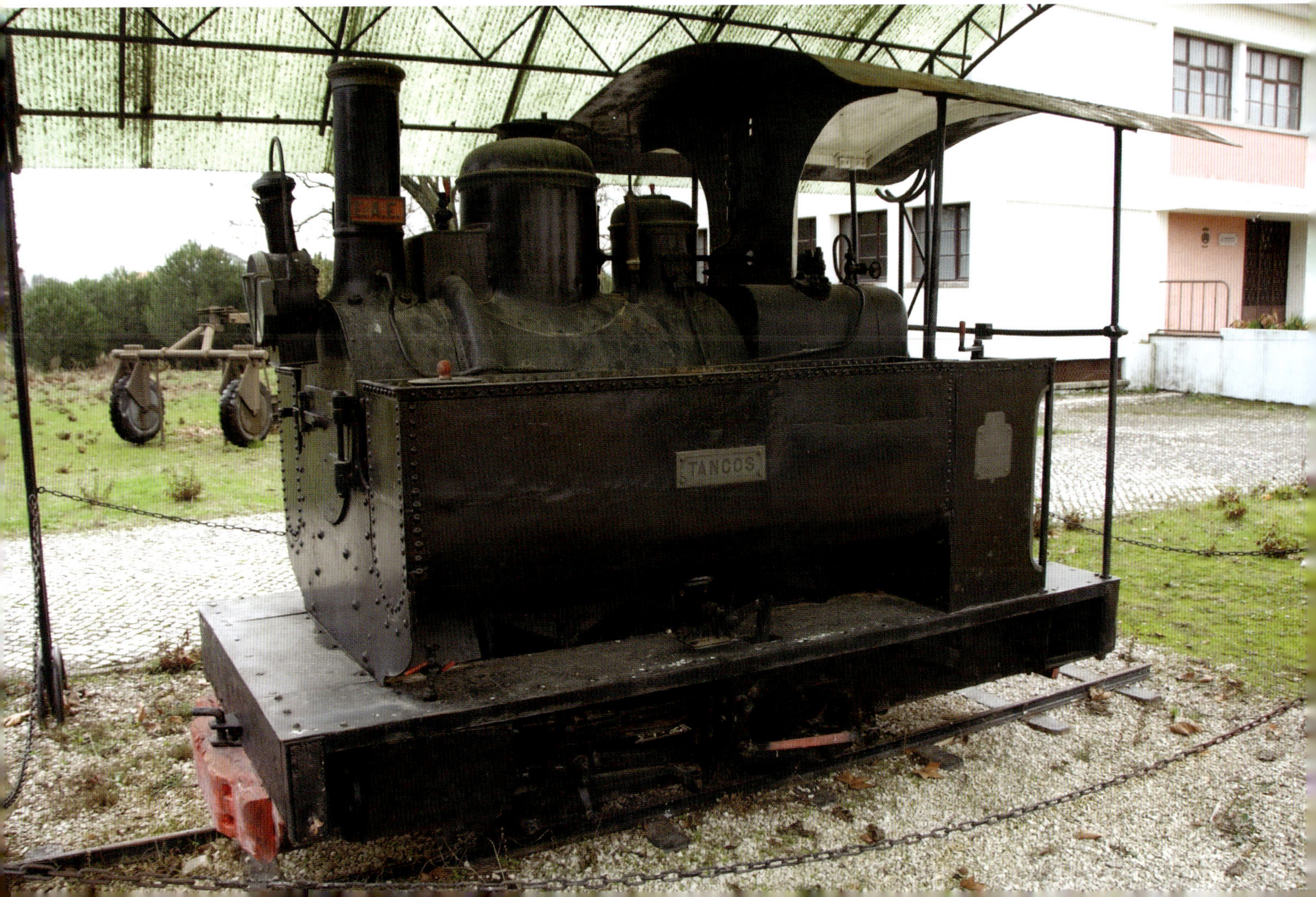

A Leap Day treat! Madeira's metre gauge Riggenbach-rack CF do Monte opened in 1893 and ran from Pombal station in Funchal up to Monte, a genteel village rather like the Indian hill stations, where wealthy residents could escape the heat of the island's capital. In 1912, it was extended further up the hill to Terreiro da Luta, nearly 4km from Pombal. It closed in 1943 but its memory lives on, not least in this splendid azulejo or blue tile painting, very typical of Portugal, which graces the wall of the Café Ritz in central Funchal. In the foreground a toboggan makes its way down the hill from Monte. In 1954, Ernest Hemingway described a ride on one of these as amongst the most exhilarating experiences of his life. They are still a major tourist attraction, but nowadays the slippery cobbled roads have been tarred over and progress is much more sedate! The CFM was worked by four Esslingen 0-4-0RT's built between 1893 and 1912, and in 1925 it bought the last of the eleven Abt-Brown type III 0-4-2RTs built by SLM. The trackbed is intact and there are occasional proposals to rebuild the railway. 29 February 2020.

SPAIN

A railway version of the three wise monkeys! Nos 4 (Couillet 544/1881), 6 (Couillet 545/1881) and 5 (Couillet 479/1880) are three of six tiny 550mm gauge machines which worked at Barruelo colliery in Palencia. It was owned by the Norte railway company and later by Renfe, its nationalised successor. The colliery provided coal for many of Spain's mainline locos; the decline of steam sounded its death knell and it closed in 1972. Today much of the site forms a most informative museum of the old mining days. The locos must have been by far Renfe's smallest machines! These three are amongst the twenty-one beautiful narrow gauge steam locos from all over Spain collected by the late Sr López at Industrias López Soriano, a metal recycling business in Zaragoza, where I saw them on 9 September 2011. The firm is now run by his son who does not share his father's passion for the locos, though he respects their historical value. A similar Barruelo loco forms the only narrow gauge steam exhibit at the Museo del Ferrocarril in Madrid.

Many of the early steam locos on the metre gauge system in Spain's Basque country were British-built. Here are three at Trenbidearen Euskal Museoa, the region's fine railway museum. 0-4-0ST *Espinal* (RS 2631/1887) came from the FC Orconera, a mineral line west of Bilbao. Behind her is FFCC Vascongados no 104 *Aurrera* (NW 551/1898). She started out life working for the FC de Elgoibar a San Sebastián, which later merged with other lines to form the FFCC Vascongados. At the rear is FC de Amorebieta a Guernica y Pedernales 0-6-0T no 1 *Zugastieta* (SS 3435/1888). They stand at the southern end of Azpeitia station, next to the town's steelworks, on 13 October 2018.

The museum operates about 5km of the old metre gauge FC del Urola, which ran through hilly country of great beauty. It was one of Spain's first electrified railways when it opened in 1926, and its last train ran sixty years later. The wires have gone, though the electrical control equipment at Azpeitia now forms an important part of the museum display. Much of the old line's route is now a *Vía Verde*, a long-distance footpath increasingly popular with the region's many tourists. The Urola's buildings were designed to replicate features of the region's distinctive architecture. The northern end of Azpeitia station presents a delightfully rural appearance, in contrast to the steelworks to the south. Here *Aurrera* arrives with a well-laden train on 12 October 2018. The Vascongados operated the regional mainline between Bilbao and San Sebastián which was electrified in the late 1920s, and *Aurrera* was one of the few steam locos which they kept on. She shunted at their Durango works for many years. The two leading coaches came from the Urola, and were probably built for its opening.

Above: On 13 October 2018 *Zugastieta* heads towards Lasao, the northern terminus of the museum railway. Her old line formed a branch off the Vascongados, and she worked there for her entire life until being withdrawn in 1960. Its principal station and engine shed were at Guernica, but fortunately she was elsewhere when the notorious bombing raid on the town brought death and destruction on an unprecedented scale during the Spanish Civil War.

Opposite above: Four of these 0-6-0Ts were the first locos supplied to the FC Vasco-Asturiana, a compact metre gauge system around Oviedo. No 21 *Nalon* (Hunslet 783/1902) has survived thanks to being sold in about 1961 for industrial service at Figaredo in the Asturias coalfield. She is now one of many locos preserved at the Museo del Ferrocarril de Asturias at Gijón, another fine museum. 7 July 2012.

Opposite below: The greatly loved 750mm gauge FC de San Feliu de Guíxols a Gerona opened in 1892 and was one of Spain's most delightful narrow gauge railways. Its closure on 10 April 1969 caused much sadness, somewhat lightened later that year by the rescue of this train, including 0-6-2T no 6 (KM 5267/1905), which Sr Josep Maria Bregante Ventura and his wife kindly showed me on 8 September 2011 at their home near the old line at Cassa de la Selva. It was bought by Sr Bregante's father, and they've looked after it since he moved away to México City. The loco carries the lined green paint scheme introduced by the SFG in the 1950's. Six of these 0-6-2Ts were built for the railway from 1890. While smaller, it's easy to see the resemblance they bear to the three 0-6-2Ts which Krauss built the previous year for the Steyrtalbahn, Austria's first 760mm gauge railway (see page 165).

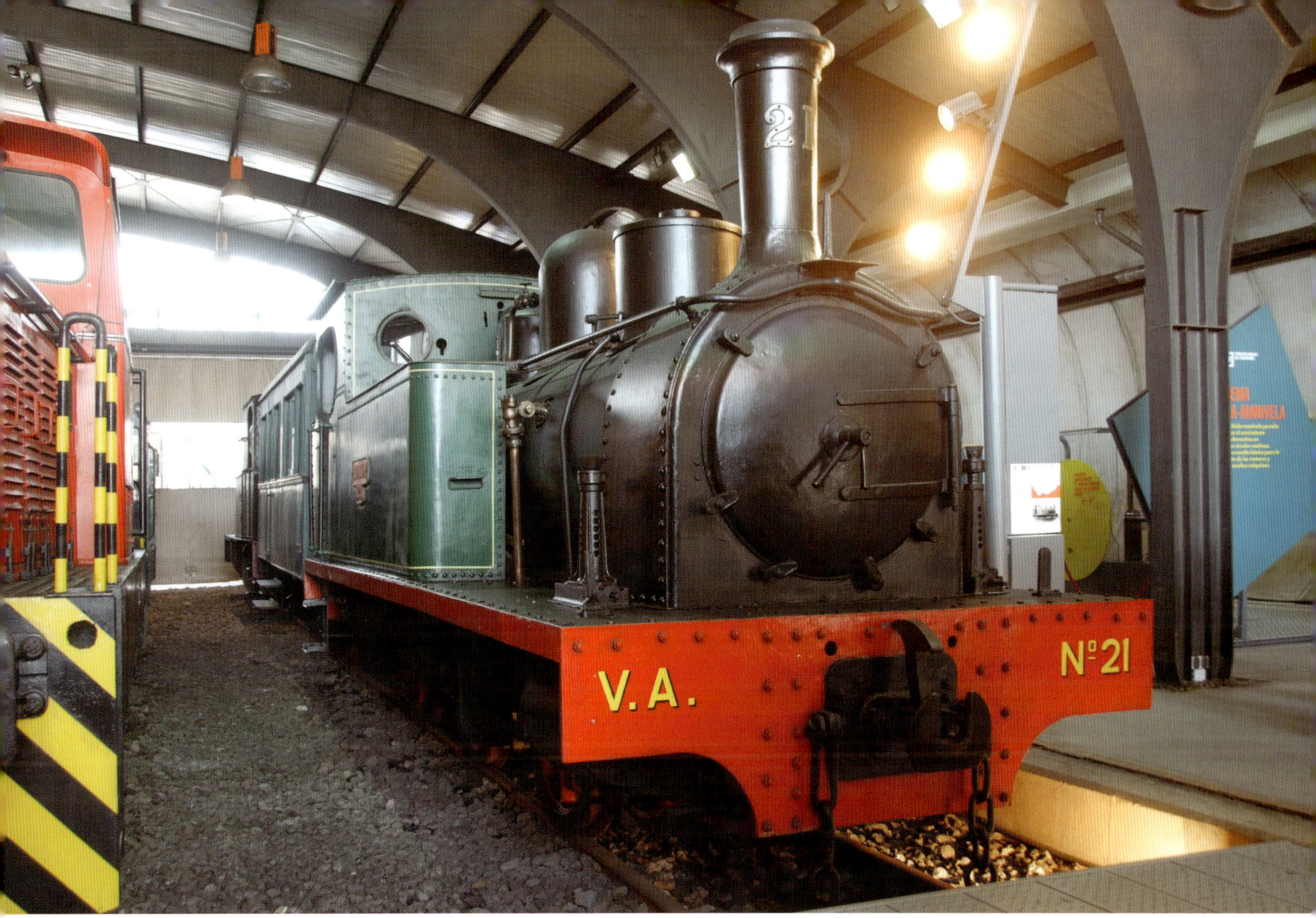
V.A.
Nº21

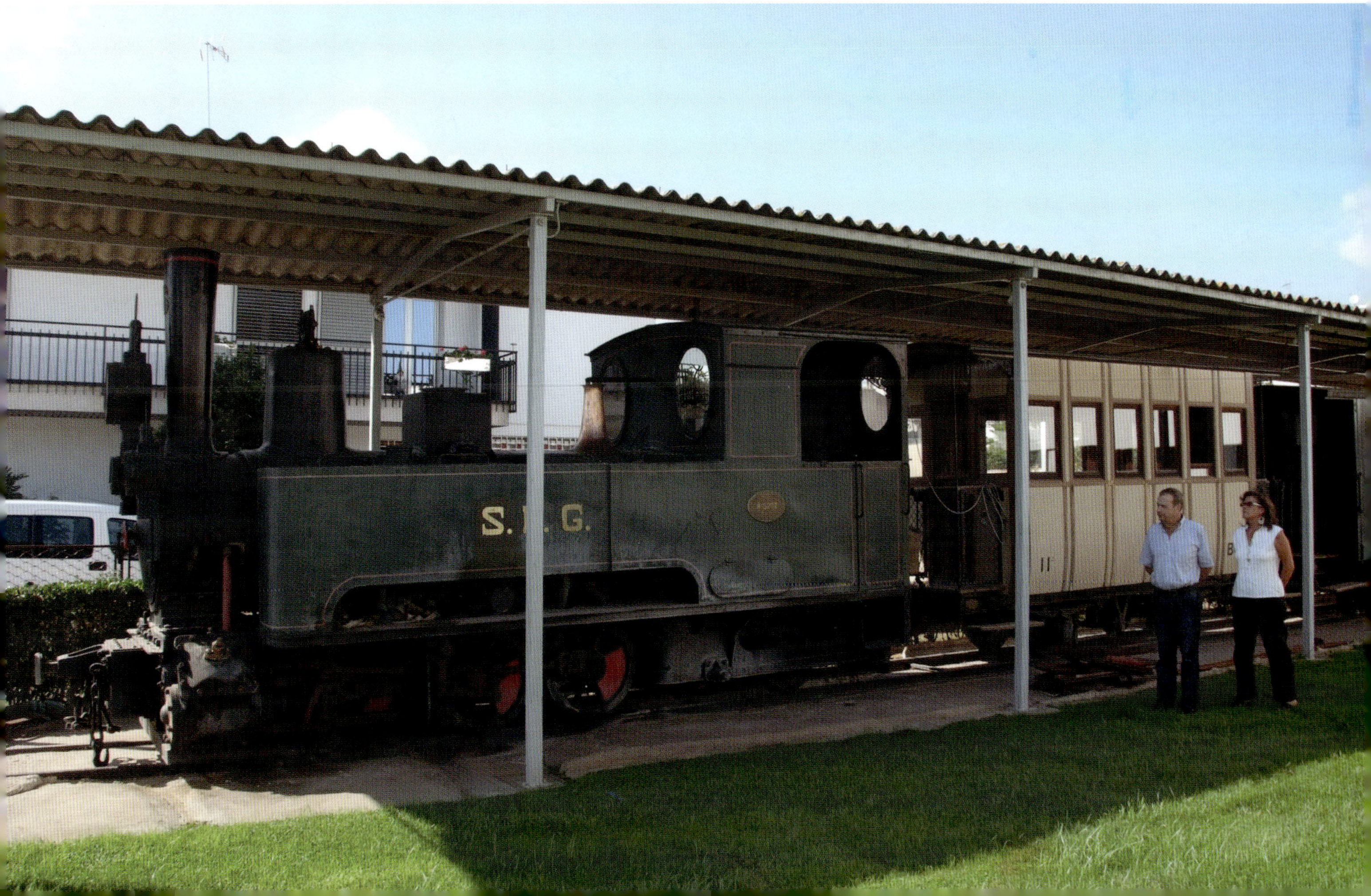

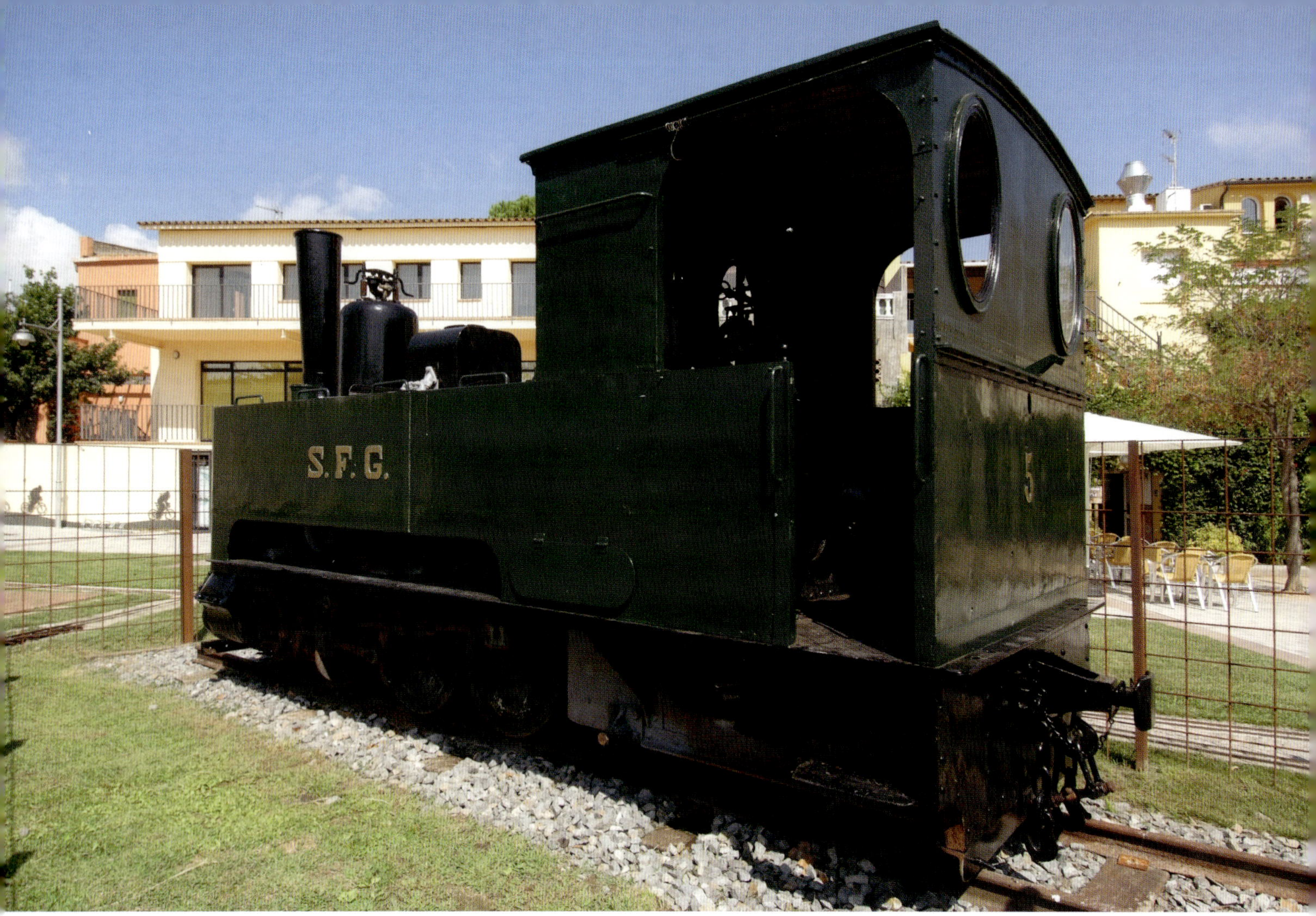
S.F.G.
5

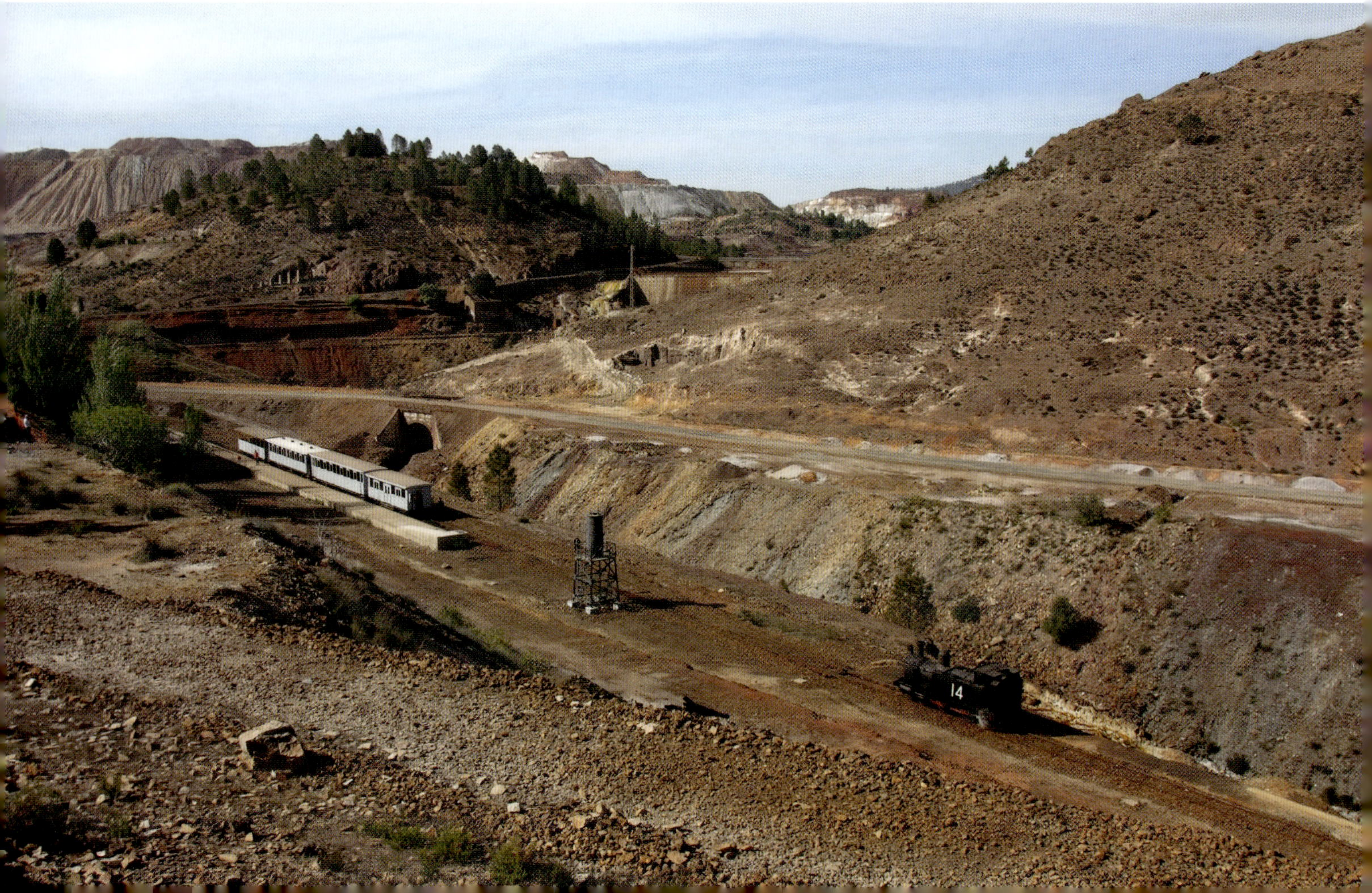
14

Opposite above: Eight other SFG locos were stored at San Feliu after the closure, and eventually all but one were rescued. Catching up with 0-6-2T no 5 (KM 2826/1893) was a reunion for me, as I first met her running round her train at Gerona in 1968. When I visited on 8 September 2011 the local authority had recently turned the old SFG station at Castell d'Aro into a museum and acquired her as its principal exhibit. She had just been repainted, in the same unlined dark green livery she carried after her final overhaul back in 1962.

Opposite below: The enormous Río Tinto copper mining operation once found work for more than 120 locos on its 3ft 6ins gauge railway, which opened in 1875 to carry the ores down to Huelva on the Río Odiel. A short part of the old line has become a heritage railway and here C class 0-6-0T no 14 (BP 1439/1875), the oldest working loco in Spain, runs round her train on 5 April 2009, surrounded by Río Tinto's post-industrial dereliction. Several of its locos have survived, including no fewer than nine at the López yard at Zaragoza.

I class 0-6-0T no 50 (Dübs 1515/1881) was trapped many years ago by a rockfall on one of the galleries at the vast Corta Atalaya pit at Río Tinto. She was still there on 6 April 2009 and can just be seen right of centre in this photo. Río Tinto's mines were first worked in Phoenician times, but later lay abandoned for more than 1,000 years before they were reopened in 1727. The railway closed in the early 1980s.

The Tharsis copper mines lay to the west of Río Tinto. The Scottish company which owned them operated a 4ft gauge railway to carry the ores to Corrales, on the Río Odiel opposite Huelva. No 1 *Odiel* (Dübs 231/1867), its first loco, is one of three survivors of the ten B class 0-4-0Ts which were built for it between 1867 and 1869. On 6 April 2009 she stood on a roundabout in the outskirts of Tharsis, superbly restored in the railway's attractive green livery, but has since moved to Corrales. Another B class loco lives in the main square at Tharsis, and there is a third one at a mining museum in the town. The López yard in Zaragoza is home to three more modern Tharsis 0-6-0Ts. The line opened in 1868. It was remarkably long-lived and its last train didn't run until 1999. There were plans to reopen part as a heritage railway, but most of what's left is now highly derelict.

Here is another Spanish 4ft gauge 0-4-0T but she's far away from the mainland. No F6 (Henschel 20320/1924) was one of five supplied between 1924 and 1928 to the port authority at Santa Cruz de Tenerife. They had Scottish managers, and this perhaps explains the gauge as the Scots seem to have had a fondess for it; in addition to the Tharsis line the Glasgow Subway is also 4ft, as was at least one railway in Sweden with Scottish connections. These locos hauled stone from a quarry at La Jurada for construction of the port's South Pier. The railway dated from about 1890 and had previously been worked by OK locos. No F6 was kept on until 1965 to help with maintenance and spends her retirement next to the port. She may include significant parts of sister loco no F5 (Henschel 20319/1924).
16 February 2016.

140 • NARROW GAUGE PANORAMA

Above: Most of Spain's sugar came from its colonies in Cuba, Puerto Rico and the Philippines until it lost them in 1898. Domestic production then stepped up all over the country, mostly using sugar beet. No fewer than thirty-seven factories opened by 1904. One of them was at La Poveda, near Madrid, served by the FC del Tajuña, and also by an extensive internal 600mm gauge system. The factory closed in 1972, but several of the 600mm locos have survived including one at the López yard. A preservation society now occupies part of its site, and runs trains over a short section of the old Tajuña line. This little 0-6-0T (Henschel 20605/1925) has steam to spare on 13 December 2015 as she stands next to the factory's perimeter wall, its only surviving structure. She previously worked for a construction company at Gijón.

Opposite: Although most of Spain's sugar had been imported until 1898 some was produced within the country since the Moors brought sugar cane to the district around Malaga centuries ago. The delightful little 600mm gauge 0-4-0T *Lirio* (OK 173/1896) spent most of her working life at a sugar factory in the city. It closed in 1977 as a consequence of trading arrangements when Spain joined the European Union. *Lirio* was rescued for preservation on a short railway at Mataró, near Barcelona, where I was introduced to her on 28 July 2011 by the very hospitable Jordi Comella, one of her owners. Here she finds her way between Mataró's fishing boats.

SPAIN • 141

LUXEMBOURG

Above: Esch-sur-Alzette was home to several steelworks, which were major contributors to Luxembourg's economy until the last blast furnace closed in 1997. This chunky metre gauge 0-4-0T no 21 (Hanomag 5921/1911) is one of four which worked at Esch-Belval steelworks and is now preserved in the town. She looks well-suited to a steelworks environment! 12 September 2010.

Opposite: 600mm gauge *Mosi oa Tunya* (Precirail 4/2005) was visiting the heritage railway at Fond-de-Gras, in south western Luxembourg, on 11 September 2010. She is a replica of Decauville's second design of 3.5 tonne 0-4-0T and was built for the Feldbunn Dol, a garden railway run by Marcel Barthel and Simone Bianchy at Dahl in the north of the Grand Duchy. Marcel was the shedmaster at Luxembourg City but came originally from southern Africa; the loco carries the name of the Victoria Falls in the local language which means *The Smoke that Thunders*.

GERMANY

In 1904, the metre gauge Bergheimer Kreisbahn bought two 0-4-4-0 Mallet tanks of Humboldt's type M.105. One of them soon moved to the Brohltlbahn and became their no 10sm. The railway connects communities in the Eifel Hills with Brohl, a small port town on the left bank of the River Rhine between Koblenz and Bonn. They were so pleased with her that they bought two more, nos 11sm and 12sm. No 10sm was withdrawn as long ago as 1934, but the other two remained in service until diesel locos arrived in 1965. No 11sm (Humboldt 348/1906) was sold to a museum society in 1968 but returned in 1989 and was later restored to working order. In this photo, she pauses at Brenk quarry on 21 April 2018. Phonolite, a mineral used in the manufacture of coloured glass, is mined here. It is despatched by rail, some of the last freight still conveyed on the narrow gauge anywhere in Germany.

The Brohltalbahn's 1:20 section from Oberzissen through Brenk to Engeln was rack-worked until 1934. It is still known as the *steilstrecke*, or steep section, and has special operating rules. On 21 April 2018, no 11sm has nearly reached the top as she approaches Engeln. Her offset standard gauge buffers enable her to haul mainline wagons over a mixed gauge section between a yard near Brohl station and the quay on the River Rhine.

Above: The metre gauge Mittelbadische Eisenbahn used 0-4-0Ts in line service for many years. One of the most modern was no 101 (KM 17627/1949), which it bought second-hand from the Oberrheinische Eisenbahn in 1958. Two generally similar locos were bought by ME in 1948, but unlike no 101 they were fitted with steel fireboxes which proved unsatisfactory. All three were reportedly built as 900mm gauge locos and must have been regauged almost immediately. No 101 was sold for preservation in 1969. Now she runs on the Selfkantbahn, a heritage railway close to Germany's border with the Netherlands north of Aachen. I saw her heading away from Schierwaldenrath on 27 September 2019.

Opposite above: ME had its origins in the street tramways of Strasbourg, in the days when Alsace was a part of Germany and they crossed the Rhine into Baden. Their 0-4-0T no 46 (SACM 4805/1897) was one of eleven generally similar locos built between 1891 and 1901 which betrayed their tramway origins with their inside cylinders and skirting. Here she stands in the engine shed at Schierwaldenrath on 27 September 2019.

Opposite below: This loco started out life as 0-6-2T no 3 (KM 4113/1899) of the Kreisbahn Rathenow-Senzke-Nauen in the old East Germany. She became Deutsche Reichsbahn's no 99 4511 and moved in 1961 to the Rügensche Kleinbahn. Four years later she was taken to Görlitz works and became the last loco to be subject to DR's narrow gauge reconstruction scheme. Most locos involved in this emerged looking something like they did when they went in, but not so no 99 4511! She became a 0-6-0T with new frames, axles, wheels, motion, boiler, tanks and cab, mostly with different dimensions - and even new numberplates. It's hard to see that anything old was left. In 1966 she moved to the extensive 750mm gauge Prignitzer Kleinbahn, which opened in stages from 1885, and stayed during the final years before it closed between 1969 and 1971. She was popular there and worked one of the trains on the system's last day. On 8 May 2018, she runs through fields of oilseed rape near Brünkendorf, on a section of the Prignitz system which has been rebuilt by enthusiasts. In preservation, she lives elsewhere, but often makes visits to her old haunts.

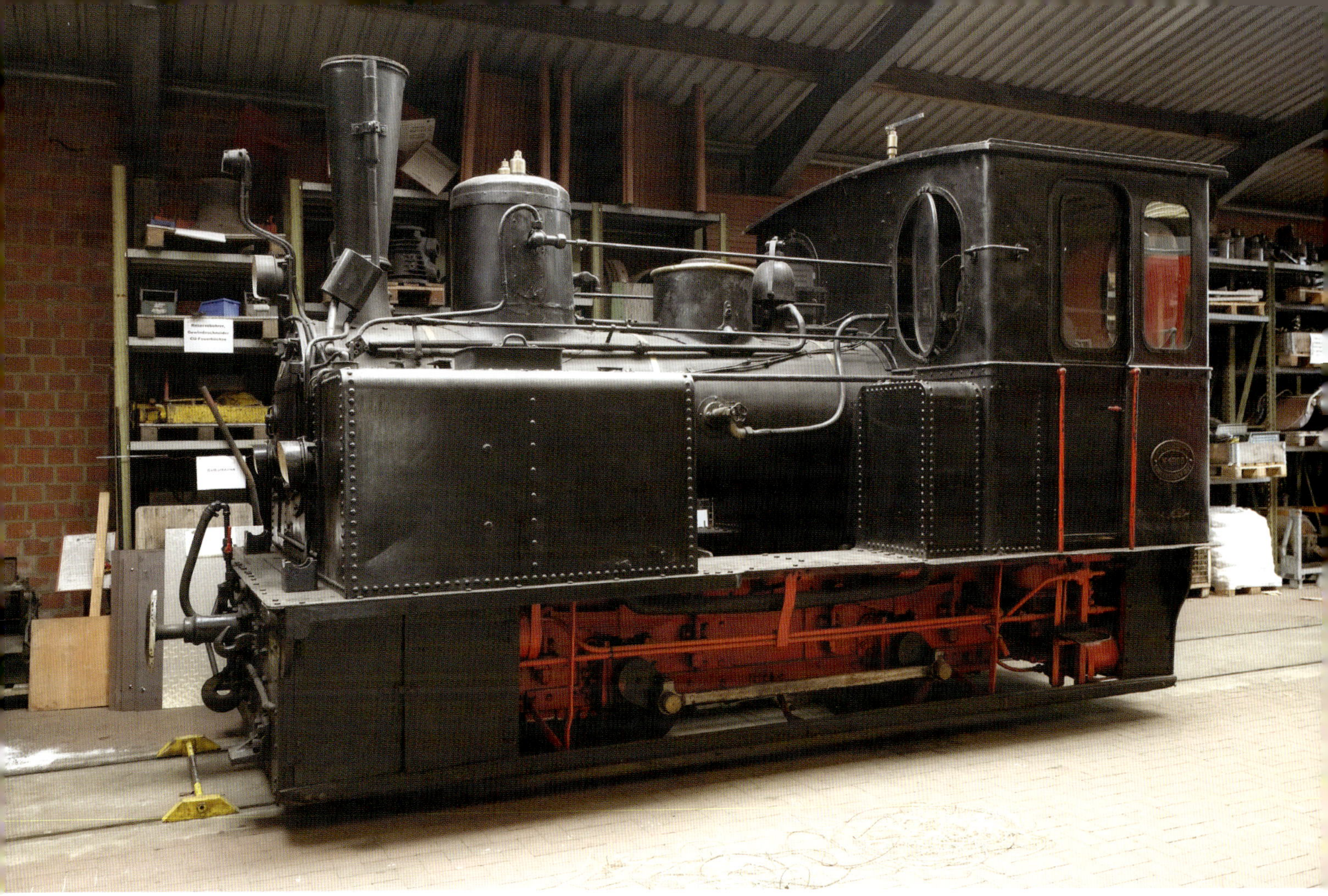

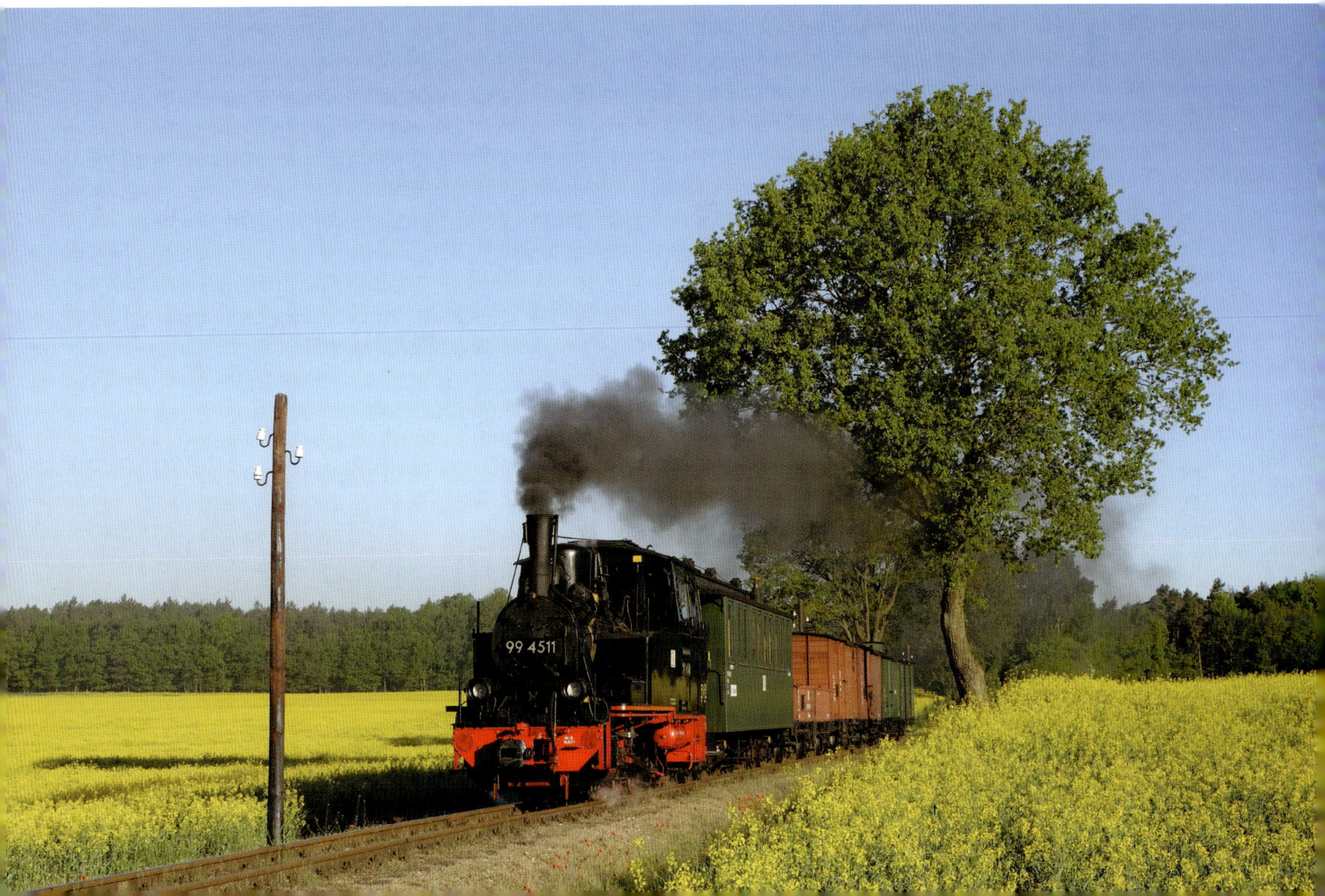
99 4511

Above: The prototype of the GR class 750mm gauge 0-8-0s built in East Germany for the Soviet Union remained in the country and became DR's no 99 1401. She worked on the Prignitz system for some years but was eventually scrapped. This loco is Soviet no GR-320 (LKM 15417/1951) and was carrying the old loco's number on this occasion during a visit to the preserved Prignitz line. She crosses a minor road near Vettin on 8 May 2018. The very stylish car is a Wartburg 311 Coupé, a type built in Eisenach between 1956 and 1965. Not all East German cars were Trabants! It was only available with a 0.9 litre 3-cylinder engine so maybe its performance didn't match its looks!

Opposite above: It is just moments before sunset on 7 May 2018 as no 99 4511 approaches Lindenberg, the preserved railway's southern terminus. Note the train's Heberlein overhead brake cable.

Opposite below: No 12 (Esslingen 3711/1913) was one of two 0-4-0Ts built for the metre gauge Härtsfeldbahn, in eastern Württemberg, which opened in 1901. They were thoroughly modern machines for their day and, like ME no 101, were superheated and intended for mixed traffic. They were kept on for a few years after diesels arrived in 1956, and both had been preserved by the time the line closed in 1972. Volunteers have been rebuilding a part since 1996 and some years ago returned no 12 to service. On 20 October 2019 she passes the Benedictine monastery at Neresheim with its magnificent baroque chapel – the size of many cathedrals. The coach came from the Stuttgart Rack Railway and is similar to some which ran on the old line.

148 • NARROW GAUGE PANORAMA

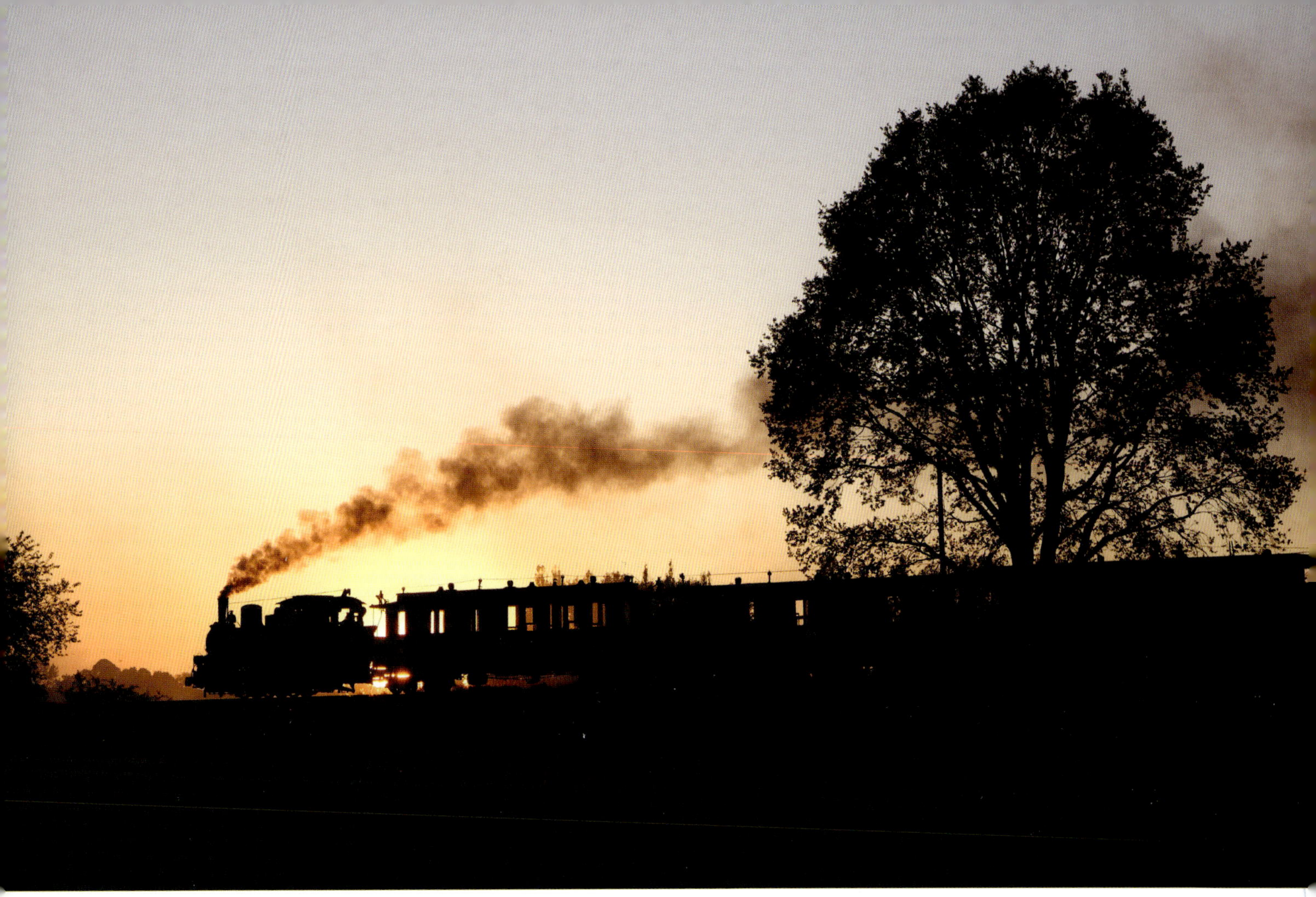

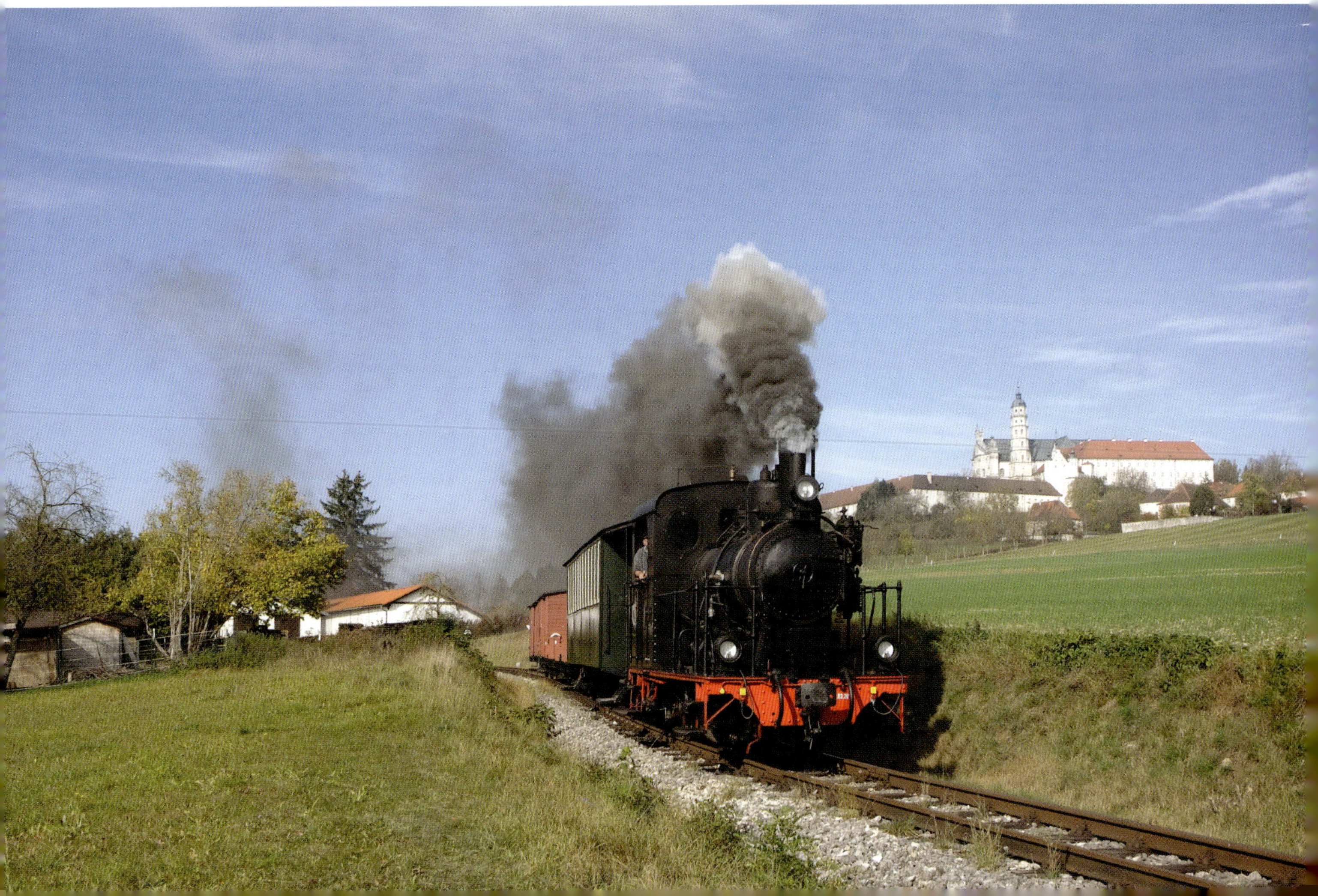

The volunteers kindly left no 12 outside her shed on the evening of 2 September 2018 so that I could take night photos of her. What a pretty little loco and an equally pretty and friendly little railway!

The Mecklenburg-Pommersche Schmalspurbahn, in the north of the old East Germany, operated more than 250km of 600mm gauge lines. They opened between 1892 and 1927 and the final section closed in 1969. The second no 1 *Jacobi* (Jung 989/1906), later DR no 99 3351, was the first of eight 0-6-2Ts built for the system between 1906 and 1914. She spent many years in museums in the US before moving to the Frankfurter Feldbahnmuseum where she is now a star exhibit. Here she stands outside their engine shed on 13 June 2009. Another 0-6-2T, no 5 *Graf Schwerin Löwitz* (Jung 1261/1908), later DR no 99 3353, has worked at the Brecon Mountain Railway for many years. On the right is Decauville 1593/1915, one of nineteen Progrès 0-6-0Ts sent to Greece during the First World War. This one later worked at the Domokos chrome mines in Thessaly, was sabotaged by a group of British soldiers in March 1944 and reportedly lay on her side for thirty-eight years until being rescued for the museum. She was one of several French, British and German military locos which had begun their working lives on the Salonica front during the First World War and remained in the region after peace returned.

This 0-4-0T (Heilbronn 393/1900) was built as a 720mm gauge machine for a salt works at Friedrichshall, on the River Neckar near Heilbronn. By 1939, she had moved downstream to a cement factory at Lauffen am Neckar and been converted to 600mm gauge. Here she runs through allotments on the Frankfurt museum's extensive railway on 13 June 2009. German allotments have lawns, summerhouses and flowerbeds and are places of leisure; they would scarcely be recognised by vegetable-growing allotment-holders in the UK!

Three 600mm gauge OK locos at the Frankfurt museum on 7 December 2019. A few of these 0-4-4-0 Mallet tanks were supplied to railways in Germany and elsewhere in Europe, but most worked in the Javanese sugar industry including this one, no 4 (OK 3902/1909) of the Pabrik Gula Gending, near Probolinggo. Next to her is 0-4-0T (OK 9244/1921), a standard 40hp machine which started her career at Mönchengladbach and later moved to Mayen, where she saw use on autobahn construction. The third loco is a 0-10-0T with Luttermöller axles at each end, a military type intended to augment the Brigadelok 0-8-0Ts but this one was the Japanese army's no E103 (OK 11073/1925). She was one of three which ended up with the Seibu Railway, or Tetsudō to use the Japanese term, a busy 3ft 6ins gauge electrified system serving the northwestern suburbs of Tōkyō. They worked at its ballast quarry at Ahina. She is one of two of them to have survived, the other, no E18, being preserved close to Shin-Egota metro station on the Toei-Oedo line and not much further away from Ekoda station on the Seibu's Ikebukuro line in Tōkyō.

SWITZERLAND

The metre gauge Rhätische Bahn owned twenty-nine relatively modern 2-8-0s when its electrification was completed in 1922. Twenty-three were sold while the other six, nos 102 and 104-8, were kept on, mainly for work when the catenary was unavailable. Between 1949 and 1952 nos 102 and 104-6 were also sold, leaving just nos 107-8 which are now part of the railway's heritage fleet. No 108 (SLM 1710/1906) runs through the Engadine's winter snow near Zernez with a train of the railway's historic coaches on 19 February 2008. These 2-8-0s were developed from four built by SLM in 1902-3 for the CF Ethiopiens which operated the metre gauge line between Addis Ababa and Djibouti. One of them made trial runs on the RhB before moving to Africa.

Most of the RhB's large roundhouse at Landquart houses its electric locos and, like many things in Switzerland, is squeaky clean. Not so the two bays at its northern end, which were screened off when I visited on 20 February 2008 and formed a working steam depot with the attendant coal dust, oil and dirt. The RhB's first loco, 2-6-0T no 1 *Rhätia* (SLM 577/1889), was awaiting overhaul and to her right is 2-8-0 no 107 (SLM 1709/1906). *Rhätia*, double-heading with no 3 *Davos*, worked the system's first train between Landquart and Klosters in 1889. She was one of sixteen similar machines which were built until 1908, three of which have been preserved.

SWITZERLAND • 155

The 800mm gauge Pilatusbahn, near Luzern, has a maximum gradient of 48 per cent and has always been the world's steepest rack railway. After it was electrified in 1937 two of its old 0-2-2 steam railcars were kept on for many years to help maintain the line before becoming museum exhibits. Her transverse-mounted boiler is prominent in this view of no 9 (SLM 563/1889) at the Luzern Verkehrshaus. 12 September 2009.

156 • NARROW GAUGE PANORAMA

No 10 (SLM 1309/1900) is at the Deutsches Museum in Munich. This view, on 1 October 2010, shows the ingenious drive system which uses a horizontally-mounted rack rail with teeth on each side, the wheel underneath the rack rail which prevents the car from lifting off the track, the outside flange on the carrying wheel and the unusual suspension. These two cars are only on loan to the museums, and there are occasional reports that the railway may recall one and restore it to working order.

The Waldenburgerbahn, in the canton of Basel-Landschaft in north western Switzerland, opened in 1880 and has always been the country's only public 750mm gauge railway. Regular steam operation ended when it was electrified in 1953 but 0-6-0T no 5 *G Thommen* (SLM 1440/1902) was kept on as a static exhibit at Liestal station, the railway's mainline junction, and was restored to working order for its centenary celebrations in 1980. She remained in use for occasional steam specials which became greatly valued by local residents, but they came to an end in 2014 following a change in management. They returned for one last day on 23 September 2018, shortly before the only remaining steam driver reached compulsory retirement age. Early in the morning 0-6-0T no 5 *G Thommen* (SLM 1440/1902) raises steam at Waldenburg.

No 5, richly bedecked with flowers, passes St Peter's church at Niederdorf on 23 September 2018. The steam trains went out in style. Large numbers of well-wishers turned out and the railway's frequent electric service was suspended so that *G Thommen* had sole possession of the line. By the end of October, the railway had built a new display hall alongside the line at Talhaus and installed the entire train there. This coach was built in 1937. Several other historic vehicles, including an 1882-built coach, have moved to Romania for preservation. In 2016 the railway was taken over by the public authority which operates the extensive metre gauge tramway system in Basel, and became the tramway's route 19. Now it is to be converted to metre gauge and ten new railcars are on order. All the present ones will be sold to the 760mm gauge Čiernohronská Železnica in Slovakia (see pages 176-177) which intends to change from a heritage railway to an electrified public service operation.

AUSTRIA

At daybreak on 11 August 2006 I looked out of my hotel room overlooking Vienna's Prater gardens and was surprised to see movement on its 15ins gauge railway. It turned out that Pacific no 2 (KM 8442/1928) was preparing to move her sister no 1 (KM 8441/1948) from the running shed to the workshop for overhaul, a happy opportunity to see them out in the sunshine together. These locos were designed by Roland Maertens, the chief engineer of Krauss's light railway division. Their styling was inspired by the Bavarian State Railways' S3/6 Pacifics. Officially Krauss designated them as their K3/6 class, but they were often just called *Liliputloks*. Fifteen were built between 1925 and 1950 and saw service in several European countries, while one even reached New Delhi! Maertens was a close friend of Henry Greenly who designed the Pacifics on the 15ins gauge Romney Hythe & Dymchurch Railway and there are many mechanical similarities.

The metre gauge Achenseebahn opened in 1889 and is Austria's oldest surviving rack railway. On 25 July 2019 0-4-0RT no 4 *Hannah* (nominally Floridsdorf 704/1889, reconstructed in 2006) climbs through the outskirts of Jenbach on her way to Eben, the summit of the line, where the rack section ends. There she will run round her train and continue her journey over the non-rack section down the gentle hill through Maurach to the shore of the Achensee at Seespitz. The old no 4 was withdrawn in 1930 and used as a parts donor for other locos, and although *Hannah* is regarded as a rebuild, it is hard to see that much of the original material can have been reused. The two open coaches in this train were built in Graz for the opening and have been in service ever since. There are also four closed coaches which are only a little younger.

Above: On 24 July 2019 *Hannah* has arrived at Seespitz station on the Achensee and is ready for her return journey to Jenbach. Many of the passengers she has brought up from the Inn valley are boarding the lake ferry just visible on the right.

Opposite above: On 25 July 2019 *Hannah* approaches Burgeck station, midway along the rack section, with a descending train. The station remains much as originally built.

Opposite below: *Hannah* has set off from Maurach which can be seen in the background. It is the largest community on the line apart from Jenbach. I took this photo on 26 July 2019 from what was for many years the terrace of the Seespitz Hotel, a superb establishment which was separated from the lake shore only by the railway, but sadly it was closed in the 1980s and turned into an operational base for the local hydro-electric company. Management and funding problems at the railway came to a head early in 2020, and operation was suspended even before the COVID-19 outbreak. At one point it was suggested that all the locos, stock and track would be moved to Madeira for use in the reopening of the Funchal-Monte railway (see page 130), but now the regional government has taken it over and plans to reopen it in 2022.

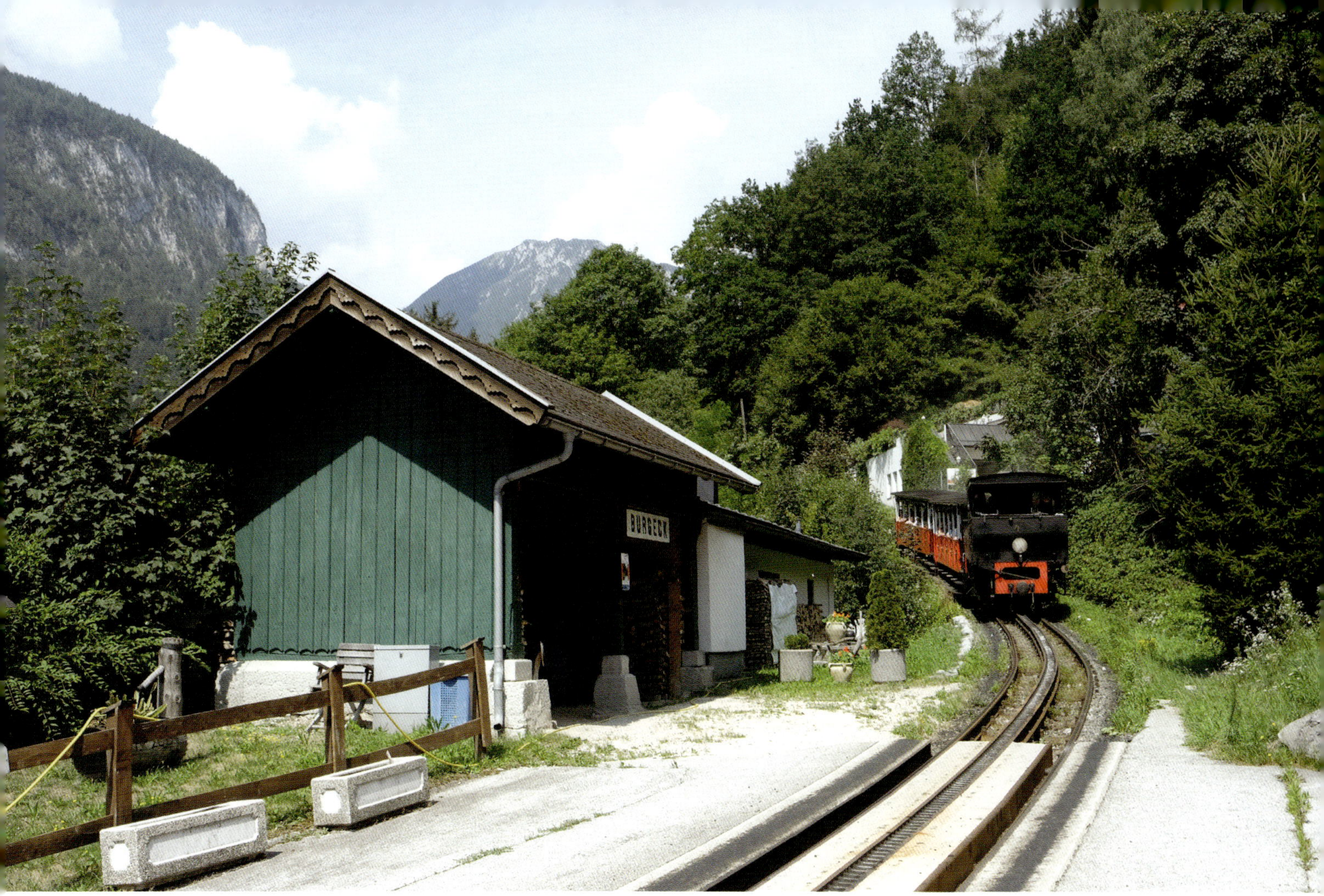
BURGECK

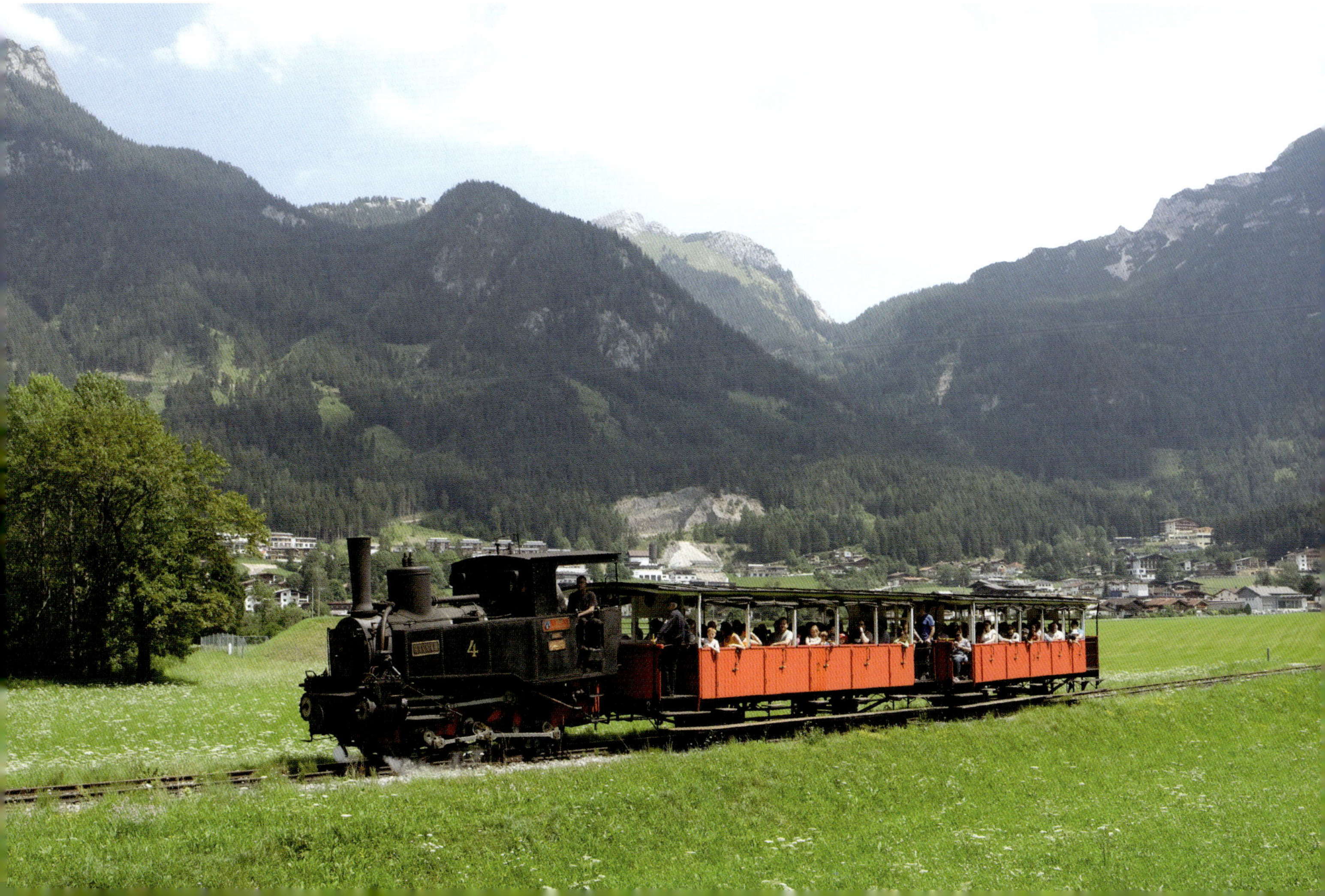
4

Above: There is still snow on the mountains on 1 August 2013 as Engerth 0-8+4 no Mh3 (KL 5433/1906), formerly no 399.03 of the Österreichische Bundesbahnen, heads away from Zell am See on the 760mm gauge Pinzgaubahn. The railway runs for 53km, mostly through the foothills of the Alps, and opened throughout in 1898. Back in steam days services were worked at first by 0-6-0T's and later by the celebrated U class 0-6-2Ts, though these Engerths occasionally stood in for them.

Opposite above: On 1 August 2013 no Mh3 heads up the valley between Mittersill and Krimml, beside the River Salzach with the grey/blue colour characteristic of many Alpine rivers. After many years of operation by ÖBB energetic local management was installed by the Salzburgerland regional government in 2008. Freight services were reintroduced almost immediately after a ten-year absence, and there is now a flourishing passenger service, including summer-time heritage trains.

Opposite below: The Steyrtalbahn was Austria's first 760mm gauge line when it opened on 14 August 1889, and 0-6-2T no 2 *Stierning* (KL 1994/1888) hauled its first train. She is now the only survivor of its first three locos and stands outside Grünberg engine shed exactly 125 years later, ready to work an anniversary special. Like several of Austria's early 0-6-2T's she was fitted with elongated frames to support an unusually long smokebox, and over the years her tanks have been extended both upwards and forwards. Originally, they looked similar to those on the SFG locos in Spain, though the latter were somewhat smaller.

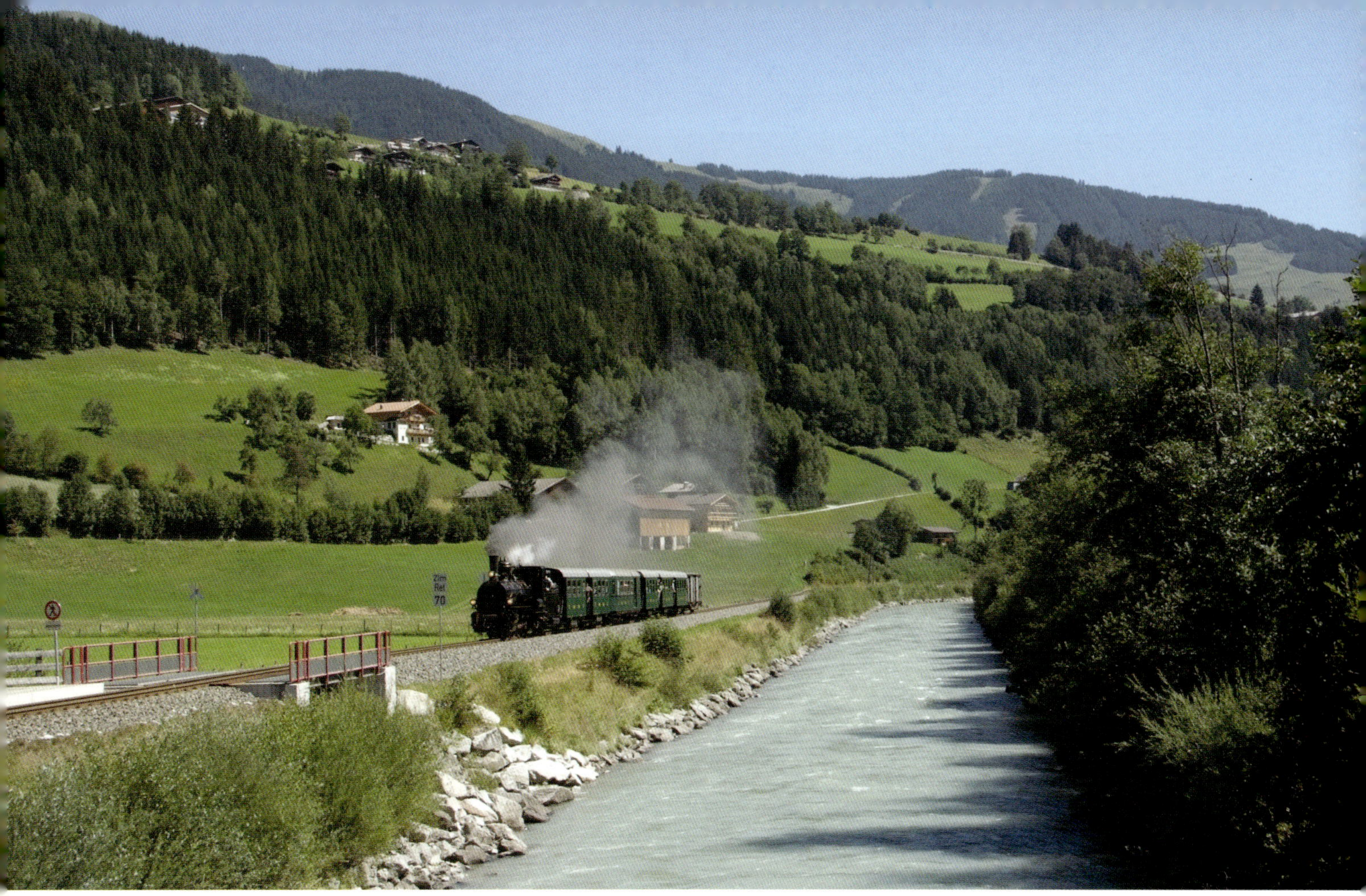

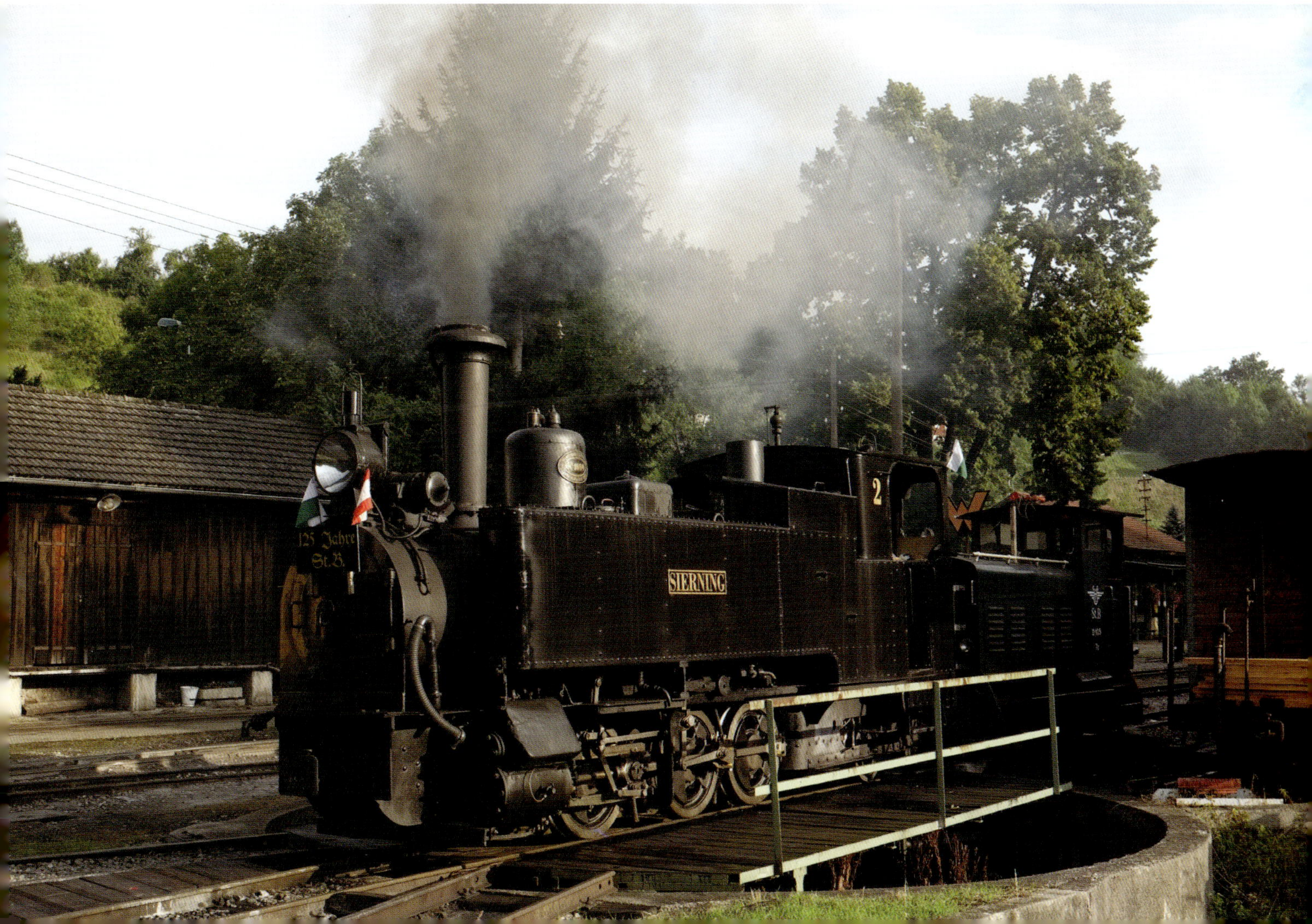
125 Jahre
St.B.
2
SIERNING

The 760mm gauge Salzkammergut Lokalbahn, which opened in 1890, ran through the superb Alpine countryside east of Salzburg. Its closure in 1957 was greatly lamented, but in a small way it lives on as many of its locos have been preserved. On 3 October 2012, no fewer than three SKGLB 0-6-2T's, nos 9 (KL 2821/1893), 5 (KL 2342/1891) and 4 (KL 2341/1891) stand in its old engine shed at Mondsee, now part of a fine museum. Like *Stierning* nos 4 and 5 feature extended smokeboxes though they are not apparent from this angle. No 5 was requisitioned by the Austrian military in 1917 and spent more than fifty years in Bosnia. The other two always worked on the SKGLB.

SKGLB 0-6-2T no 12 (KL 5513/1906) raises steam in Mautendorf engine shed on the enthusiast-run Taurachtalbahn on 2 August 2013. By the time she was built, the railway had abandoned extended smokeboxes on its new locos.

HUNGARY

760mm gauge 0-8-0T no 490,039 (Budapest 5260/1942) climbs towards Széchenyihegy on the Budapest Children's Railway on 15 June 2019. The line has always been operated by MÁV, Hungary's state system, and is one of the most successful of the pioneer railways built throughout the old Eastern bloc in socialist times. It provides the principal means of access to the Buda hills, a hugely popular recreational district for the city's inhabitants, and regularly carries more than 350,000 passengers each year. Its peak service requires more than 100 children to operate it, and the only adults involved are operating supervisors, footplate crews and people providing the children's pastoral care. No 490,039 was one of three steam locos used when it opened in 1950, but diesels took over the following year and she didn't resume active service there until 2007. Now she is one of two of MÁV's 490 class or Budapest type 70 locos on the line, and steam trains often run at weekends.

No 490,039 returns to the railway's operating yard north of Hűvösvölgy station at the end of the working day on 16 June 2019. The coaches came from the Lillafüred forest railway in northeastern Hungary and carry its attractive livery; the railway also has one of Lillafüred's historic diesel railcars. 142 type 70 locos were built was between 1905 and 1950, though there was a lull in production after the First World War when Hungary lost two thirds of its territory and almost all its state-owned narrow gauge railways. The country temporarily regained some of them in 1940, and construction of an updated version of the type 70s began two years later.

Nagycenk lies close to the Hungarian shore of the Neusiedler See, the large shallow lake which straddles the country's border with Austria. On 18 August 2019 0-8-0T *András* (Budapest 4756/1924) approaches Nádtelep station on the 760mm gauge Nagycenki Széchenyi Múzeumvasút. This museum line was built by GySEV, an international system which serves western Hungary and south eastern Austria and has always managed to remain independent of either country's state railway. GySEV had no narrow gauge of its own, but Hungary's little lines were closing at an alarming rate and it set out to preserve something of them before it was too late. The first section opened in 1970.

András is a type 85 0-8-0T, MÁV's 492 class, smaller that the type 70s. She arrived at Nagycenk in 1952 and previously worked at a colliery at Balinka. Ninety type 85s were built between 1908 and 1949. Here she makes her way around a sharp curve between Barátság and Nagycenk on 18 August 2019. The coaches come from several of Hungary's narrow gauge lines. This is another children's railway, though it is a low-key operation compared to the one at Budapest.

Nagycenk's first locos were two Budapest type 106 0-6-0Ts, MÁV's 394 class. Forty of these wood-burning locos were built at the Budapest factory between 1916 and 1950. In 1999 no 394,057 (Budapest 5785/1949) moved to the Szilvásvárad Forest Railway in northeastern Hungary which has become a popular tourist line. I saw her in its engine shed on 12 August 2010. She was still in working order then but now needs major repair.

CZECH REPUBLIC

A 600mm gauge railway opened between 1919 and 1922 to carry shale and low-grade coal from deposits in the Hřebečov hills to a fireclay factory at Mladějov, near the border between Bohemia and Moravia. The route was twisty and included a steeply-graded section between Mladějov and Nová Ves, for which a powerful loco was needed. The solution was provided by Krauss's Linz factory, which rebuilt an almost-new ex-Austrian army First World War RIIIc class 0-6-0T as a 0-6+2 Engerth. In addition to the rear truck the work involved adding an additional ring to her boiler. No 1 (KL 7485/1920) proved to be a great success and is still in service 100 years later. Here she climbs the incline between Mladějov and Nová Ves on 9 September 2018.

Above: Another view of no 1 between Mladějov and Nová Ves on 8 September 2018. The line remained largely unchanged for many years until it closed along with the fireclay factory on 31 December 1991. Happily moves began immediately to turn it into a heritage railway. It is now operated as the Průmyslové Muzeum Mladějov and provides a boost to tourism in this somewhat neglected part of the Czech Republic.

Opposite above: Further south the line runs mostly through woodland. No 1 passes orchards near Hřebeč on 8 September 2018. Diesels arrived in the 1980s but were too heavy and couldn't be used until the track had been relaid. This work was still in progress at the time of the closure.

Opposite below: In 1929 the railway ordered 0-6+2 Engerth no 5 (KL 1518/1929), a much larger machine which was built from new. Here she stands in Mladějov's dilapidated engine shed as no 1 returns after her day's work on 9 September 2018.

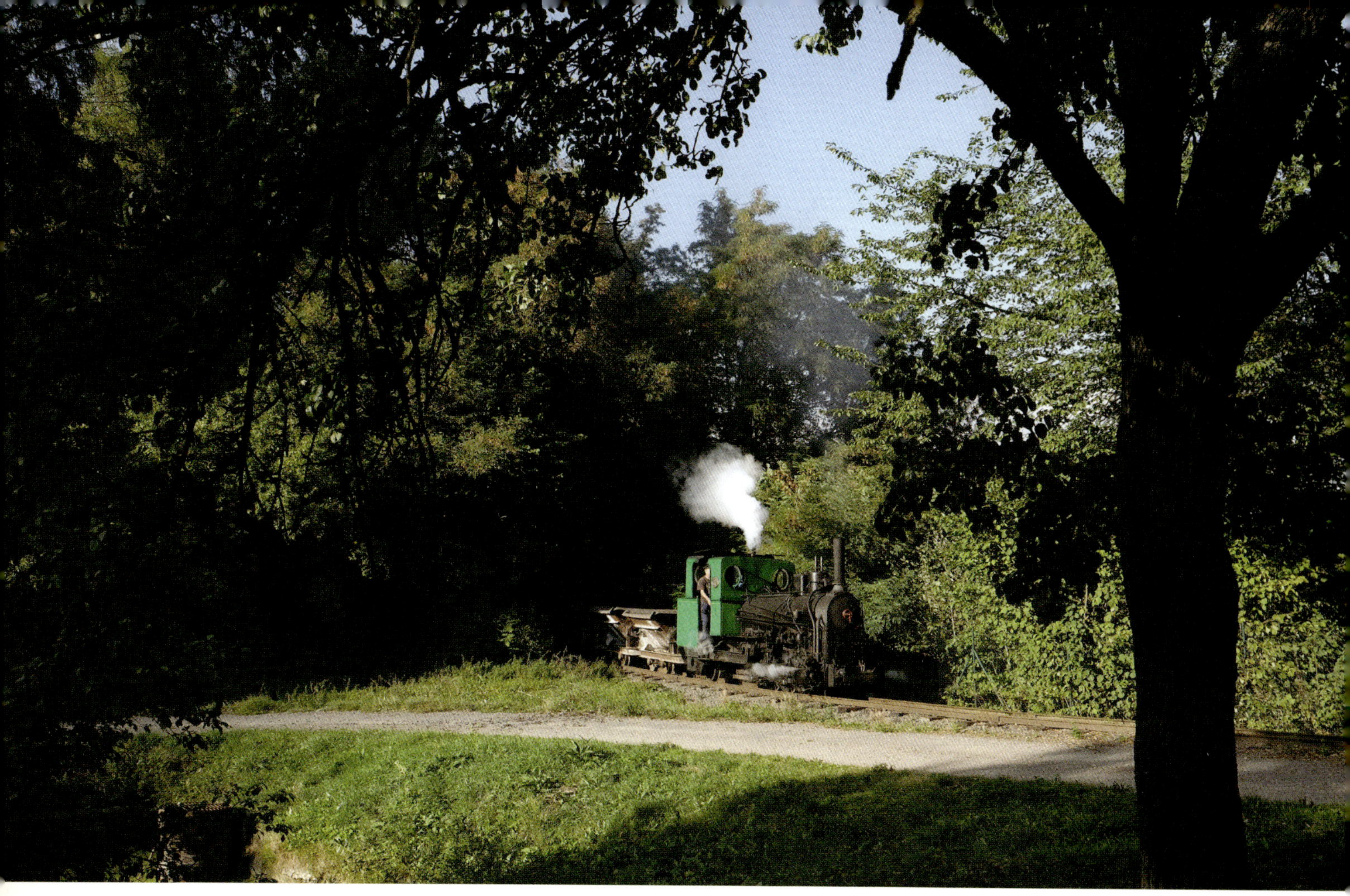

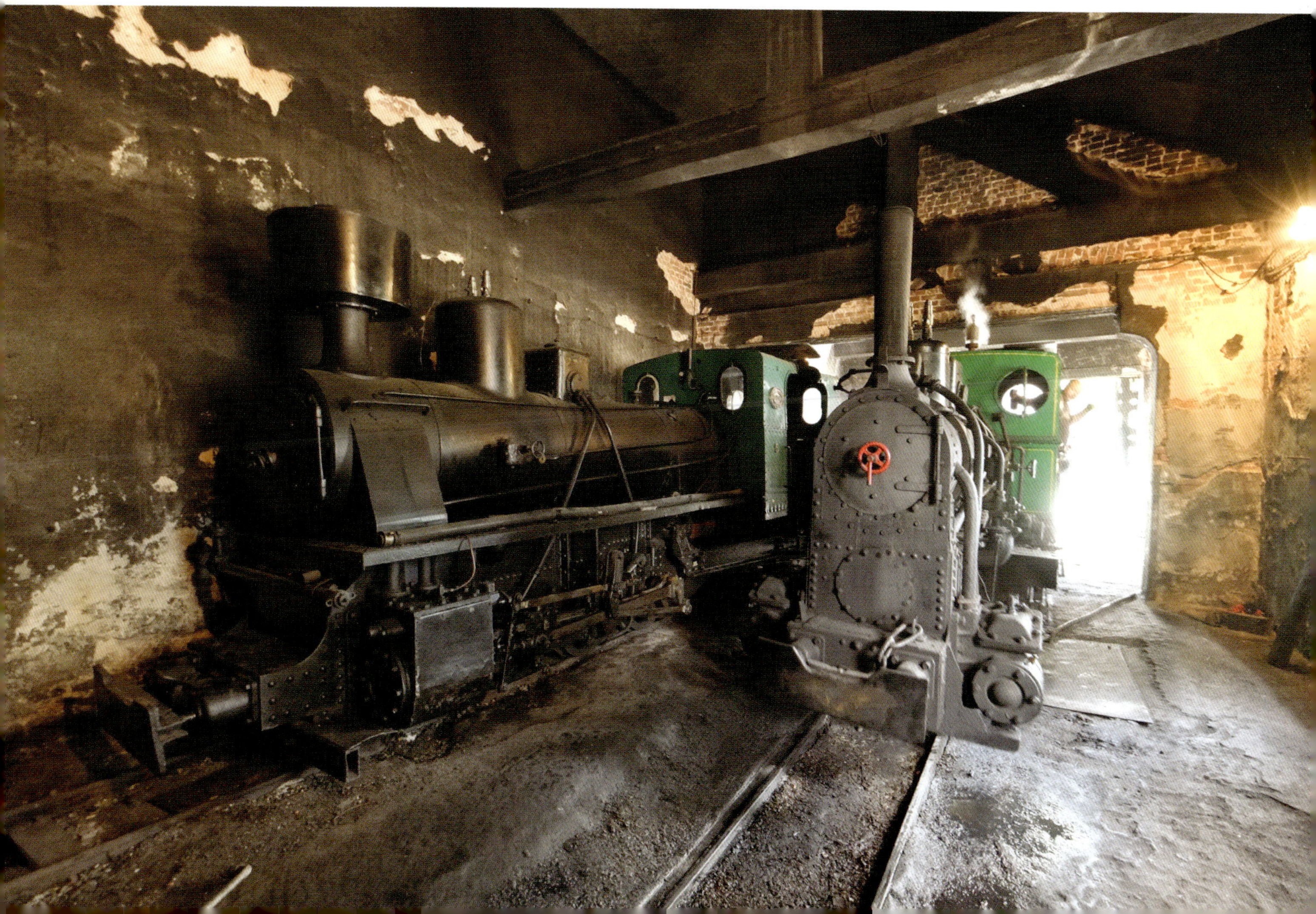

SLOVAKIA

Above: The 760mm gauge Čiernohronská Železnica was one of the largest of about forty forest railways which operated in Slovakia. It closed to commercial traffic in 1982 and heritage operations began in 1993. 0-6-0T No 3 (Schmoschewer 625/1918) is a RIIIc class loco. She was regauged from 600mm after being discovered in a shed at Modřice in 1984, but is otherwise more or less as built. She makes an interesting comparison with the reconstructed Mladějov machine. Here she backs towards the engine shed at Hronec in the evening of 11 August 2010.

Opposite above: The Povážská Lesná Zeleznica was another of Slovakia's major 760mm gauge forestry railways. Its 0-8-0T no 2 or U45.903 (Budapest 4280/1916) is another type 85 like *András* at Nagycenk, and not a type 70 as I mistakenly wrote in my first book. She now runs on the ČŽ, and here shunts one of its old workmen's coaches at Hronec before setting off for Čierny Balog on 12 August 2010.

Opposite below: No 2 crosses the Čierny Hron river, near Hronec, on 12 August 2010.

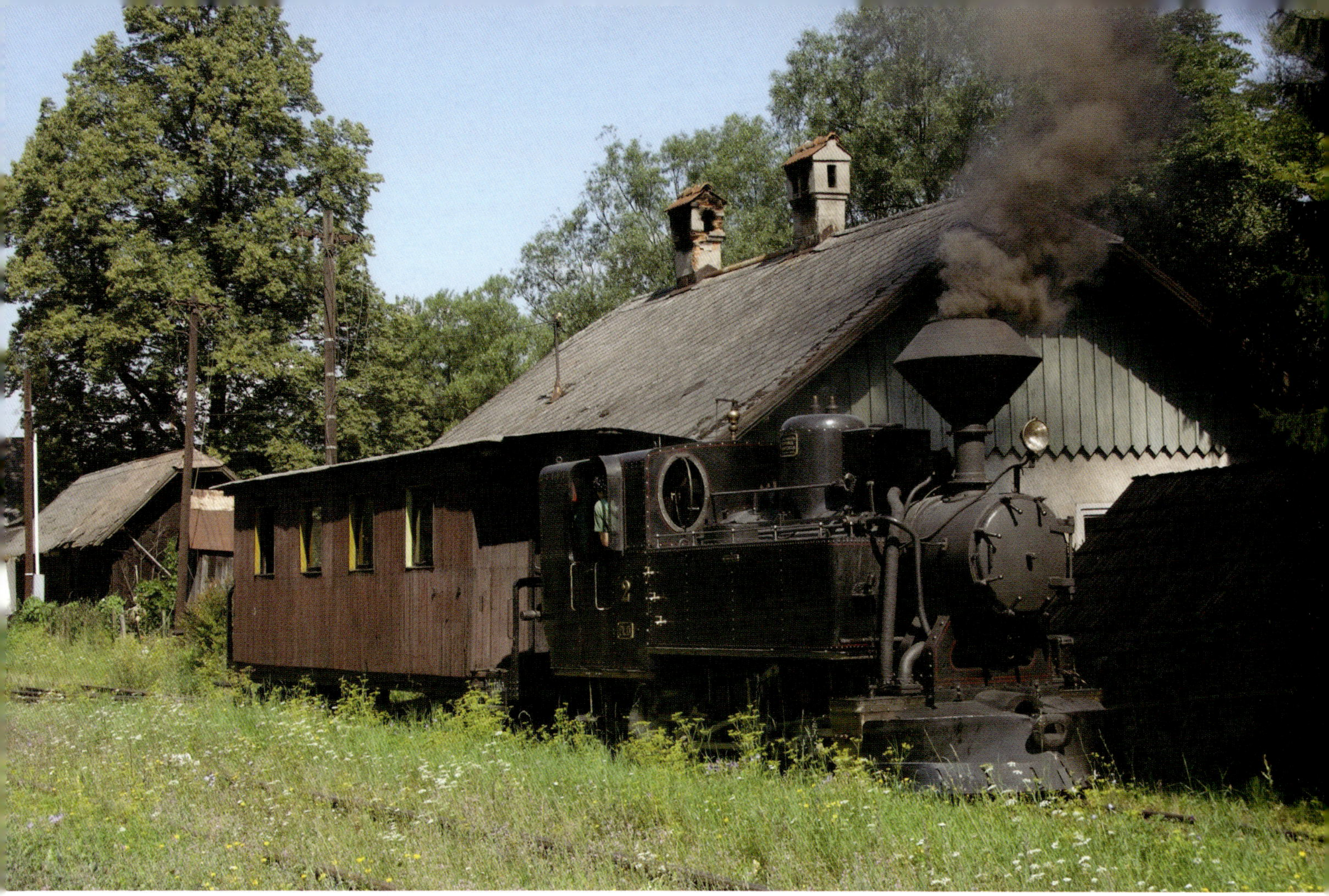

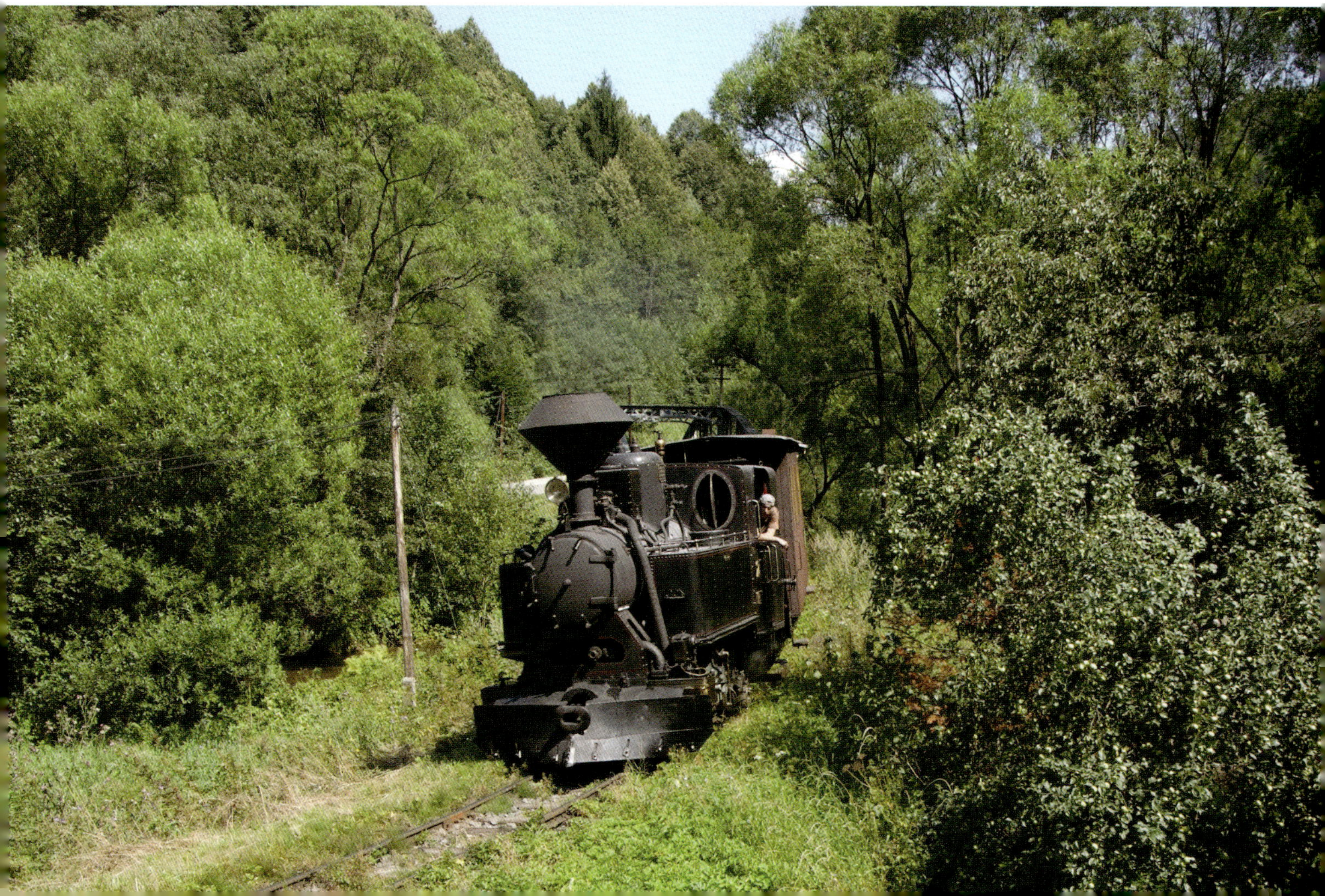

The 760mm gauge forest railway over the Beskyd pass, in north-western Slovakia, was built in 1926 to transport logs to the mainline at Krásno. East of the pass there is a stiff climb, while the western side is even steeper and incorporates zig-zags. It was sufficiently unusual to be declared a listed monument after it closed in 1969. This loco (ČKD 1441/1928) is one of several similar 0-8-0Ts. They were intended to supplement the Budapest locos which had been built to serve Slovakia's forestry railways before the First World War, when the country was a part of Hungary. She now operates tourist services on the eastern section of the line. When I visited on 12 May 2019 and asked if she could be posed next to one of the old timber wagons the helpful staff went much further and took her and a short train consisting of tree trunks on bogies up to this attractive spot near Tanečník.

UKRAINE

Sun, steam and fully ripened grapes on the vine! 750mm gauge GR class 0-8-0 no Gr-280 (LKM 15377/1950) waits at Haivoron station on 5 October 2010. At least 417 GRs were built at the old OK plant at Babelsberg in East Germany as reparations for the Soviet Union.

No Gr-280 crosses a minor road at Ustya en route from Haivoron to Bershad on 5 October 2010. This railway, based at Haivoron, opened in 1899. It is the only surviving section of a network more than 800km long in central Ukraine which was built at a time when the country was a part of the Russian empire in Tsarist times, and has outlived all the numerous public 750mm lines in Russia proper other than its children's railways. The Ukrainian government has made several attempts to close it, but so far public opinion has ensured that it has remained open. No Gr-280 was based at Haivoron for many years in the days when the line's regular services were steam-worked. She was transferred away in 1978 after diesels took over and was withdrawn in 1984. More recently she has returned as a heritage loco.

RUSSIA

On 1 November 2009 no Gr-185 (OK 15285/1949) was running on the 750mm gauge Rostov-on-Don Children's Railway in southern Russia. She's the oldest survivor of her class, and the only one to have been built as an OK loco. When the East German authorities broke with the old company, they renamed its factory as the Lokomotivbau Karl Marx.

PT-4-type 0-8-0 no Kp-4-430 (Chrzanów, probably built in 1957) heads away from Rodina, on the 750mm gauge Nizhny Novgorod Children's Railway, on 1 August 2009. She's one of more than 5,500 generally similar locos, most of which were built for service in the Soviet Union or in China, and has spent her entire life at Nizhny Novgorod. The large pipe on the right serves the city's communal heating system.

ITALY

The old 950mm gauge Ferrovie Mediterraneo Calabro-Lucane served much of southern Italy. 0-8-0T no 353 (Borsig 11940/1926) approaches San Nicola-Silvana Mansio, the highest station anywhere in the country at an altitude of 1,404m, on 13 September 2008.

After many years out of action, no 353 resumed service in 1991. On 13 September 2008, she had just been turned at San Giovanni in Fiore, the far terminus of the Sila line from Cosenza which now forms part of the Ferrovie della Calabria, owned by the Calabrian regional government. It was a sunny afternoon but the clouds in this photo were precursors of a hailstorm! The railway here was built as recently as 1956 to promote development of this impoverished part of Italy. It was planned to extend it further, but this never happened.

SERBIA

Not quite what it seems! The Sargan 8 railway in Serbia was completed in 1925 to connect the Serbian and Bosnian 760mm gauge systems and to provide a through route between Belgrade and Sarajevo. Golubići station looks old but was only built in the early 2000s as a prop for Emir Kusturica's epic movie *Zivot Je Čudo* or *Life Is a Miracle*, a thriller and love story set in the 1990s Bosnian war. No 83-173 (ĐĐ 129/1949) enters the station on 9 June 2008.

Above: The magnificent eighteen-road roundhouse at Kostolac was built in about 1950. By the time I first visited, it had become seriously dilapidated, and most of its residents had long since departed. 900mm gauge 0-8-0s nos 13 and 12, two of Davenport 2881-3/1945, are both in steam while outside no 9 (Davenport 2885/1945) is under repair on 8 November 2005.

Opposite above: Everyone's concentrating hard as no 9's tubes receive attention outside the roundhouse on 7 November 2005.

Opposite below: Up at Klenovnik pit lignite is tipped into no 13's train by one of its enormous dragline diggers. 7 November 2005.

SERBIA • 187

At the end of the day's operations on the 900mm gauge Kolubara railway on 19 April 2009 0-6-0T no 53-017 (Decauville 5317/1952) rests at Vreoci's loco preparation point. Lignite is a low-grade fuel and it is easy to see why it is sometimes called brown coal. The line dates from the early 1950s. Decauville supplied thirty of these 0-6-0Ts to Yugoslavia and several ran at Kolubara until the railway was electrified some years later. A few were retained, mainly for maintenance work on the overhead line.

BOSNIA

The 760mm gauge Steinbeisbahn crossed the mountains of western Bosnia. No 1934 (Škoda 1934/1949) is one of six 0-10-0s built for it three years after it was taken over by JŽ. On 24 March 2011 she looked as though she had just rolled down the long hill into Prijedor in the Republika Srpska, the part of the country whose people identify with Serbia, though in fact she has been there for many years as part of a memorial to local people who died in the 1990s Bosnian war.

BOSNIA • 189

Above: Like no 83-173 at the Sargan 8, no 83-158 (ĐĐ 53/1948) is a member of JŽ's celebrated class of 0-8-2s which dominated operations on Bosnia's 760mm gauge system for very many years and were affectionately called Čiros by railwaymen. 178 were built between 1903 and 1949. She was one of six of the youngest 83s which began a second life in 1971 at the Banovići colliery railway near Tuzla after newly-built diesels arrived on JŽ's narrow gauge lines. Here she shunts in Oskova yard on 11 November 2007. She carries the smart lined green livery used throughout the old Yugoslavia for industrial locos.

Opposite: The steam locos collect loaded trains at Oskova station and take them a few hundred metres down the valley to a yard where the coal is screened and transferred to mainline trains. On 11 November 2007, no 83-158's friendly driver welcomed me on board there for a ride back to the station.

BOSNIA • 191

An all-out effort as 0-6-0T no 25-33 (ČKD 2533/1949) takes her train through the unloading shed on 10 November 2005. Ten of these locos were built for Banovići and nowadays nos 25-30 and 25-33 share work with the two remaining serviceable 83s.

JŽ had closed most of its narrow gauge railways by 1978, and several of its diesels followed the 83s to Banovići to take over its line work. Steam operation is now normally confined to the Oskova shunt. Generally one of the 83s is active while the other is overhauled, and it's a rare treat to see both in action. On the snowy morning of 25 February 2012, nos 83-159 (ĐĐ 54/1948) and 83-158 head a special train through the western outskirts of Banovići.

The Banovići railway is double track as far as a colliery complex at Turija, after which a single track continues through the countryside to a terminus at Grifice colliery. Near Grifice the exhaust from the two locos catches a glimpse of the setting sun to brighten up what was otherwise an almost black and white scene on 25 February 2012.

GREECE

On 6 March 2010, 2-6-0T no 101 *Miliai* (Tubize 1339/1903), the last working steam loco on the 600mm gauge Mount Pelion Railway, emerges from a tunnel at Gatzea while working a special arranged by the Athens Railway Club.

Above: A little later, *Miliai* crosses a long single-span girder bridge over a ravine shortly before arriving at Miliai. Sadly, her climb into the mountains proved too much for her; she burst a tube on arrival and has not run again.

Opposite above: 0-4-0T's nos 2 (Jung 11734/1952) and 4 (Jung 12856/1957) of the metre gauge Aliveri mine railway on Evia or Euboea are survivors of the few steam locos to have run on any of Greece's many islands. The line was built in 1952 to connect lignite mines with a newly-constructed power station. Six of these Jung machines were used until being replaced in 1971 by four Nippon-built diesels, some of the very few Japanese locos to have run in Europe until recent years. The small diesel came from OK and the underground electric from AEG. The railway replaced a 600mm gauge line which dated from about 1922 and which initially used two ex-British army Baldwin 4-6-0T's; in 1942 they were joined by two Decauville Progrès class 0-6-0T's. 4 May 2010.

Opposite below: 0-6-2RT no Dk 8.001 (Cail 2343/1891) has just left Kerpini, on the 750mm gauge Diakofto-Kalavryta Abt-rack and adhesion railway, on 4 November 2016. She had been restored to working order for the line's 120th anniversary celebrations the following day. This superbly scenic line connected with the metre gauge Peloponnese system, and no fewer than five of its six steam locos are still there. The sixth lives at the railway museum in Athens.

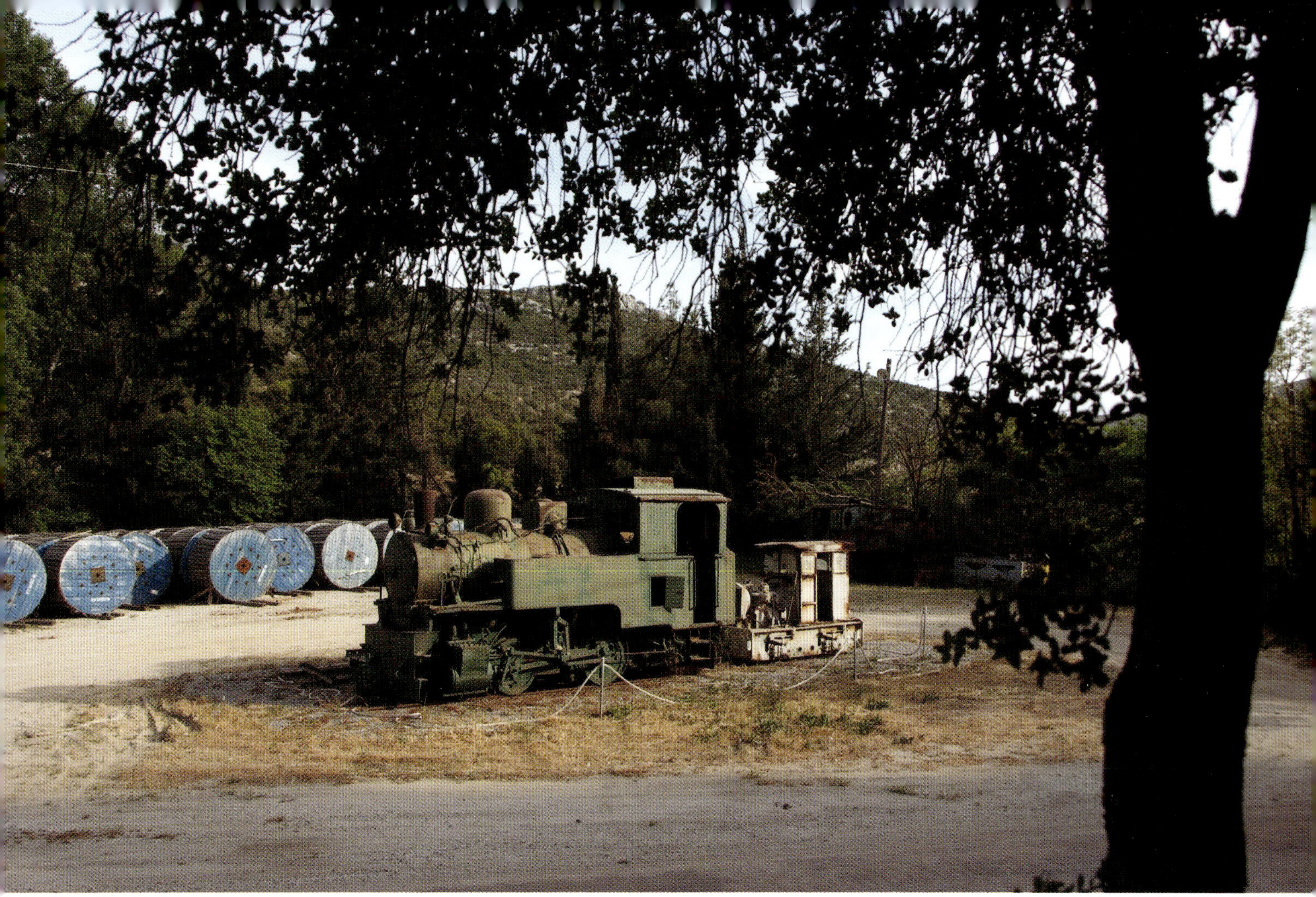

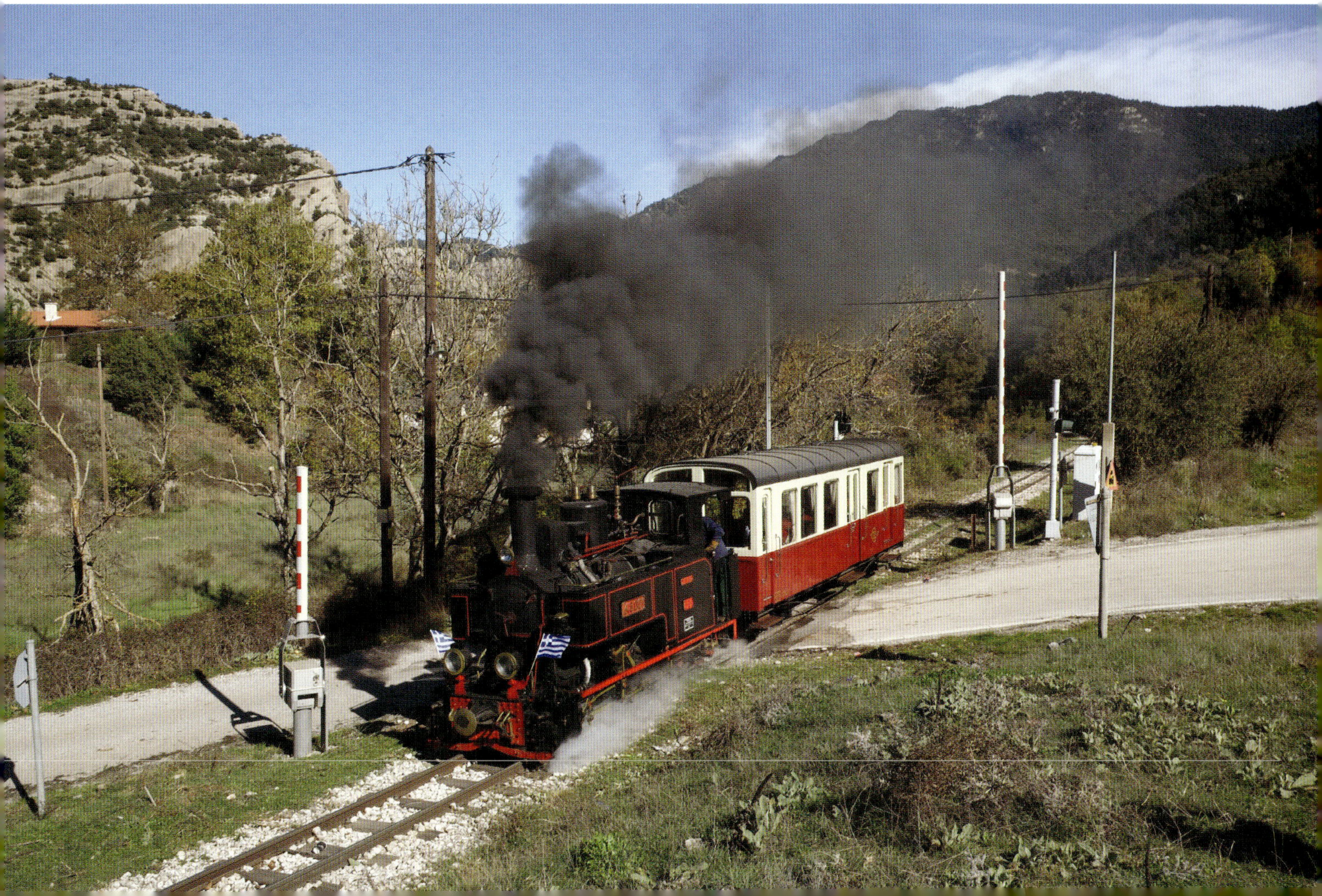

Those who know the adventures of Ivor the Engine in the top left-hand corner of Wales will recognise what is going on here at Kalavryta engine shed, though no Dk 8.001's contribution seems to be too *fortissimo* for at least one member of the town's band! 5 November 2016.

Most of the Peloponnese's magnificent metre gauge system fell victim to Greece's austerity programme in 2011, and, as I write this, it is intact but still hasn't reopened. Es class 2-8-0 no 7.721 (LHW 3034/1925) was one of the locos which worked the last steam train in the early 1980s. She still looked well cared-for at Patras engine shed on 5 May 2010 though she would benefit from a fresh coat of paint!

ROMANIA

Romania used to be home to many forestry railways. They were mostly 760mm gauge and invariably ran through beautiful countryside. Closures began under a plan introduced in 1962, and now only the long 760mm gauge line serving the timber factory at Vișeu de Sus still carries logging traffic. It runs through the remote, steep-sided Vaser valley in the north of Transylvania, close to the Ukrainian border, and the huge cost which would be involved in building even a rudimentary road has always ensured its survival. Many of the logs arrive at its stations by horse and cart. On 7 August 2006 0-8-0T no 764.211 (OK 3980/1910) shunts at Coman, at the eastern end of the line. She worked at Margina between 1962 and 1970, and then at Berzasca from 1971 before moving to a museum at Bucharest in 1993. A Swiss enthusiasts' group which used to support the railway brought her to Vișeu in 2005.

Romania's logging industry expanded hugely in the 1950s. Many new railways were built, and by 1960 they had reached a total length of about 6,000km. The Reșița factory built at least 110 of these 0-8-0T's for them between 1951 and 1958, along with more for other users, and they soon appeared on all but the most lightly laid forestry lines. Another twelve were built between 1983 and 1987 in the central forestry workshops which had been established at Reghin in 1953. The design of all these locos was developed from the 1942 version of the Budapest type 70s, ten of which had been supplied to the country in 1949. On 9 August 2006 0-8-0T no 764.469 (Reșița 2253/1956) heads a train near Ihoat on the Novat valley branch, with lumbermen as passengers. The branch was built in 1953, but much of it was destroyed by a catastrophic flood in 2008 and has not reopened. No 764.469 has been a Vișeu loco since 1962 but has recently been set aside in need of major overhaul.

Several of Romania's forestry railways had been on Hungarian territory until the end of the First World War and featured typical Hungarian locos. 0-8-0T no 763.313 (Budapest 4680/1921) was put out to grass at Vişeu engine shed in 1990 after she suffered cylinder damage. She is notable for being one of the few survivors anywhere of the pre-1942 version of the type 70s. Note her outside Stephenson valve gear. 9 August 2006.

0-6-0T no 763.193 (KL 1219/1921) sucks up water from a lineside pond near Novat on 8 August 2006. This has always been an essential way of watering locos on many forestry railways. Construction of the Vișeu line began in 1932, probably using track materials left behind from a strategic railway built by the Austrian army over the Prislop Pass during the First World War. In addition to Romanians there are still many ethnic Hungarian people in the district. It is also home to some of the Zipser Germans who headed east in the 1700s and later settled here. Romanian, Hungarian and German are all commonly spoken on and around the railway. The Swiss group encouraged the development of tourist traffic on *Mocănița*, as the line is known locally, and tourists now provide a significant amount of its business. No 763.193 was one of two similar locos built for the Greco-Oriental Religious Fund of Bukovina, the largest landowner in this region which today is divided between Romania and Ukraine. Its headquarters were at Chernivtsi and the locos probably spent all their working lives on northern Romania's forestry railways. In the 1960s no 763.193 was at Falcău and by the 1980s had been transferred to Moldovița where she stayed until the line there was closed. She moved to Vișeu in 2004, and is still there even though heritage trains now run at Moldovița.

ERITREA

0-4-4-0 Mallet tanks nos 442.54 (Ansaldo 1364/1938) and 442.59 (Ansaldo 1369/1938) make their way up the steep and winding section of the superbly scenic 950mm gauge Eritrean Railway between Arbaroba and the summit near Asmara on 7 March 2005. The eight 48.2 tonne 442s were the final steam locos supplied to the country, and probably the most successful of the fifty-seven Mallets which ran there. Fifteen coaches were built for the railway in 1887, and another seventeen in 1913, probably all in Italy. Only five survived intact after Eritrea's long war for independence from Ethiopia ended in 1992.

The coffee ceremony is an important custom in Eritrean society. It is always prepared by a lady and usually accompanied by the burning of incense. Elsa Tesfamariam was pouring the coffee on a train bound for the Red Sea at Massawa on 5 March 2005. In her day job she was the railway's head of HR.

At Nefasit no 442.59 takes a pause from her journey to Massawa to shunt these wagons on 5 March 2005. Although no coaches were built after 1913 there was a large influx of freight stock in the 1930s. Seventy five more came from Krupp in Germany in 1966 including the grey van in this photo. This train ride was advertised as a day trip from Asmara. As the afternoon wore on it became apparent that this was meant more literally than some of us had expected as it didn't involve going back! Happily, one of the passengers, a Italian lady doctor on secondment to the country, knew her way around its public transport system, hitched a lift for three of us to Massawa bus station on the back of a pick-up truck and soon had us on our way back into the mountains. Only four 442s survived the independence war. The reconstruction of the railway in the 1990s and 2000s without outside help was a remarkable achievement.

No 442.54 crosses a fine viaduct just before the summit on 6 March 2005. Only four of the 442s survived the country's long war of independence from Ethiopia. The leading coach was once a luxurious saloon for use by the Italian colonial governor but was later downgraded. The turquoise-coloured building at the top left is the Bar Durfo. It stands on a ridge looking out over the scenic valley and the railway above Arbaroba, while from its other side the view towards the Great Rift Valley is even more spectacular. It is hard to think of a more delightful place to sit back and enjoy the sunset, perhaps accompanied by one of its pizzas, some of the best outside Italy, and a glass of Melotti's Asmara lager! The tunnel mouth to its left leads briefly to the other side of the ridge with the spectacular view before the railway doubles back into the Arbaroba valley.

KENYA

The metre gauge East African Railways' 2-8-4 no 3020 *Nyaturu* (NB 27466/1955) has just left Naivasha, in Kenya's Great Rift Valley, shortly after sunrise on 19 May 2011. The railway runs along the valley for about 100km from Nakuru to Longonot. In the left background is Ol Doinyo Eburru, a group of volcanoes north west of Lake Naivasha which rise more than 900m above the valley floor. The two coaches are third class vehicles and formed part of a large group introduced after 1953 when traffic was rising rapidly, but the railway had been unable to obtain new ones since the Second World War.

Nyaturu pauses at Suswa station later that morning amidst some of the region's exotic flora. The twenty-six 30 class locos were fitted with extra-large tenders for the waterless stretches of what is now the Tanzanian central railway. While visiting Nairobi works for overhaul in 1976 *Nyaturu* became stranded in Kenya after political tensions led to the closure of its border with her home country. She has been based at Nairobi ever since.

Near Longonot on 19 May 2011, *Nyaturu* makes her way up the escarpment which forms the eastern wall of the Great Rift Valley. Her enormous tender comes in very useful now that the railway's watering facilities are few and far between. EAR used this red and cream colour scheme for its coaches since its formation in 1948. It lasted until a short-lived privatisation scheme took effect in 2006, by which time it had become one of the last reminders of the steam era. Brake vans like the last vehicle are always called cabooses, a curiously North American term for what was once a quintessentially British railway!

Right: Waiting for the train at Nairobi station on 21 May 2011. The coach, with the distinctive ribbed sides typical of Swedish practice, is one of twelve built jointly by Kalmar Verkstad and SJ. They were funded by Swedish grant aid and handed over in January 1979, not long before regular steam operation in Kenya came to an end.

Below: Metre gauge was chosen for the Kenyan railways when construction began in the 1890s because it was already in use in India, and in their earlier years they were to some extent treated as being an appendage to the Indian network – even down to some of the rail supporting the awnings at Nairobi station which predates the first line by several years. EAR's 2401 class 4-8-0s shared many features with their Indian cousins. The signalman at Makadara, in the eastern outskirts of Nairobi, takes a break as no 2409 (VF 3581/1922) runs round her train on 21 May 2011. The sidings to the right used to serve Nairobi's diesel depot, but it had closed by the time of this visit.

The diesels are now serviced at the fine old steam shed at the east end of Nairobi station. When I first visited in 1976 it was an all-steam establishment, and several of the magnificent 59 class 4-8-2+2-8-4 Garratts would normally be in residence along with many smaller locos. When no 5918 *Mount Gelai* (BP 7649/1955) passed through on 20 May 2011 she provided a fleeting reminder of how good things used to be there. The thirty four 59s were the world's largest metre gauge steam locos. No 5918 became well known for the excellent condition in which she was kept by Kirpal Singh and Walter Pinto, her regular drivers. In April 1980 she was the last to be withdrawn, when Kirpal drove her from Mombasa to her new home at the Nairobi Railway Museum, his final trip before retiring. He returned in 2001 to drive her once more when she was refurbished to work tourist trains. Alas, this was to be her last outing as she suffered a major superheater failure and has never been repaired.

SOUTH AFRICA

It's a really damp afternoon on 30 November 2014 at Kloof station on the Umgeni Steam Railway as South African Railways 3ft 6ins gauge 19D class 4-8-2 no 2685 (Borsig 14736/1938) sets off for Inchanga. This twisting mountain railway was once the mainline inland from Durban before a heavily engineered direct route was built.

Above: 3ft 6ins gauge GMA/M 4-8-2+2-8-4 Garratt no 4074 (Henschel 28703/1954) was in steam at Creighton engine shed in KwaZulu Natal on the evening of 30 November 2014. For several years she has been the only active mainline Garratt anywhere in the country.

Opposite above: Sappi Saiccor's 19D no 3 (RSH 7280/1947), formerly SAR no 2767, arrives at their mill at Umkomaas on the coast of KwaZulu Natal with a train of eucalyptus logs on 1 December 2014. This was South Africa's last commercial steam operation and ended in 2015. The mill processes eucalyptus into chemical cellulose or dissolvable wood pulp, an environmentally messy process which attracts criticism within South Africa and beyond, not least from local residents who have to live with the pollution it produces.

Opposite below: Snenhlanhla Mthembu stands on the running board of Umtwalume Valley Estates 2ft gauge 0-4-2T no 2 (Avonside 2065/1933) on the early evening of 29 November 2014. He is directing shunting operations at Allwoodburn station on the Paton's Country Railway as NGG11 class 2-6-0+0-6-2 Garratt no 55 (BP 6200/1925) approaches on an adjoining track. Umtwalume no 2 is one of the many small steam locos which used to work in the sugar industry of KwaZulu Natal.

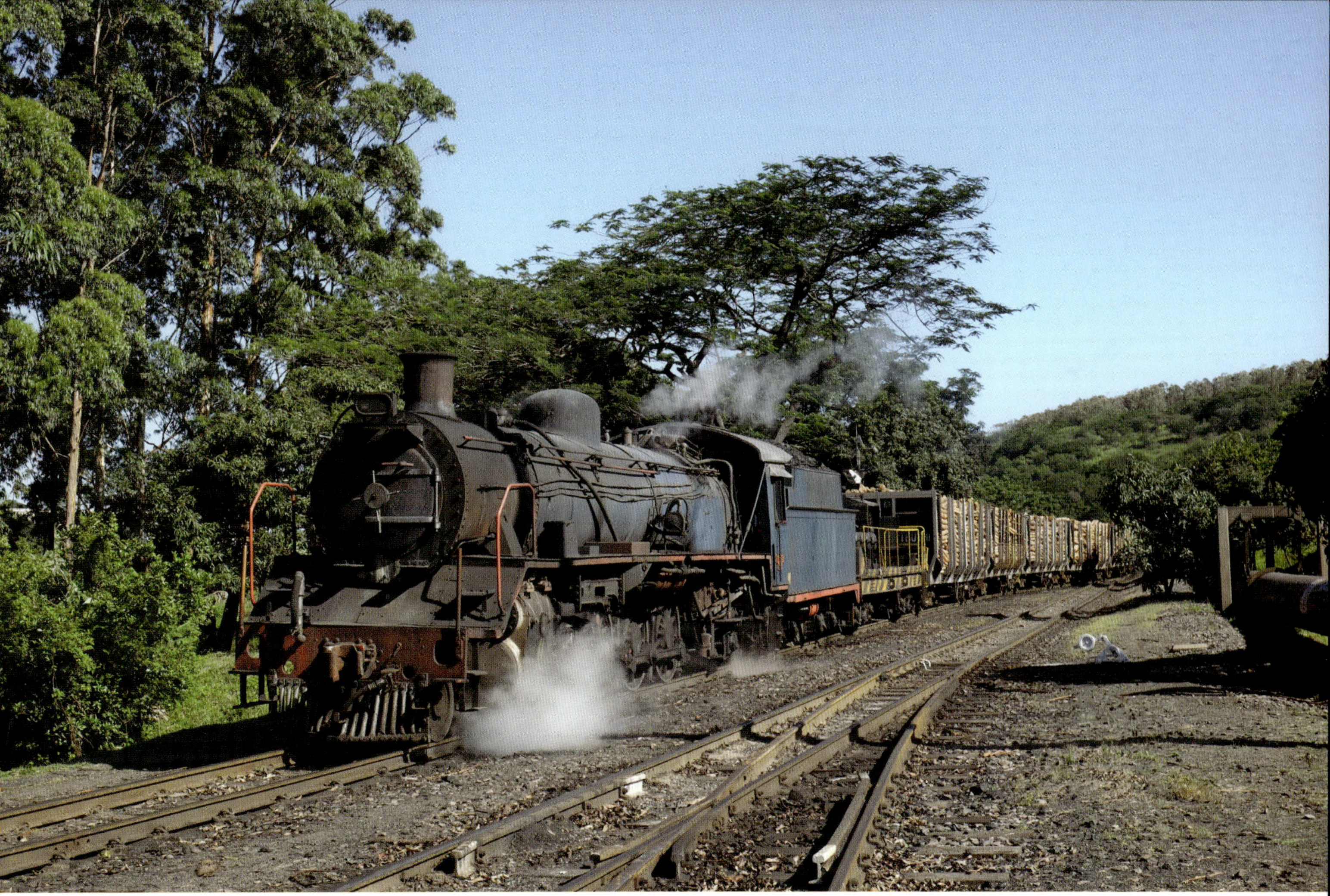

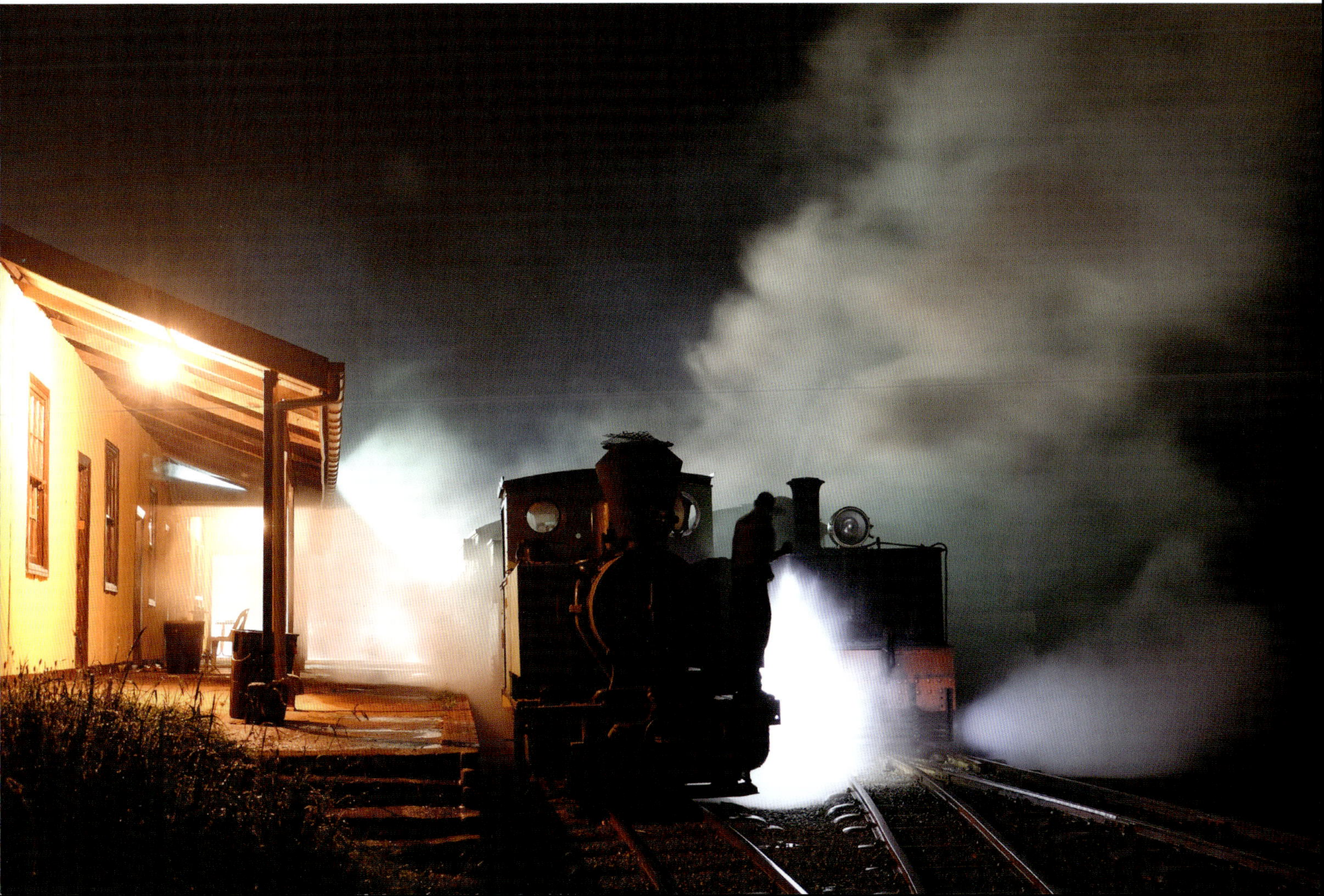

No 55 stands at Allwoodburn at the head of a short freight train on 29 November 20. She was one of the earliest of South Africa's many 2ft gauge Garratts. The railway runs over what was once a branch from Ixopo, on the Umzinto-Donnybrook line, down into the Umzimkulu valley which was movingly portrayed in Alan Paton's book *Cry, the Beloved Country*. Much of the track on the Donnybrook line was lifted for reuse in the construction of the Welsh Highland Railway, but fortunately the branch was mostly left intact.

SYRIA

The Hedjaz Railway's 1,050mm gauge 2-8-0 no 90 (Hartmann 3039/1906) arrives at Ain Al-Fijeh station in the outskirts of Damascus, on the line which once ran to Beirut, on 25 May 2005, though by then this was the most westerly point still in use. It was originally run by a French company and predates the Hedjaz; it opened throughout in 1896.

The Hedjaz was promoted by the Ottoman empire to convey Muslim pilgrims to the holy places in what is now Saudi Arabia, though the military had at least one eye on its ability to move troops swiftly to some of the empire's more restive regions. The northern terminus used to be in central Damascus. The magnificent station building there still stands but when I visited the rails ended at Cadem in the southern outskirts of the city. On 26 May 2005, 2-8-2 no 260 (Hartmann 4029/1918) sets off for the south and passes sister loco no 262 (Hartmann 4031/1918) which was acting as the shed pilot. 116 coaches were built for the railway in its early years. Most came from western Europe, but there were three built in Istanbul, including a travelling mosque with a retractable minaret. The break-up of the railway after the First World War and the renumbering of stock makes it difficult to identify the survivors, but the leading coach is probably one of forty supplied by Baume & Marpent, whose factories were in Belgium and northern France.

On 27 May 2005 0-4-4-2 Mallet tank no 962 (Hartmann 3001/1906), originally the Beirut railway's no 62, crosses bridge no 13 on the branch through the Yarmuk gorge, which once ran from the Hedjaz mainline at Dera'a to Haifa on the Mediterranean coast. In the foreground is a vineyard, a surprising sight in what was mostly a desert environment. Between the two world wars, Syria was administered by France and, in 1924, the Syrian section of the Hedjaz was brought under the control of the French company which ran the Beirut line. The country's railways were nationalised in 1956 and were reorganised as the CF Syriens in 1965. I rode in the third coach in this train, a luxurious first class vehicle with roomy compartments and leather upholstery, though the latter had seen better days with springs uncomfortably close to the surface! It was probably built by the Nürnberg factory, now part of the giant MAN engineering combine. The second coach, with wooden seats, was probably from Ammendorf, another German builder.

On 19 October 2007 Hedjaz 2-8-0 no 160 (Borsig 9009/1914) leaves a tunnel on the Yarmuk line, close to where the borders of Syria, Jordan and Israel meet. She was built as a metre gauge loco for the Peloponnese railway, but was regauged and diverted to the Hedjaz soon after the outbreak of the First World War.

JORDAN

Jordan was administered by the UK as part of Palestine between 1920 and 1946, and its railway system was known as the Palestine Railway. The Jordanian part is now state-run as the Hedjaz Jordan Railway. Pacific no 82 (Nippon 1610/1953) was one of five built for the metre gauge Thai railways. They weren't delivered, and five years later were regauged and sold to the HJR. Here she runs through the desert south of Amman on 20 October 2007. The Bedouin horsemen were an unexpected sight in this remote place. The railway once had thirty seven baggage vans. The leading one here came from Ammendorf, and the second from Roeulx in Belgium. The third and fourth vehicles were probably Beaune & Marpent and Nürnberg products but may have been rebuilt.

A look of intense concentration as the driver makes adjustments to his loco, 2-8-2 no 71 (HSP 2144/1955), on 21 October 2007. In the 1950s HJR bought 2-8-2s from German and British builders and both 2-8-2s and 2-6-2Ts from HSP, as well as the Thai Pacifics, and were able to replace all the old Hedjaz locos.

No 71 climbs through the southern outskirts of Amman on 21 October 2007. The young lad dressed in yellow and red is getting ready to throw a stone at the train, sadly an activity which seems to be widespread in the city. I am far from being the only person to experience a broken carriage window there.

PAKISTAN

Late in the afternoon of 1 December 2004 SP class 4-6-0 no 138 (KS 4120/1921) attracts admirers as she arrives at Nawabshah, on a metre gauge branch north from Mirpur Khas, and runs beside the Karachi-Rawalpindi broad gauge mainline. The branch was opened as far as Khadro in 1912 and extended to Nawabshah in 1939. These 4-6-0s were built for the Jodhpur Railway, which operated the metre gauge system around Mirpur Khas from 1900 until the 1947 partition, and for nearly another year thereafter until the Pakistani state took over. They carried the same numbers for all their long lives and were being kept in service because the YD class 2-8-2s, which worked most metre gauge trains out of Mirpur Khas, were too heavy for the Nawabshah line.

The metre gauge mainline ran east from Mirpur Khas through the inhospitable Thar desert to Khokhrapar, near Pakistan's sensitive border with India. There was very little civilian traffic and it was kept open mainly to serve the Pakistani military. I overslept on the morning of 2 December 2004 and arrived at Mirpur Khas station to find YD no 518 (VF 4401/1929) and this train of tanks which looked far too wide for the metre gauge. In the distance my fellow travellers, most of whom came from Germany, were being led away under the watchful eye of a gentleman who looked every inch a Raj-era British army officer. I greeted him with a cheery 'Good morning' and was amazed when he said how good it was to meet 'a Britisher' and how he had just sent away 'a group of foreigners'. Taking my chances, I said something about 'Don't mention the war', whereupon he fell about laughing and was happy for me to photograph the loco with his tanks. Three cheers for Basil Fawlty!

A donkey pauses from his travels to watch no 518 later that morning, as she heads away from Tando, on the Jhudo loop line which served an arid district south east of Mirpur Khas. Trains for Khokhrapar left on Mondays and returned on Tuesdays. A train also ran anticlockwise around the loop every Thursday (but never in the other direction) and the Nawabshah line operated only on the 1st and the 15th of each month. The trick, therefore, was to visit when these dates fell on a Wednesday! The loop line left the main Khokhrapar railway at Jamrao Junction and was opened as far as Jhudo in 1909. In 1935 it was extended northeastwards to rejoin the Khokhrapar line at Pithoro Junction. When India was partitioned in 1947 the Mirpur Khas YDs were based in East Pakistan (now Bangladesh), and moved west in 1954. The coaches in these photos were built by Linke-Hofmann-Busch at Braunshweig in 1953; I did not see any earlier ones anywhere on the Pakistani metre gauge.

SP class 4-6-0 no 127 (Hanomag 7141/1914) has just returned from heavy repair at Moghalpura works at Lahore and awaits recommissioning at Mirpur Khas engine shed on the evening of 30 November 2004. Note the chalk marks to guide the cabside lining which are still in situ. The railway east from Hyderabad, through Mirpur Khas as far as Shadipalli, was opened as a broad gauge line in 1892. It was converted to metre gauge in 1901 after the remainder of the line through Pithoro and Khokhrapar to Luni, near Jodhpur, opened the previous year. The last metre gauge trains ran in 2005, but some of the locos are believed still to be at Mirpur Khas.

INDIA

0-8-0ST *Lilian* (HC 1644/1930) worked at Riga sugar factory, in northern Bihar, which was served by a branch from the metre gauge mainline at Riga station. She came second hand from an oil company at Digboi in eastern Assam, and here stands outside the station on 17 March 2004, passed by a bullock cart carrying sugar cane. The factory and the branch opened in 1932. The mainline was converted to broad gauge in 2014 and the branch has closed, but recent satellite photos suggest that *Lilian* is still safe and well at the factory's loco preparation point. It's not clear quite when she moved from Assam to Riga, but in litigation about shunting charges in 1967 it was stated that the '[sugar] Company had an engine of its own for a number of years and a second engine was purchased by the Company in the year 1962.' There was also a small diesel at the factory which had previously worked on construction of the Kut barrage in Iraq which was completed in 1939. If the diesel then moved to Riga, then maybe *Lilian* was the 1962 loco.

Above: The 2ft gauge Darjeeling Himalayan Railway's thirty-four B class 0-4-0STs were built between 1889 and 1927, and in recent years fourteen have been in in stock. On 18 March 2004 no fewer than six of them stood at Siliguri engine shed, then newly-built as the land occupied by its predecessor was required for construction of a new broad gauge line to Assam. The five nearest ones are nos 782 (SS 4561/1899), 780 (SS 3883/1892), 802 (NB 23678/1927 and the last B class loco to be built), 790 (NB 20639/1914) and 792 (Baldwin 44912/1917). Barely visible on the farther track is the top of no 787 (NB 20143/1914) which had been radically rebuilt as an experiment with oil firing that was eventually abandoned. Note that nos 782 and 780 are fitted with old round-topped fireboxes, whereas nos 802 and 790 have the newer Belpaire type.

Opposite above: 0-4-0ST no 805 (NB 23300/1925) takes a short test train around Agony Point loop near Tindharia on 18 March 2004. She is one of five B class locos which were built for the Raipur Forest Tramway as their no B1. This 68-mile line was built between 1924 and 1927, mainly to transport sal, a hardwood used for making railway sleepers. Its traffic fell away as steel sleepers came into more general use in India and had closed by 1943, when its four remaining locos moved to Darjeeling. No 805's stay at Raipur was much briefer and she arrived at Darjeeling in 1927.

Opposite below: 0-4-0ST no 788 (NB 20144/1913), on the left, had just joined no 786 (NB 16212/1904) at Kurseong engine shed on the evening of 18 March 2004. My hotel was by the railway and next to it a cheerful sign read "Hurry Burry Spoils the Curry", providing food for thought for diners and travellers alike!

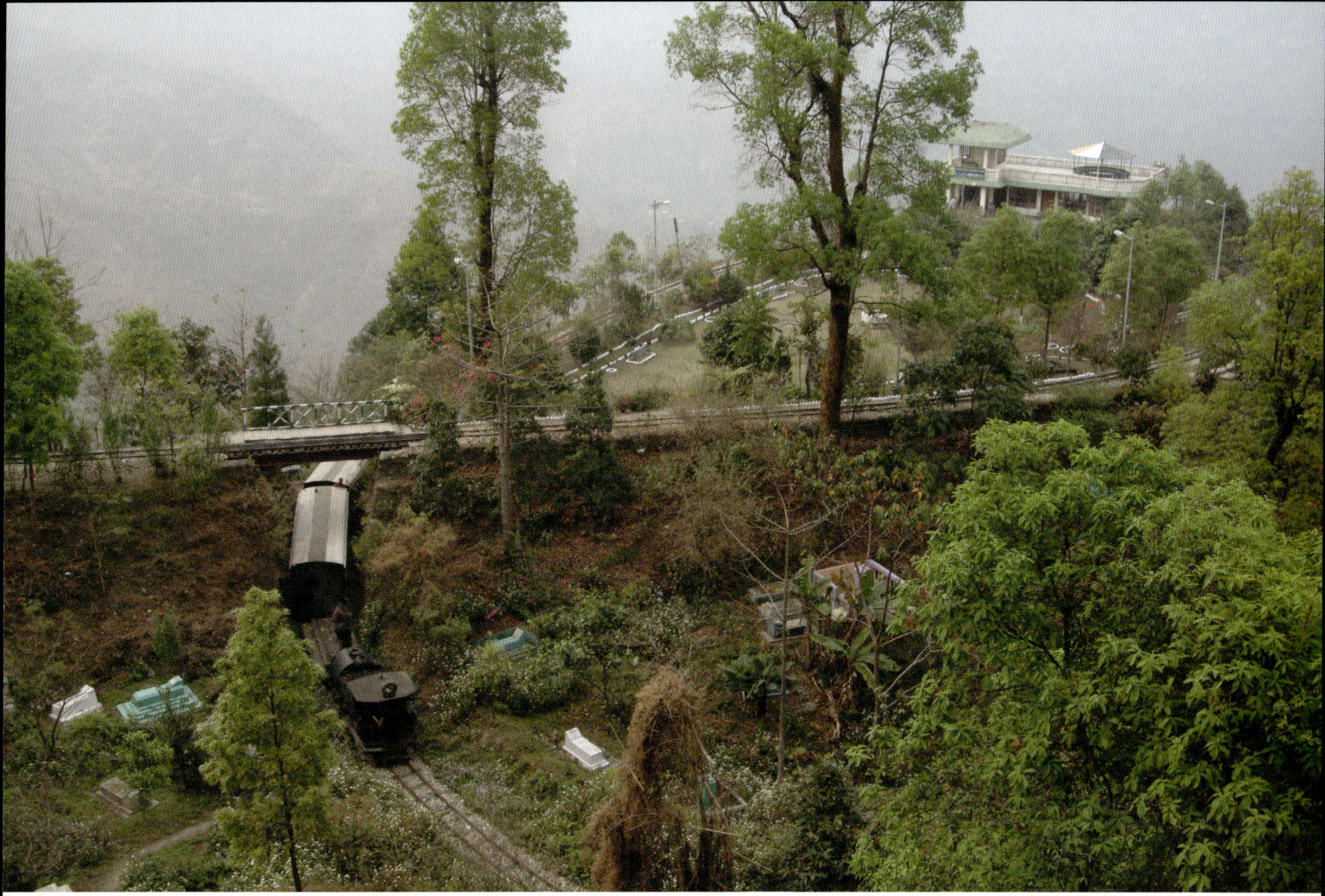

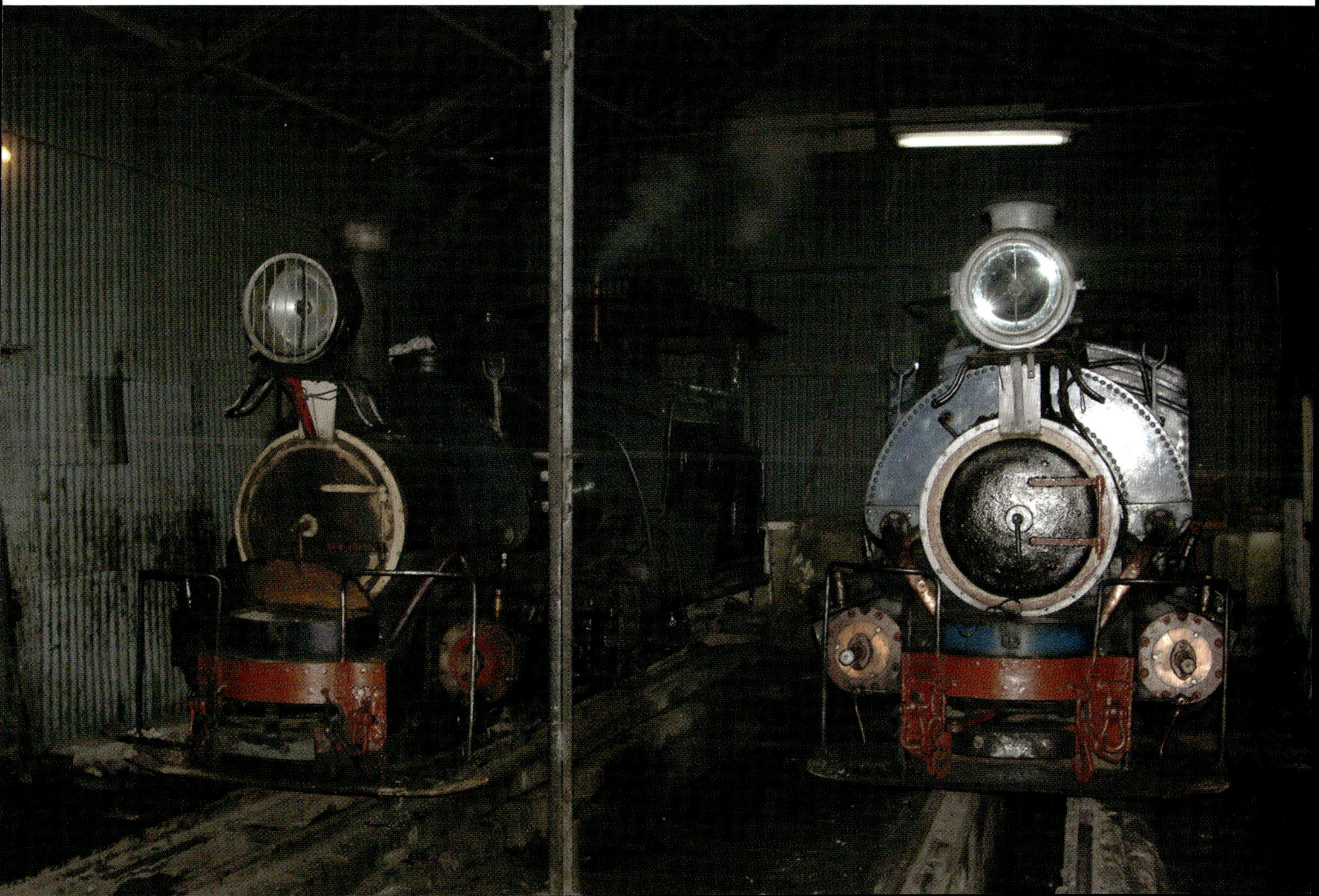

230 • NARROW GAUGE PANORAMA

Opposite above: Steam working was suspended the following day and Ashok Sharma, our resourceful guide, arranged an impromptu visit to DHR's Tindharia works. This gentleman is working on the firebox of 0-4-0ST no 791 (NB 20640/1914).

Opposite below: We were also shown the railway's oldest coach, no 124 *Himalayan Princess,* built in 1917, which only sees very occasional use for important visitors. Its observation end features this elaborate wooden carving.

Shimla was the summer capital of British India and was also the capital-in-exile of Burma during the Japanese occupation between 1942 and 1945. Now it is the capital of the state of Himachal Pradesh. It occupies a spectacular position up in the mountains. The sun has yet to rise and there is mist in the valleys below the station as 2ft 6ins gauge KC class 2-6-2T no 520 (NB 16819/1905) raises steam on 26 February 2016. The railway runs up from a junction with the broad gauge system on the plains at Kalka, some sixty miles away, and was opened in 1903.

Above: Early that afternoon, no 520 has returned to Shimla after working a train down the line to Taradevi, and backs towards the shed by way of the double slip midway along the station's long platform. The station is built on a hillside ledge with no room for a second platform, and the slip enables two trains to come and go independently. These locos were built with side tanks holding only 650 gallons; they were later enlarged upwards to hold 1,250 gallons, giving the locos their familiar, if unconventional, appearance.

Opposite above: 2ft gauge 0-4-0ST no 789 (NB 20638/1914) was one of four Darjeeling B class locos which moved to Tipong colliery in eastern Assam in 1968. It is a rainy day as she runs alongside the Tipong Pani river on 23 March 2004. She has been rebuilt with some surprising-looking features, but her origins are still clearly recognisable. The start of a cable-worked incline up to an opencast mine can be seen over the river, beyond the flimsy-looking Second Jhulna Suspension Bridge.

Opposite below: 0-4-0ST *David* (Bagnall 2134/1924) takes water at Tipong engine shed on 22 March 2004. She is the last survivor of a series of these 7x12ins cylinder Bagnall locos which had worked all traffic ever since the colliery opened in 1924 until the Darjeeling locos arrived. She was kept on because the newcomers were too heavy for a bridge on the branch which led to the cable incline. With the clay used to seal her smokebox door, and the cogwheel instead of a chimney cap, she has clearly seen better days though, as I write this sixteen years later, she is believed still to be steamed occasionally.

232 • NARROW GAUGE PANORAMA

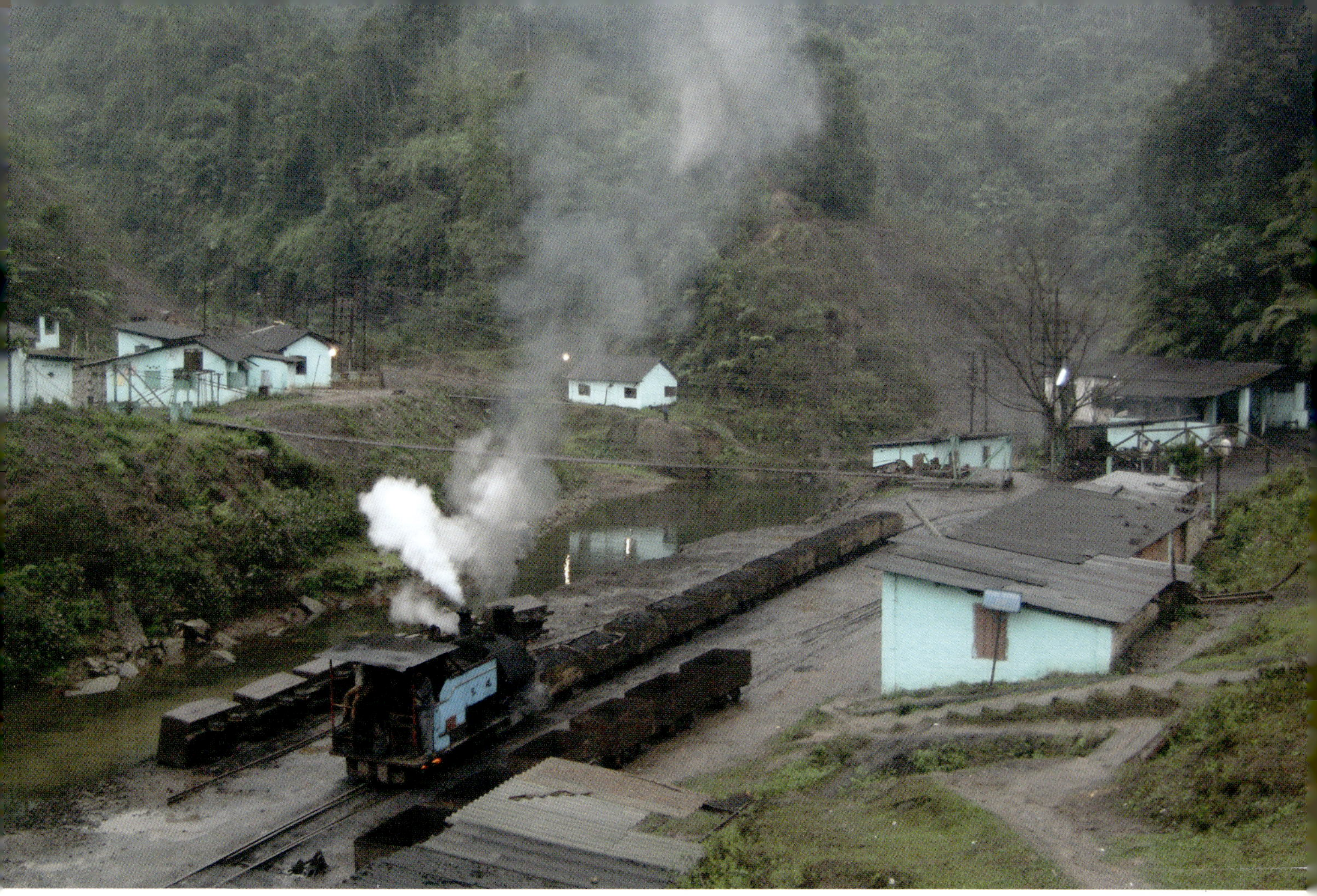

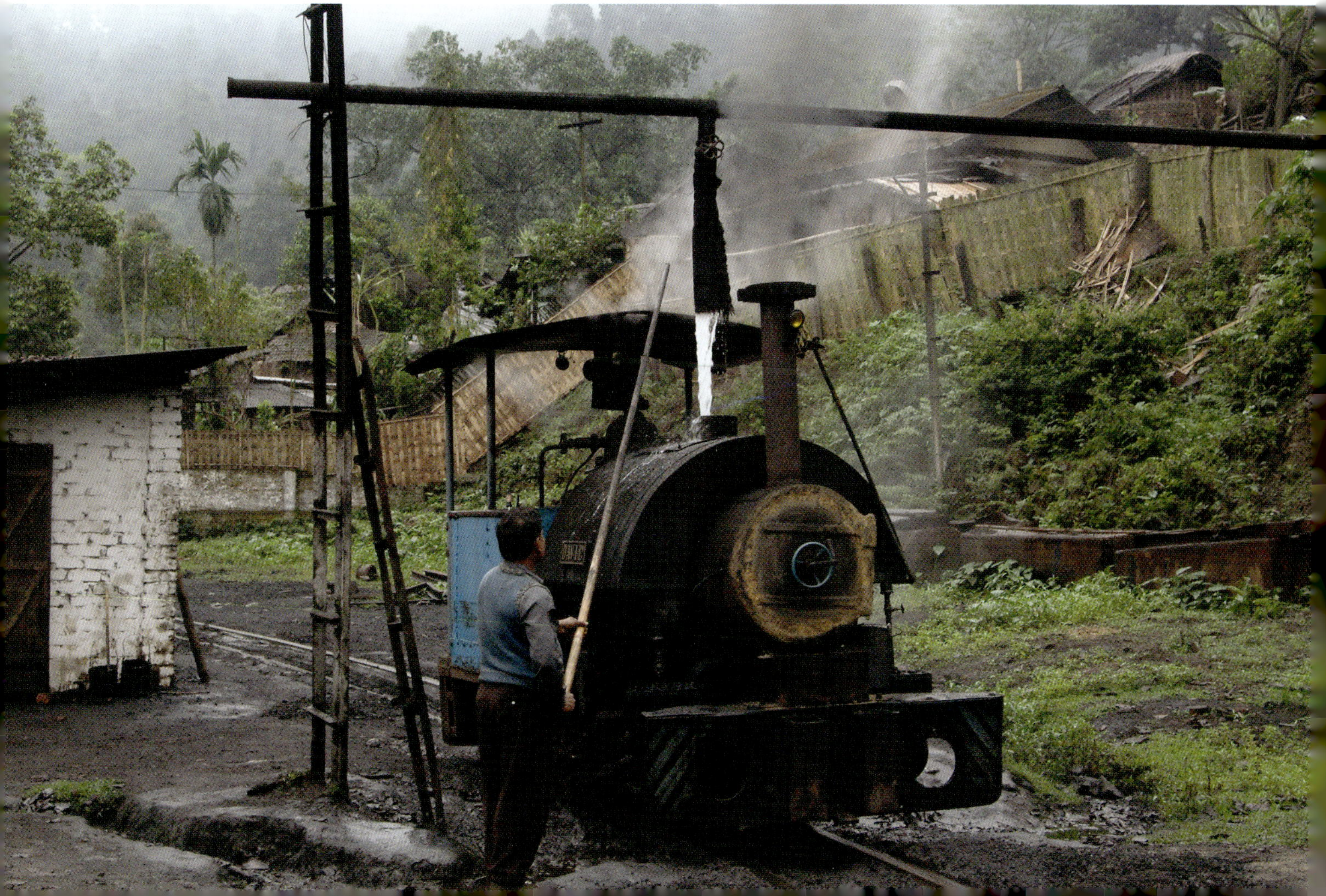

Above: X class 0-8-2RT no 37389 (SLM 3000/1925) receives attention outside Coonoor engine shed on the metre gauge Nilgiri Mountain Railway on 30 March 2004. Sister no 37391 (SLM 4069/1952) is the nearest loco inside the shed. The railway opened as far as Coonoor in 1899, and reached its eventual terminus at Ooty, as it is unofficially but nearly always called, in 1908. The line beyond Coonoor isn't rack-equipped, though by normal standards it's still steep and trains are pushed uphill. For many years now diesels have worked this section, but there is a movement in Ooty campaigning for the return of steam.

Opposite: High up on the side of the valley above Hillgrove 0-8-2RT no 37393 (SLM 4071/1952) works the one daily train to Ooty, on the Abt rack section between Kallar and Coonoor, on 27 March 2004. Thirty one coaches were in service on the line in the early 2000s, all built in 1931 and 1932, of which twelve had been rebuilt with new steel bodies, including the second coach in this train. Since my visit many coaches have been more drastically rebuilt, and few if any of them now resemble their original appearance. In 2019 the first of three sets of entirely new lightweight coaches was delivered.

INDIA • 235

236 • NARROW GAUGE PANORAMA

Above: A rural scene at Mettupalayam station in the late afternoon of 29 March 2004. X class 0-8-2RT no 37386 (SLM 2735/1920), the oldest loco still in service, has just arrived with a special working to collect redundant permanent way materials; after a little negotiation on Ashok's part my group was kindly invited to ride for the equivalent of a first class fare – just over £1! We were also treated to cab rides and runpasts at locations which are normally inaccessible – real Indian hospitality! The railway's first rack locos were four 0-4-2RTs built by BP in 1897, but they were seriously underpowered. NB built two 0-6-2RTs in 1905 and four 0-8-2RTs in 1910, but they were also unsatisfactory. It wasn't until the first eight X class locos arrived in 1920 that the railway settled down to trouble-free operation. Four more were built in 1925 and SLM delivered a final batch of five in 1952, mainly to replace four of the 1920 locos which were worn out and had already been withdrawn. In 1907 four adhesion-only 0-4-4-0 Double Fairlies arrived to work the new line to Ooty; they'd been in store since 1887, originally with eleven others, most of which moved on to Burma in 1896. They were built by Avonside in 1880 for military service in Afghanistan but never arrived there. None of the early locos lasted long after the first Swiss ones arrived.

Opposite: 0-8-2RT no 37395 (SLM 4073/1952) climbs up the gorge leading to Coonoor with the daily train to Ooty through hazy early morning sunshine on 30 March 2004. Shortly before my visit she was rebuilt with oil-burning apparatus as a prototype for four new locos which have recently been built at Golden Rock workshops. The old SLM locos no longer work regular services.

The 2ft gauge Matheran Light Railway, in the ghats southeast of Mumbai, opened in 1907. It was built by the Peerbhoy family, and they continued to own it until it was nationalised in the 1950s. At only twelve miles, it is very short compared with the country's other hill railways. OK built two big 0-6-0Ts in 1905, and two more in time for the opening. They were fitted with Klien-Lindner axles to cope with its notoriously sharp curves, and some remained in use until 1982. Two are still at the railway, one is an exhibit at the National Railway Museum at New Delhi, and this one, no 740 (OK 2343/1907), came to the UK and was restored to working order at the Leighton Buzzard Railway where I saw her on 22 June 2005. She has since moved away and needs major overhaul before she can run again. Members of the Peerbhoy family take a keen interest in what they still regard as their railway and have been lobbying vigorously for one of the 0-6-0Ts in India to be put back into service. Wouldn't it be marvellous if they succeed!

The first section of India's metre gauge system opened in 1873 between Delhi and Rewari Junction, where a four-road engine shed was built in 1893. It became a live steam museum in 2002, and is still home to three metre gauge YG class 2-8-2s and one YP class Pacific, though they no longer have much track on which to run as all the lines through the town have been converted to broad gauge. On the left are YG class no 3438 (Telco 719/1963), YP class no 2151 (Telco 131/1955) and YG 4252 (Telco 377/1959). On the right YG no 3415 (Telco 695/1963) is under repair. By the time construction finished in 1972, no fewer than 871 YPs and 1,074 YGs had been built. 28 February 2016.

The Ewing monorail system was designed to be laid alongside a tarred road. It involved locos and stock with a large balancing wheel which ran on the road while 95 per cent of their weight rested on the single rail. The result was cumbersome but much less expensive to build than the Lartigue lines serving Ballybunion and Panissières with their raised running rails, balancing arrangements on both sides, turntables instead of points and lifting bridges at crossings. In the Punjab, two lines were built for the Maharajah of Patiala in the early twentieth century. A circuit of monorail track was laid at the Delhi museum when it was set up in the 1970s, for use by Patiala 0-3-0T no 4 (OK 3358/1909), the museum's only operable steam loco. This is her non-road side as she stands at her preparation point on 15 March 2004. Her sister no 5 (OK 3359/1909) is preserved at Amritsar. They are remarkable survivors since the last Patiala line closed as early as 1927.

The Patiala railways were intended to provide employment for some of the 300 or more mules which the Maharajah kept to assist the British army in time of war. Steam traction was introduced to maintain services while the mules were away. There were four OK 0-3-0Ts, and at least one smaller loco which may have been geared, as well as an early petrol car. On 31 March 2004, no 4 stood inside her old shed which travelled with her from Patiala and was re-erected at New Delhi. The gentleman on the left regarded himself as her guardian and relished the opportunity to tell me about her history.

BURMA

The Burma Mines Railway's 2-6-2 no 42 (Bagnall 2338/1928) heads south through the outskirts of Namtu on 12 February 2006. This 2ft gauge line, about 80kms long, connected with the metre gauge Burma Railways' Lashio branch at Namyao, in Shan state in eastern Burma. It was built between 1907 and 1909 to serve silver, lead and zinc mines at Tiger Camp and Bawdwin, in the hills beyond Wallah Gorge. Its operating base has always been at Namtu and, in 1912, a smelter was built there. The ore was previously taken away for smelting at Mandalay.

In steam days the line north from Namtu on the climb to Tiger Camp and Bawdwin was generally worked only by tank locos. It includes this loop just before Wallah Gorge station which Huxley class 0-4-2T no 13 (KS 2383/1914) is negotiating on 11 February 2006. Beyond Tiger Camp there is a zig-zag section; there is also a network of underground lines between Wallah Gorge and Tiger Camp which are worked by overhead electric locos built from 1920. The Bawdwin mines had been worked by the Chinese between the fifteenth and nineteenth centuries, but they were only interested in the silver and they dumped the lead and zinc ores. The Burma Corporation assumed control in 1907. The company was led by Herbert Hoover, then a mining engineer who much later went on to become the US president and is best remembered for the construction of the gigantic Hoover Dam near Las Vegas. Other than a hiatus during the Japanese occupation of Burma between 1942 and 1945, the company remained in charge until the mines and railway were nationalised in 1965.

On the evening of 11 February 2006, no 13 simmered at Namtu engine shed, under a full moon which was so bright that it picked out the clouds in this picture, unusual for a night photo. Note the boiler on the right from no 17 (NB 2116/1915), one of six 0-6-0s supplied between 1908 and 1915. The railway once possessed no fewer than forty seven steam locos, from nine different builders. Sadly many of them were scrapped in about 2000. At least five boilers were lying around the engine shed, including one marked as being a spare for no 42 and another from a group of three ex-WDLR Hunslet 4-6-0Ts nos 353-5. There were also two complete tenders from the 2-6-2s, and also a treasure trove of cylinder blocks, axleboxes and smaller parts. By the time of my visit, road transport was being used to bring in coal for the Namtu smelter and to take away the finished product. The ore was still being brought down to Namtu by rail, but in 2010 the mines were sold to private interests and production is now only sporadic.

The extensive yard at Namtu is home to a large community which runs all sorts of stalls and eateries. People constantly come and go, here with no 42 as a backdrop soon after sunrise on 12 February 2006. This young lady's face is covered in thanaka, a yellowish-white paste made from ground tree-bark which is commonly used throughout Burma as a sunscreen and cosmetic. The local people belong to an ethnic minority group. Access to Namtu for foreigners has long been difficult, and as I write this is forbidden altogether while the Burmese army carries out what it calls 'operations' against ethnic groups. The language is chillingly similar to that used to justify the recent Rohingya genocide. There are known to be no fewer than four camps in Namtu for people displaced by its activities and another near Bawdwin, and armed drug growers and dealers have moved in to exploit the breakdown in law and order. In the absence of more detailed reports from the region, and with no-one in government prepared to speak out in public against the persecution of minorities, one can only hope that these people are safe.

On the metre gauge line which runs south from Bago into the finger of land between Thailand and the sea YD class 2-8-2 no 962 (VF 5727/1949) shunts at Mokpalin station on 14 February 2006. She was the only serviceable steam loco at Mokpalin's small engine shed and was kept spotlessly clean and well-polished. The helpful shedmaster at Bago had tipped me off that she was being hurriedly steamed to take over a freight train after the diesel just visible on the left had failed. Regular steam working on Burma's mainline system ended in 2008, but some locos have recently been restored to operate special trains.

THAILAND

Three out of what were then five operable steam locos on Thailand's metre gauge railways rest at Thonburi engine shed in Bangkok on 9 February 2006. To the left are 2-6-0s nos 713 (Hitachi 628/1935), carrying her old Japanese number C5615, and 715 (Nippon 374/1935) formerly Japanese no C5617. They are two of the ninety of these locos converted by the Japanese from their 3ft 6ins to metre gauge for use on the notorious Thailand-Burma railway during the Second World War. 164 C56s were built between 1935 and 1939 and were developed from Japan's C12 class 2-6-2Ts. In the foreground is Pacific no 824 (Nippon 1524/1949), mecahnically similar to the locos which ended up in Jordan (see page 221).

Left: Looking after the locos in Bangkok's heat is tiring work! 9 February 2006.

Below: Outside Thonburi shed on 4 December 2007 2-8-2 no 953 (Hitachi 2051/1950) is being prepared to work an excursion to Ayutthaya the following day. Just over the water is the Royal Barge Museum, one of Bangkok's major tourist attractions.

248 • NARROW GAUGE PANORAMA

A tin of Brasso works wonders on no 953's polished metalwork!

250 • NARROW GAUGE PANORAMA

Opposite above: On the next morning nos 824 and 953 show off the results of all that hard work with the Brasso as they arrive at Bang Sue Junction in the northern outskirts of Bangkok.

Opposite below: Freshly-cooked food is available everywhere in Thailand, and the trains are no exception! Monks with their distinctive saffron-coloured robes are also to be seen throughout most of the country and command wide respect. Many boys and young men become monks; most return to their families after a few months but some follow their calling for the rest of their lives. 9 February 2006.

It is 9.00pm on 26 March 2008 and no 824 stands under the magnificent roof at Bangkok station after her day's work. She is about to return light to Thonburi engine shed. As the crow flies Thonburi is not much more than 1km away across the Chao Phraya River but it's much further by rail as the Rama VI Bridge, which provides the only connection over it, is a long way upstream. I was treated to a footplate ride – well over one hour of sheer bliss!

Above: Near Bangkok airport on 4 December 2010, Pacifics nos 824 and 850 (Nippon 1547/1950) head towards Chachoengsao, and pass under bridges carrying a motorway and the airport's electrified standard gauge railway. This was the start of a three-day festival of steam around the city. The two Pacifics have now been rebuilt with new boilers but no 953 has been left as she was. She was kept in steam as spare loco during the festival, and it is believed that she hasn't seen use since then.

Opposite above: The two Pacifics cross the Rama VI Bridge on 6 December 2010 as they head west to Nakon Pathom. Forty of these locos were built between 1941 and 1950. In Japan they were known as the CX50 class, the X perhaps standing for *Export*. The 2-8-2s were DX50s. The majority of both types were supplied shortly after the Second World War in exchange for rice, which has always been one of Thailand's principal exports but was then in desperately short supply in Japan.

Opposite below: Although steam locos last worked in everyday service in Thailand nearly four decades ago, the railway continued to operate steam breakdown cranes for many more years, and possibly still does. No 25 (TS 11208/1930) was at Lampang engine shed on 6 December 2010.

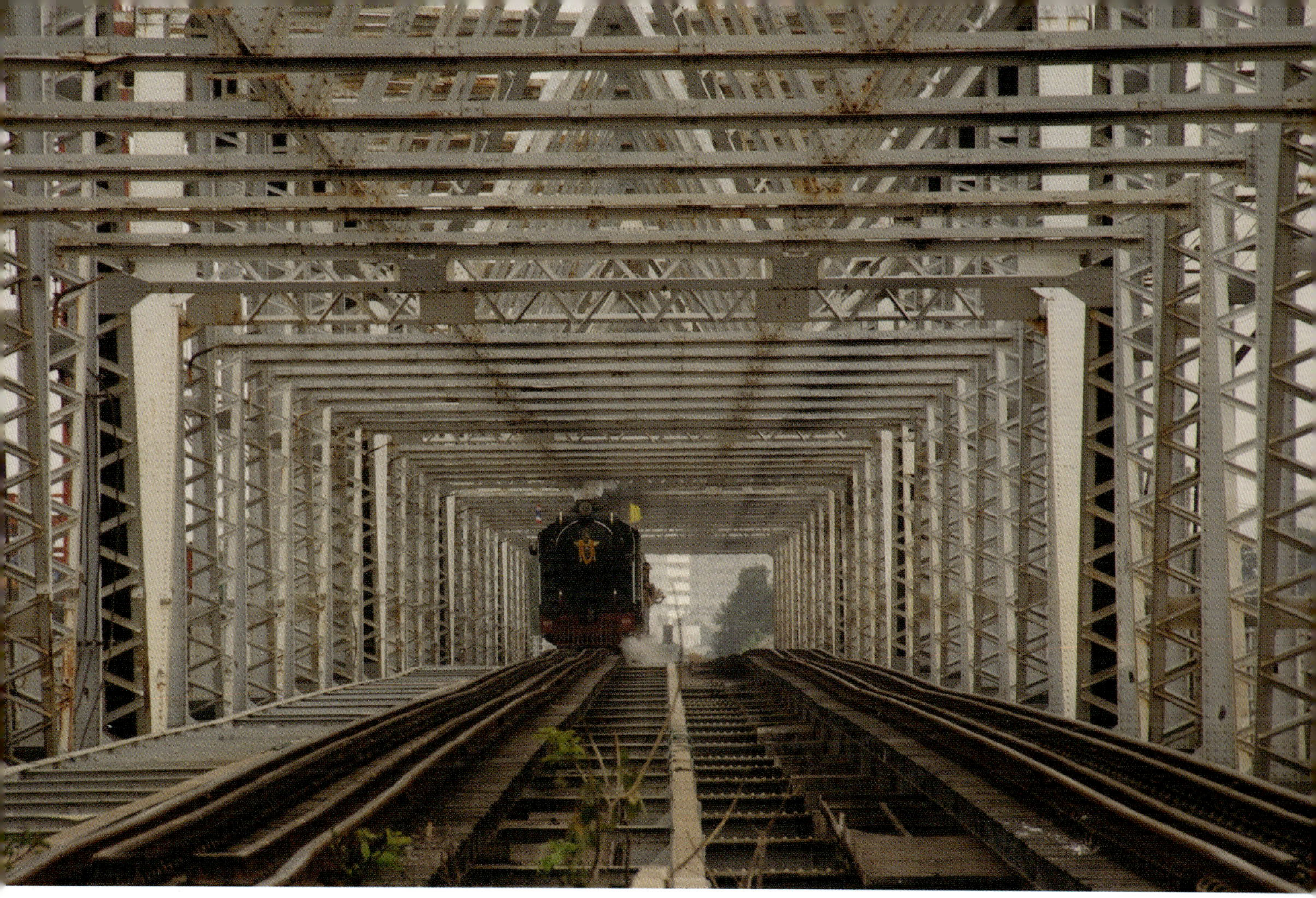

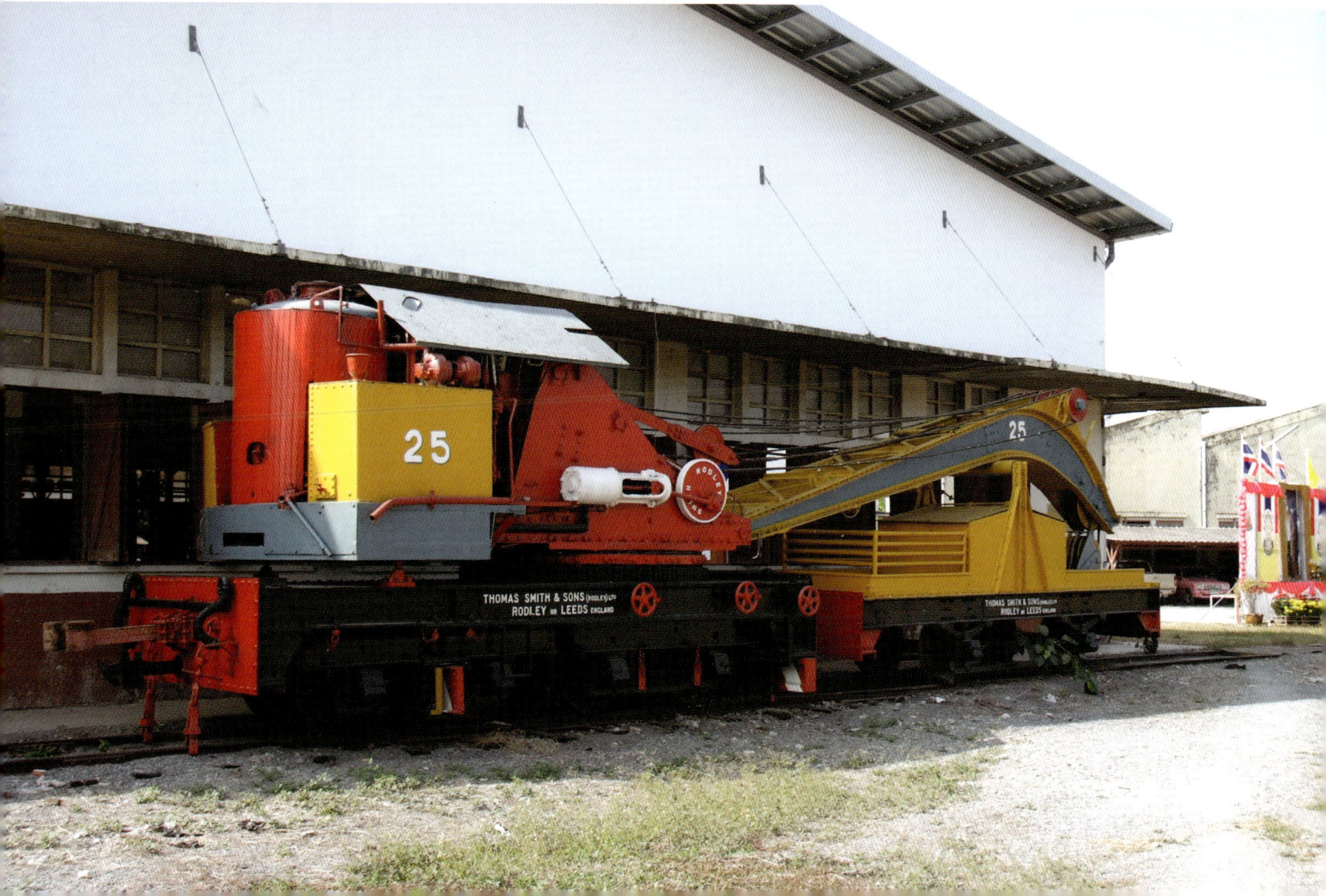
25
25
THOMAS SMITH & SONS (RODLEY) LTD
RODLEY NR LEEDS ENGLAND

In 1926, the Thai railways bought from the Rhätische Bahn the twelve youngest 2-8-0s made redundant by its electrification. They were sufficiently pleased with them to buy six more the following year, all that the RhB had left for sale. They ran mostly on the hilly main line between Uttaradit and Chiang Mai in northern Thailand. RhB no 118 (SLM 2208/1912), Thai no 340, which I saw at Chiang Mai station on 6 December 2010, is one of two survivors in the country. The other sixteen there were scrapped between 1950 and 1965. Two of the RhB's twenty-nine 2-8-0s went to Brazil in 1924 and seven went to the FC de La Robla in northern Spain, three in 1920 and the others between 1949 and 1952. I saw two of them out of use on the Robla in June 1970, just before its many remaining steam locos were cut up.

2-8-2 no 351 (Nippon 475/1935) was the first of the ninety-eight Japanese-built 2-8-2s supplied to the Thai railways until 1950. In the early 1920s large mixed traffic locos were required, and they experimented with 2-8-2s from several builders. After 1926, the eighteen Swiss locos filled the need until a further growth in traffic in the early 1930s led to the purchase of the Japanese ones. These proved much better than anything which had gone before. After being withdrawn in the early 1970s, nos 351 and 353 (Kisha, possibly 1390/1935) began a second life as stationary engines powering milling machinery at the Asia Rice Mills near Rangsit, in Bangkok's northern outskirts. A staff dormitory building was later erected around them. Guardian spirits or *phi* occupy a prominent place in Thai religious belief. These two locos are considered to be the homes of the spirits which protect the dormitory, perhaps because they were there first. They are very well looked after, even though they haven't been used for many years. 6 December 2007.

CAMBODIA

Cambodia's first railway ran northwest from Phnom Penh towards the Thai border and opened in stages between 1932 and 1933, back in the days when the country was a French colony. In 1936 it was taken over by the CF Indochinois, based in Vietnam, and they continued in charge until the state took over in 1954 after Cambodia, and the other countries in Indochina, became independent. One of the new administration's first acts was to renumber the locos and the original identities of many of them are not now known. Two of the ten French-built metre gauge Pacifics which worked in Cambodia came from the final batch of ten built for the CFI as nos 231-536 to 545 (SACM 7786-95/1947 and 1948), and it may be that the whole batch went there. Altogether, forty-five of these locos, called Super Pacifics by the French authorities, were built between 1939 and 1948. The majority spent their working lives in Vietnam, although a few were diverted to French colonies in north Africa during the Second World War and never reached Asia. Six Pacifics, one 2-8-2 and one 2-6-2, have been stored in a walled-off section of Phnom Penh engine shed for many years. Pacific no 231.504 stands under the old travelling hoist there on 27 March 2007. The shed master said that no-one had visited for a long time and he feared there might be snakes, but all we found was a group of very dusty locos!

Cambodia's railways became dilapidated after the country's involvement in the Vietnam war and the horrors of the Pol Pot years, and by the time of my 2007 visit were on their last legs. Pacific no 231.501 was the last steam loco in service but was set aside in 2004. Five years later, Toll Holdings, an Australian transport concern, took over operations and happily they soon overhauled her for heritage work. On 26 March 2014, she stood at Phlov Bambaek junction near Samrong, in the outskirts of Phnom Penh, where a line built in the 1960s to Sihanoukville, Cambodia's principal port, diverges from the old line to the northwest. The Super Pacifics were very stylish and fast machines; André Chapelon, the SNCF's gifted locomotive engineer, is reported to have had a hand in their design.

VIETNAM

258 • NARROW GAUGE PANORAMA

Above: Further along the line, no 131-402 passed this delightfully rustic general store. Her original Japanese identity isn't known. Things weren't quite how they looked since she could no longer be steamed and was being pushed by a diesel. She still carries on her smokebox the headboard awarded to her crew in 1967 by President Hô Chí Minh for efficient operation.

Opposite: Vietnamese no 131-402 is one of fifty-eight 3ft 6ins gauge C12 class 2-6-2Ts (not sixty as I wrote in my first book) which were requisitioned by the Japanese army and converted to metre gauge in 1938 and 1939 for operation in China, where they later became the PL51 class. At least forty-four, probably all the survivors, moved to North Vietnam when the last Chinese line was converted to standard gauge in the mid-1950s. Near Yen Bai the loco passes a temple of Vietnam's *Dao Mau* or Mother Goddess religion with its colourful flags carrying distinctive square patterns. It involves the worship of female goddesses and arose in the 1600s as an alternative to Confucianism, considered in Vietnam to treat women as unduly subservient. It was tolerated during the Hô Chí Minh years but only out in the countryside in temples like this, and now enjoys UNESCO-protected status.

In the late 1940s, the French authorities recognised that the Super Pacifics were not suited to the slow-going post-war conditions and production changed to 2-8-2s, not so fast with their small driving wheels but more powerful. Twenty-seven were built in France for the CFI between 1947 and 1951 along with a further eight for the Yunnan–Haiphong railway, though some of CFI ones may have been diverted to Africa like the Super Pacifics. Another of them ended up running in Cambodia and is the 2-8-2 now stored in Phnom Penh engine shed. After independence North Vietnam started to build more, though only two had been completed before US bombing made the project impossible and production moved to the Tangshan locomotive works in China. Sixty-six, or possibly sixty-seven, were built there between 1965 and 1974. They were similar to their French forebears but had much larger smoke deflectors – almost elephant-eared in shape! The Chinese called them the ZL class, short for *Zi Li*, meaning unaided. Nos 141-165 and 141-190 were in store at Hanoi engine shed on 1 April 2008. They have since been restored for the Revolution Express, a tourist service being promoted by New Zealand enthusiast Mike Gebbie.

MALAYSIA

The old North Borneo Railway, as it was called in colonial times, has lent its name to a steam-hauled tourist train operation in the Malaysian province of Sabah. This very jolly Buddha lives outside a temple in the northern outskirts of Kinarut. On 17 May 2006 metre gauge 2-6-2 no 6-016 (VF 6276/1955) is on her way to Papar from Tanjung Aru in the outskirts of Kota Kinabalu, Sabah's capital and now the sixth largest city anywhere in Borneo with a population of almost 500,000. I hope it's not disrespectful to say that with such a good view of the steam trains, it's no wonder he's happy!

Above: The tourist trains are run by the Sabah State Railway jointly with a local hotel operator. No 6-016 has just passed the temple with the Buddha as she heads towards Tanjung Aru on 10 May 2006. The line from Kota Kinabalu to Papar and on to Beaufort mostly runs near the coast. It was opened in 1902 and was later extended inland through the spectacular Penotal Gorge. The railway's earliest section, from Beaufort South to Weston, opened in 1898. It was always separated from the remainder by the River Padas.

Opposite above: An animated scene on the platform at Papar station as no 6-016 is turned on 13 May 2006. Vulcan Foundry built, and probably also designed, three of these 2-6-2s, a shortened version of the YD class 2-8-2s which they had built for Burma a few years earlier. Regular steam operation on the Sabah State Railway ended in about 1972.

Opposite below: On 10 May 2006, no 6-016 has passed through Pengalat tunnel, under the hills in this photo, and runs across the flat lands north of Papar on 17 May 2006. The leading coach originally formed part of a diesel railcar set built by Wickham of Ware in 1961 and is now used as a kitchen car where the meals served on board are prepared. The other coaches are believed to have been built in Japan in the late 1960s.

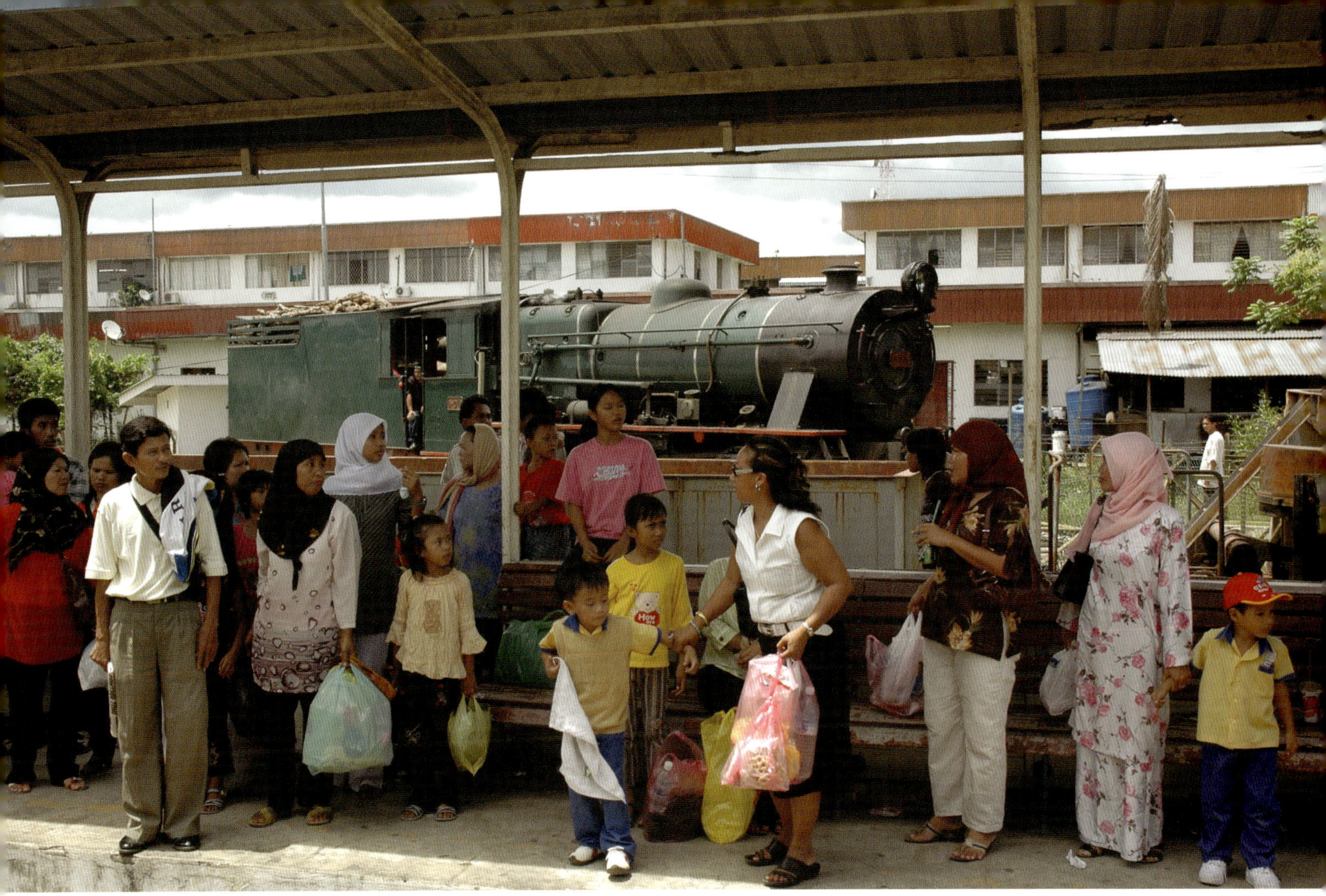

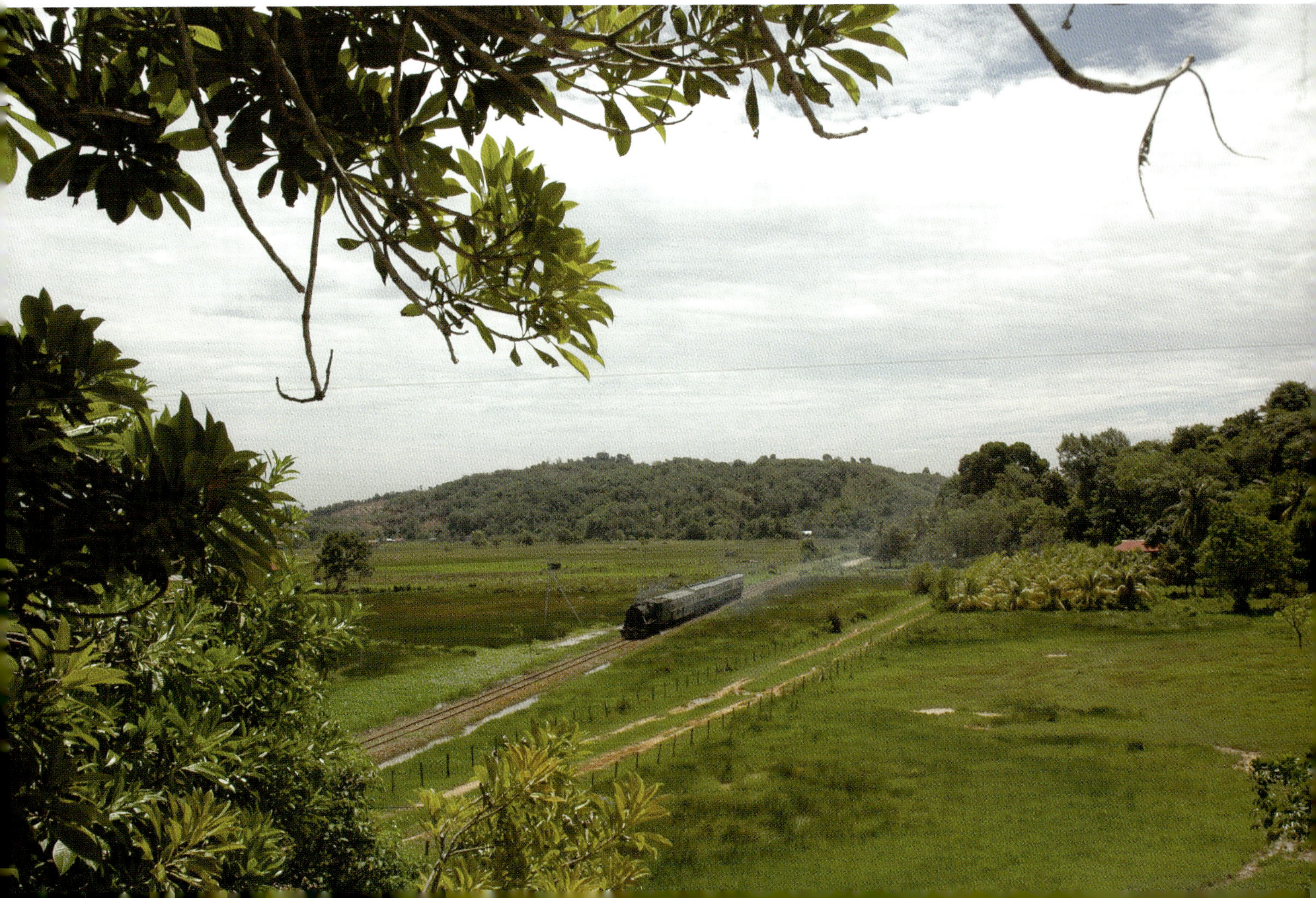

At Tanjung Aru engine shed, no 6-016 has brought her sister no 6-015 (VF 6275/1955) out into the daylight on 15 May 2006 so that her boiler can be drained down. Both locos were restored to working order when the tourist service began in 2000. No 6-014, the third 2-6-2, was stored nearby and was being used as a source of spare parts. The logs are mangrove wood which has always been used for firing the locos since the line's earliest years. It comes from a swampy area owned by the railway to the north of Pengalat tunnel, and the sweet smell from its smoke as the trains went by provided one of this trip's most enduring memories. The three 2-6-2s were originally numbered 14-16, their later numbers indicating their power classification. NBR painted its locos black until the early 1950s when the attractive green livery was introduced. At first it included lining, but this was abandoned by the time the 2-6-2s were built. Recently the running sheds and workshops at Tanjung Aru have been swept away to facilitate non-railway development. They have been replaced by a new depot in the field next to the Buddha at Kinarut – something else for him to watch!

Three of the NBR's older locos now live at the Sabah Museum in Kota Kinabalu. Here's 4-6-4T no 7 *Sir H Ralph Hone*, originally *Kinabalu*, (Hunslet 1092/1912) on 11 May 2006. The four members of this class were very successful and enjoyed long lives. *Sir H Ralph Hone* worked mostly between Kota Kinabalu and Beaufort until 1958 and was then transferred to the section through the gorge. The loco was reportedly withdrawn between 1960 and 1968 after suffering mechanical damage. The museum is also home to two other NBR steam locos. One, no 6 *Gaya* (Hunslet 1091/1912) was originally another 4-6-4T identical to *Sir H Ralph Hone*, but was converted to a 4-6-0 in 1954 and coupled to the tender from a 4-6-0 built by Kerr Stuart in 1905. The other is 0-4-0 4wVBT no 13 (Sentinel 6375/1926) which worked on the Weston line for many years and was withdrawn in 1963.

THE PHILIPPINES

The late 1910s and early 1920s saw the development of large sugar factories or centrals in the Philippines in place of smaller mills. They could be far away from the plantations which supplied them, and lengthy railway systems were built. They mostly used the 3ft gauge favoured in the US, which replaced Spain as the Philippines' colonial power in 1898 and remained in charge until 1946. La Carlota central opened in 1920. On 7 February 2007, its 3ft gauge 0-6-0T+T no 106 (Baldwin 59268/1926) works a loaded train on a branch off the Velez Malaga line in central Negros, with Mount Kanlaon as a backdrop.

No 106 rests at the terminus of a line north of the mill on 4 February 2007. This turned out to be the last season for La Carlota's railways, and as soon as the final cane train had run, they were quickly dismantled to avoid payment of further wayleave fees to the farmers whose land they crossed.

Above: The track was less than perfect. Spilt cane was a common sight and derailed wagons and locos were not unknown. On the evening of 8 February 2007, no 106 has been jacked up after coming to grief at the entrance to the factory yard. In about 2011 all La Carlota's locos were sold and left the sugar factory. No 106 and her sister no 107 were acquired for preservation elsewhere in the Philippines and their new owner has been investigating their restoration to working order.

Opposite above: This tired 3ft gauge 2-6-2T (Baldwin 57975/1924) is no 6 of the Binalgaban Isabela Sugar Company whose central lies to the south of La Carlota and was formed by merging the two businesses in its name. Their railway systems joined up – indeed all the 3ft gauge sugar systems in central and northwestern Negros were connected. The Binalbagan factory went over to diesels as early as 1937. No 6 started life at Isabela, and when my group visited on 9 February 2007, we were surprised to find she still existed, albeit completely overwhelmed by dense tropical vegetation. While we admired the mill's ancient diesels, this helpful staff member worked hard to uncover her. Here he has hacked off the plant life and is tackling the underlying soil on the upper parts of the loco. Nearby stood a 0-4-0ST (Davenport 2168/1929), possibly once numbered 2, which required similar treatment before she could become visible once more.

Opposite below: The Lopez sugar central is located at Sagay City in northern Negros. Its 3ft gauge system was notable for possessing two Shays, which were regauged from 3ft 6ins after coming second-hand from the Insular Lumber Company's logging line on the other side of the town. Lopez abandoned its railway many years ago but preserved both Shays. No 10 (Lima, possibly 2348/1910) stands outside the factory gate on 5 February 2007. I was taken there by Jayme, a retired bank manager and a most thoughtful person. He oversaw the loan accounts for farmers and others involved in the sugar industry, and made sure they weren't *pole-vaulting*, i.e., selling their product on the side without paying the bank its dues. Pitched against his encyclopaedic knowledge of the business, they can't have stood a chance!

THE PHILIPPINES • 269

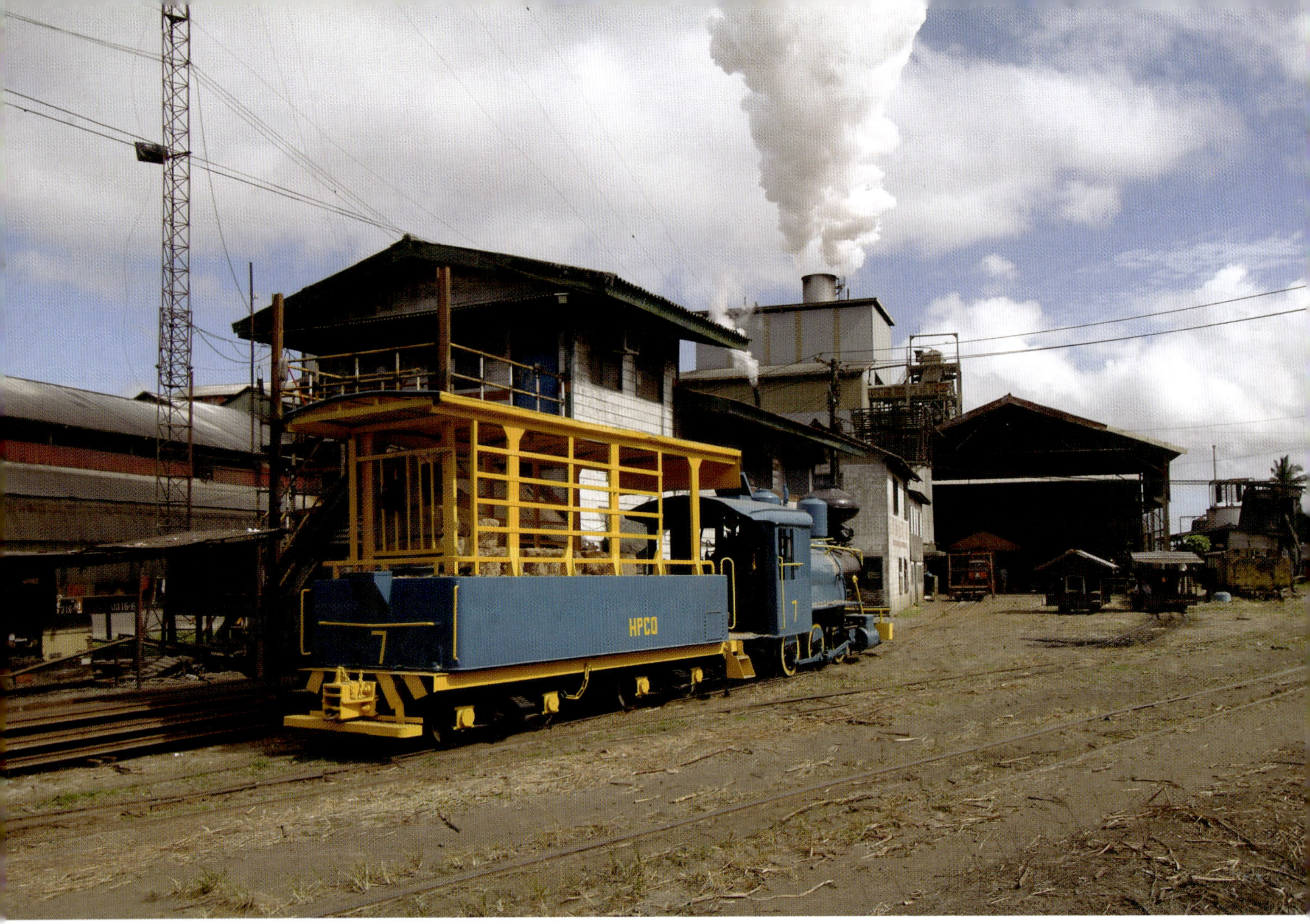
7
HPCO
7

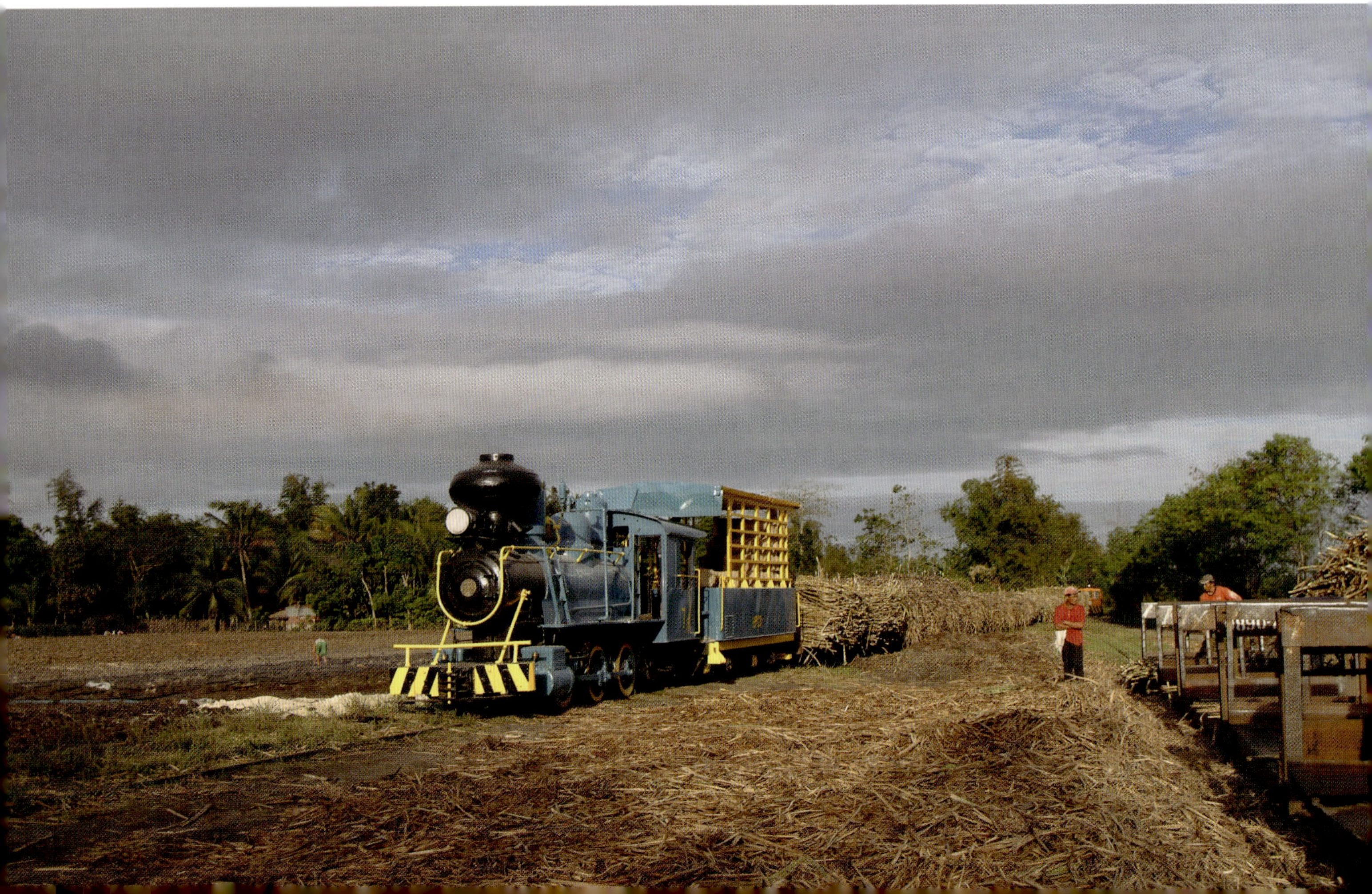

Above: In the afternoon, we headed south towards Adela. It was sunset when we reached our destination – after which we found an unexpectedly good eatery, the Vienna Kaffehaus, run by an Austrian émigré family whose schnitzels helped us celebrate a most successful day. As I write this, the Hawaiian-Philippine system is very much in use, and still home to its steam locos – but I don't know what colour they are now!

Opposite above: Back in the 1980s and 1990s the Hawaiian-Philippine central, at Silay City north of Bacolod, was well-known for its fleet of sky-blue and yellow 3ft gauge 0-6-0s. Several were still there in 2007, but no 7 (Baldwin 60677/1928) was the only one in working order. The manager had taken exception to her colour scheme and repainted her black, but was persuaded to restore her old colour for just one day provided our group paid for two repaints, one to blue and the other back to black after we'd left! Here she stands at the factory. Just visible in the shed to the right is 0-6-0 no 5 (Baldwin 52866/1920), still in blue though due for repainting. She was approaching the end of a protracted overhaul. 6 February 2007.

Opposite below: Our first trip was to loading point 78, at San Diego to the east of the factory, where no 7 stood at the head of her loaded train. Unlike the La Carlota locos, she was fired with bagasse, or cane waste, and smoke wafted from her Rushton Improved Stack, Radley & Hunter type as we were told it was, or balloon chimney as we knew it! It's a form of spark arrestor.

THE PHILIPPINES • 271

CHINA

762mm gauge C2 class 0-8-0 no 4 of the Yinghao Colliery Railway, in Henan province, approaches Yinghao on 11 October 2004. She was probably a Shijiazhuang product. The line was built to 600mm gauge and was formally opened on 12 July 1959, during Mao Zedong's Great Leap Forward. Only one year later, it was altered to the 762mm gauge commonly used for narrow gauge railways throughout the country, possibly a legacy of the days before the Second World War when significant parts of China were occupied by Japan, which used the gauge for some minor railways. The Yinghao line closed in 2007, but most of its locos have survived and are now in tourist service elsewhere in the country.

Despite his dad's best efforts, this young trainspotter seemed more interested in his bag of sweets than no 4 as she stood at Yinghao's unloading shed! 11 October 2004.

C2 0-8-0 no 3, probably also built by Shijiazhuang, was the shunter that afternoon at Xiangyang, a junction midway along the Yinghao line, where branches from two collieries joined and trains were assembled for the run to Yinghao. Someone has a novel way of drying his corn!

Like the Yinghao line, the Huangjinggou Colliery Railway, up in the hills of Sichuan, was probably built in the late 1950s. Just outside the colliery gate it ran through the village market, and traders had to move their stalls in a hurry whenever the train appeared. They no longer need to do so, as this line also closed in 2007 and was immediately demolished. Everyone looked on as 762mm gauge C2 no 31 (Shijiazhuang X1982-09 / 1982) ran through the village on 7 October 2004. The first C2s were PT-4-type locos imported from eastern Europe, but most were built locally.

TAIWAN

Taiwan's mainline system is 3ft 6ins gauge, inherited from the period between 1895 and 1945 when the island was a Japanese colony. The rather grubby no DT668 (Kawasaki 2593/1941) is a Japanese D51 class 2-8-2, and on 17 March 2015 she was awaiting repair at Dadu works, just over the Zhuoshui River from Changhua engine shed where most of Taiwan's mainline heritage locos are based.

The island's sugar industry grew enormously under the Japanese and was taken over by the Taiwan Sugar Corporation in 1945. It reached its peak in the early 1970s, when there were no fewer than forty-nine factories, nearly all served by narrow gauge railways. Most of them were 762mm gauge and many formed a single network, much longer than the mainline 3ft 6ins system or the more recent standard gauge high speed or shinkansen line. By 1952 TSC had at least 185 762mm 0-6-0Ts in stock along with several 0-4-0Ts, 0-6-2Ts, 0-8-0Ts and 0-6-0 tender locos, and they were joined a few years later by a final few locally-built 0-6-0Ts. No fewer than 237 i/c 0-6-0s arrived between 1948 and 1969. The railways didn't just carry sugar as there was also an extensive passenger service. The sugar industry collapsed as world prices fell, and now only three working factories are left. TSC has turned several old ones into tourist and educational sites, one of which is at Xihu where 0-6-0T no 346 (AFB 2654/1948) operates tourist trains most weekends. Here she stands at the loco preparation point on 17 March 2015. The loco comes from a batch of probably thirty 0-6-0Ts built under an order placed with Tubize, which subcontracted some to AFB. Twenty-six (nos 345-370) have survived, seventeen from Tubize and nine from AFB. Xihu's railway dates from 1922.

TAIWAN • 277

278 • NARROW GAUGE PANORAMA

Opposite above: The Alishan Forest Railway is also 762mm gauge, and at one time was connected to the TSC network at Chiayi. Its type B Shay no 31 (Lima 2947/1917) stands outside Alishan engine shed before dawn on 18 March 2015.

Opposite below: All those gears on a Shay consume oil by the kettleful! No 31 is prepared for an outing on 18 March 2015. The Alishan railway was built from 1907 to open up ancient forests to commercial logging, and before diesels arrived was worked by twenty Shays. Four of these met their end in accidents over the years, but the other sixteen have all been preserved.

Later that morning, no 31 heads through a park with flowering cherry trees near Zhaoping, high in the mountains. She generally only runs at Christmas and on a few days in spring each year when the cherry blossom is at its best – something as important in Taiwan as it is in Japan. Here she's watched by some of the many tourists who were visiting Alishan. The coaches are replicas of some of the line's early ones and were built in 2005.

JAPAN

In 1888, Richard Trevithick, the steam pioneer's grandson, took charge of the Kobe works of Japan's 3ft 6ins gauge Imperial Government Railway, to use its English title, and in 1890 he designed these B6 class 0-6-2Ts for freight service. No 63 (Dübs 2774/1891), was one of six bought by Nippon Tetsudō, the country's first major privately-owned railway. Its mainline between Tōkyō and Aomori, 733km away on Honshu's northern coast, was completed that year. Dübs built fifty-seven B6s between 1890 and 1902 and Sharp Stewart eighteen in 1898. Kobe produced six in 1899 and four more in 1902. No fewer than 205 were constructed by North British between 1903 and 1905, along with 168 in the USA and seventy-five in Germany; there were 534 altogether. Many of the later ones were ordered for military service in Manchuria during the Russo-Japanese war of 1904-5, though in the event older ones were sent there instead; most of them later returned to Japan. The country's main private railways were nationalised in 1906 and 1907 and merged with IGR. All its locos were renumbered in 1909; the seventeen oldest British-built B6s, with lower boiler pressure, became the 2100 class and the others built in Britain and the Kobe ones, the 2120s, the German locos the 2400s and the US ones the 2500s. No 63 was renumbered 2109, and in 1930 moved to the Seinō Tetsudō where she ran until 1966. She began a third life in 1970 at the Ōigawa Tetsudō but was too slow for the heritage services they began in 1976 and became a static exhibit. In 1992-3 she was restored once more and presented to the National Institute of Technology at Miyashiro, in the northern outskirts of Tōkyō. She is still steamed occasionally, mainly for its engineering students, and on 21 May 2016 stood outside the shed which the institute built for her.

In the 1890s and early 1900s, Japan's railways preferred 2-4-2Ts for local passenger work. Trevithick oversaw construction of one at Kobe in 1893, the first Japanese-built loco, and Kisha began mass-producing them in 1902. Sixty-three from Dübs were among 174 British-built examples. They included Ōsaka Tetsudō no 6 (Dübs 2765/1891), one of two fitted with Walschaerts valve gear long before it came into general use in either the UK or Japan. She enjoyed a long and varied career. The Ōsaka was absorbed by the Kansai Tetsudō in 1900 and they numbered her 57. In 1907 the Kansai was caught up in the nationalisation programme, after which she became IGR's no 220. She can't have been loved there since they sold her only ten years later to the newly-built Tama Tetsudō, near Tokyo, which numbered her A1. In 1927 the Tama was taken over by the electrified Seibu Tetsudō which would later become the owner of the 600mm gauge 0-10-0T now at the Frankfurter Feldbahnmuseum (see page 153). At first no A1 kept her number, but in 1944 the Seibu renumbered its few remaining steam locos and she became no 3. In 1956 she was despatched to a subsidiary line, the Nihon Nippon Tetsudō, which already had a no 3, but this wasn't a problem as a few strokes of the paintbrush turned her into no 8! Maybe the Seibu's top brass never found out since she was preserved as no 3 after her working days ended in 1965. She now lives at the Showa Tetsudō School in Tōkyō, founded in 1928 to encourage recruitment into Japan's railway industry. Note the pipe connecting the front and rear brake hoses without any connection to the cab. Was it there just for show?! 21 May 2016.

JAPAN • 281

Above: A glimpse of 3ft 6ins gauge 2-8-2 no D51 498 (Takatori 26/1940) through the cherry trees on 14 April 2015, as she passes rice paddies near Akogashima, on the Ban'etsu West line in Fukushima prefecture. She is on her way from Kōriyama to Aizu-Wakamatsu. The railway dates from 1898.

Opposite above: Further west, no D51 498 passes Mount Bandai, near the summit of the steep climb away from Aizu-Wakamatsu, on her return journey to Kōriyama on 14 April 2015. From the 1890s, Japan's state railway acquired a great many locos within a fairly small number of standard classes. The 1,115 D51s were the most numerous of all, and that total doesn't take account of the locos built for Taiwan and for the Soviet island of Sakhalin.

Opposite below: When the C10 2-6-4T class appeared in 1930, it was IGR's first new tank loco type for more than twenty-one years, and also the first to be designed and built entirely within Japan. Replacement of the early 2-4-2Ts and 0-6-2Ts had become urgent, and the C10s were prototypes before mass production began. Twenty-three were constructed; they were all withdrawn between 1959 and 1962 and only no C10 8 (Kawasaki 1363/1930) has survived. She was bought for industrial service at Miyako, on the Pacific coast of northern Honshu. After she retired again in 1986, the local authority rescued her, and she operated tourist trains from the town for some years. In 1994, she was presented to the Ōigawa and has run there ever since. Here she stands outside their engine shed at Shinkanaya on 12 April 2015.

JAPAN • 283

Above: Japan's railway system was being expanded when the world depression arrived in the late 1920s. IGR adopted an ultra-lightweight specification for minor lines and the C12 2-6-2Ts, developed from the C10s, were produced from 1932 to work them. 263 were built until 1948, though there were never this many in service at the same time because of the fifty-eight which went to China, and a few others were sent elsewhere. No C12 164 worked at the Ōigawa for many years, but now needs major overhaul. On the evening of 12 April 2015, she stood on the turntable at Shinkanaya.

Opposite: On 24 May 2016 2-6-4T no C11 325 (Nippon 1407/1946) crosses bridge no 1 on the Tadami line between Aizu-Hinohara and Aizu-Kawaguchi in central Honshu, which was built as recently as 1956. The C11s were designed in the light of experience with the C10s, and like the C12s first appeared in 1932. They made greater use of welded construction, and there were numerous small improvements which resulted in a subtly different appearance. The coaches in this train, and also in the train hauled by no D51 498 in the previous photos, come from a group of seven which are maintained for heritage service by JR East, the privatised operator of services in the part of Honshu north of Tōkyō. They were built between 1938 and 1955.

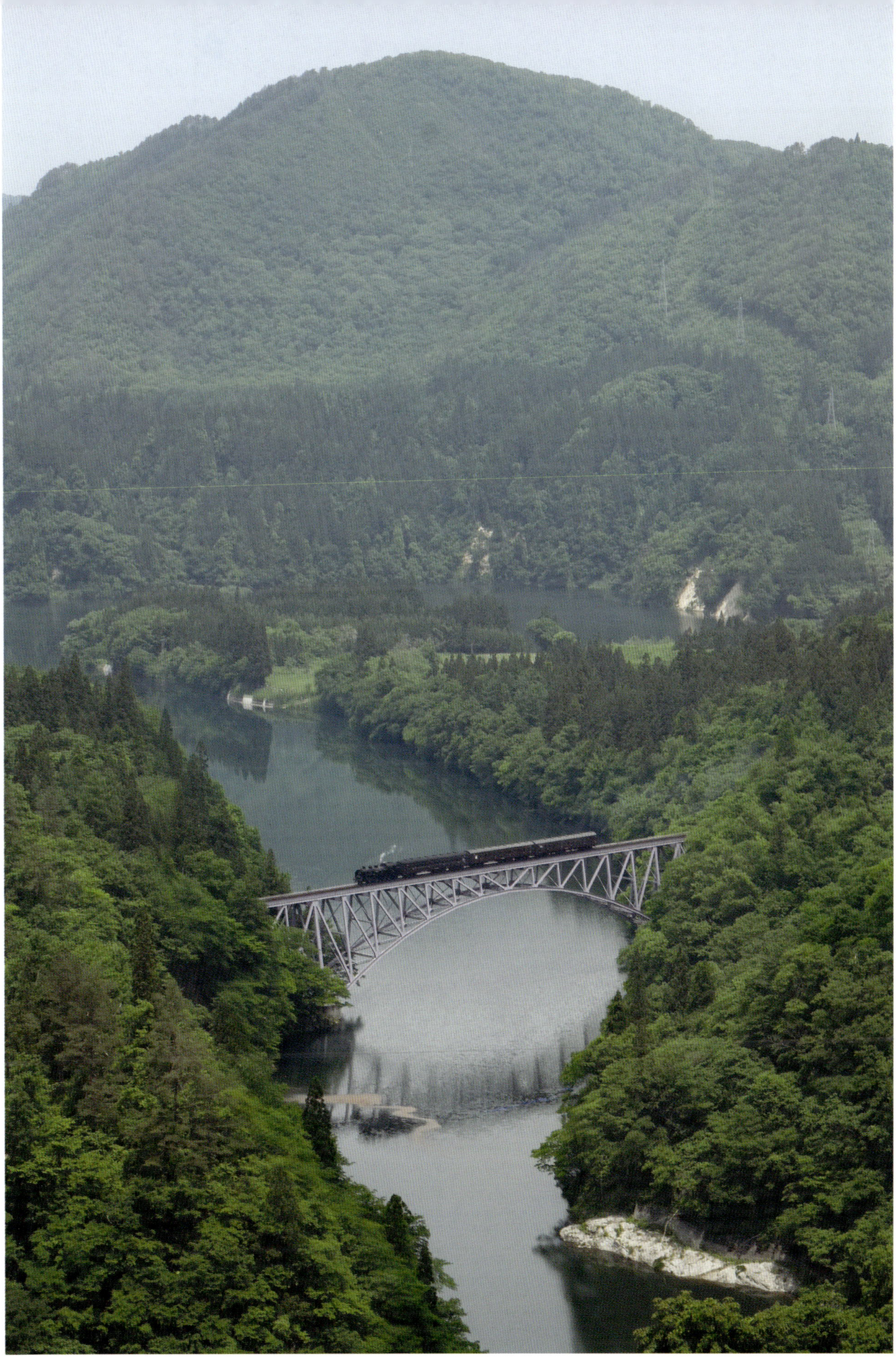

Two days later, no C11 325 leaves a short tunnel and approaches Aizu-Hinohara station. By the time production ended in 1947, 381 C11s had been built for the state railways, and a further eighteen for private lines. Unlike the C12s, none ever left Japan.

286 • NARROW GAUGE PANORAMA

AUSTRALIA

Commonwealth Railways 3ft 6ins gauge NM class 4-8-0 no 25 (Thompson 51/1925) heads south from the Pichi Richi Railway's Summit station on 12 June 2016. The leading coach, with its rounded glazed end, was built in 1929 for the use of the CR Commissioner, senior officers and invited guests. It is now a part of the railway's superb train of CR coaches constructed between the late 1920s and the 1940s, reminiscent of the old *Ghan* trains which once ran over the line on their way to Alice Springs. Fourteen NMs, nos 15-28, were built for CR in time for it to take over services from South Australian Railways on the mainline north from Port Augusta in 1926. They were close copies of Queensland Railways' C17s. Seven improved locos, nos 31-7, came in 1927 along with a final one, no 38, which had reduced coal capacity to suit it for the lightly-laid North Australia Railway at Darwin. No 25 ran for CR until 1964 and later served as a stationary boiler.

For most of her career, SAR steam railmotor no 1 (Kitson 4356/1905), with her Metropolitan-built body, was based at Quorn, now the Pichi Richi's northern terminus. She was the only piece of motive power which SAR sold to CR on the 1926 takeover and became their no NJAB1. After withdrawal in 1931, she spent nearly thirty years in store at Quorn engine shed. She was then put on show for a few years at Alice Springs station before returning to Quorn for restoration to working order. She first ran again in 1984. On 13 June 2016, she passes the site of Pichi Richi village which was abandoned many years ago. Construction of the railway began in 1878; it eventually reached Alice Springs in 1929, but never progressed further towards an intended junction with the North Australia Railway. The section through Quorn was replaced by a standard gauge line on a different alignment in 1957 and the Pichi Richi society was formed to resuscitate a part of it in 1974. Its volunteers now run a marvellous heritage operation. Most of its trains are worked by Western Australian W class 4-8-2s. Metropolitan unwittingly facilitated their survival, since the diesels built at their factory which would have replaced them were so unreliable that they worked on into the preservation era.

Victorian Railways 2-6-0+0-6-2 Beyer Garratt no G42 (BP 6268/1926) approaches Pinnocks Road crossing near Emerald on the Puffing Billy Railway, which must be by far the busiest heritage operation anywhere in the southern hemisphere. VR bought two of these Garratts, which were 2ft 6ins versions of the Western Australian Ms class 3ft 6ins locos. Passengers had been dangling their legs from these open coaches ever since the first of them arrived in 1919 but a recent accident has led to a ban, far from popular locally! 28 January 2017.

Above: On 29 January 2017, Victorian Railways NA class 2-6-2T no 14A (Newport, 1914) crosses Monbulk Creek viaduct as she heads the daily train to Gembrook. The Puffing Billy line is one of four 2ft 6ins gauge railways which opened in Victoria early in the twentieth century to encourage development of some of its poorest districts. The first two NAs were built by Baldwin in 1898 and they were followed by fifteen more from VR's Newport shops. It is easy to see the resemblence which these locos bear to *Lyn*, on the Lynton & Barnstaple, which also dates from 1898 (see pages 123-5). The leading coach, no 2NBD, is one of the first series of VR narrow gauge coaches built in 1899.

Opposite above: The old 3ft 6ins gauge Mount Lyell Railway connected the gold, silver and copper mines at Queenstown with the Tasmanian Government Railways at Strachan on the island's west coast and included two Abt rack sections. The old railway closed in 1963 but was rebuilt nearly forty years later to encourage tourism in what had become an impoverished region. On 24 March 2013 0-4-2RT no 1 (Dübs 3369/1896) stands at Queenstown station. Behind her is the goods shed, the only structure remaining there from the line's old days. Mount Owen, with an altitude of 1,146m, forms the backdrop.

Opposite below: On 25 March 2013, Tristan McMahon, one of the line's drivers, very kindly drove me in his Morris Minor to this level crossing near Halls Creek to watch no 1 pass on her way to the coast. The car was built in BMC's old factory in Sydney.

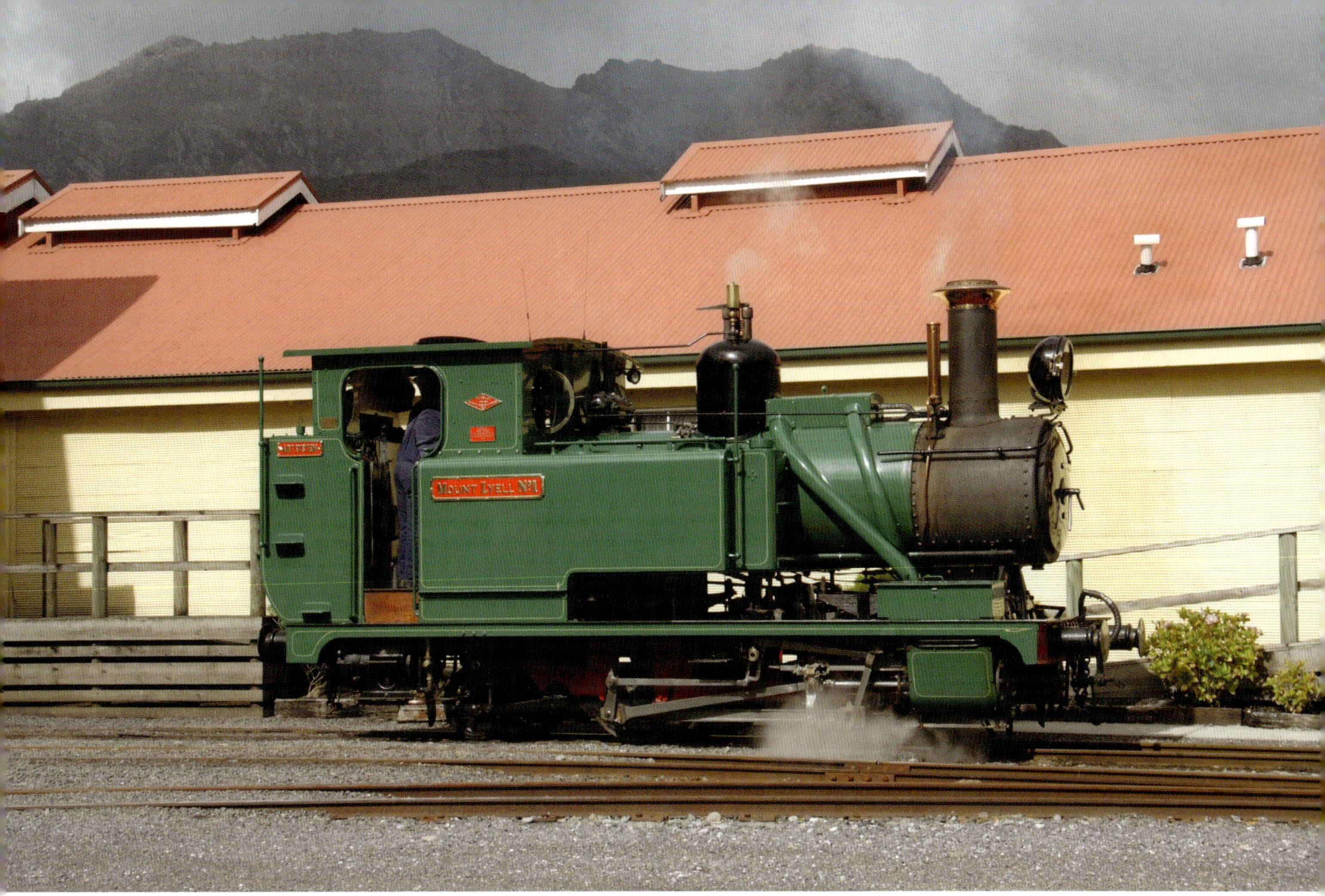
MOUNT LYELL No1

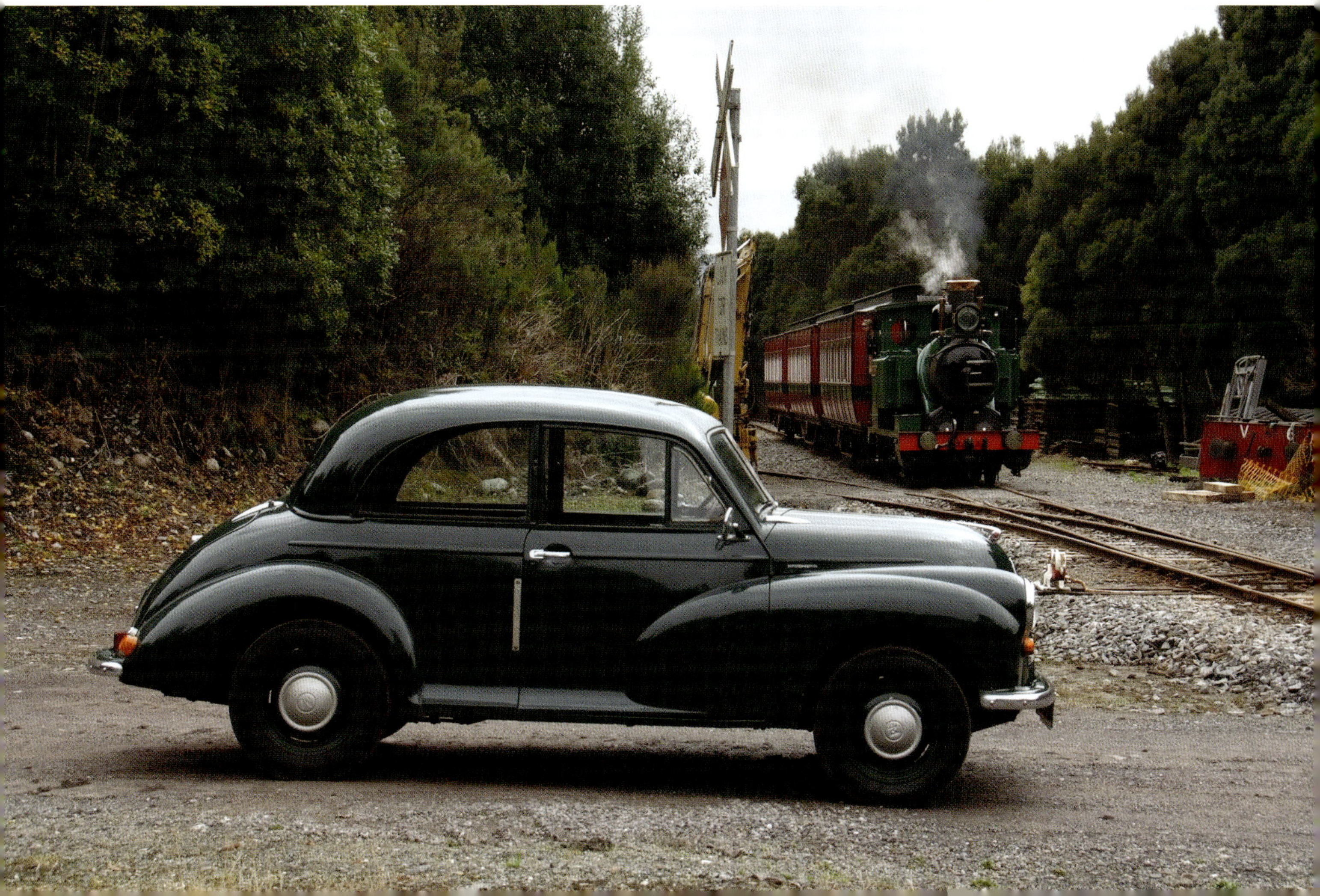

I was treated to a cab ride on 0-4-2RT no 5 (NB 24418/1938) in the late afternoon of 25 March 2013 as she worked a test train to the summit at Rinadeena after overhaul at Queenstown. On her way back she passes the Halls Creek crossing with a TGR wagon. Tristan McMahon is at the controls. The reconstruction was an enormous undertaking, since much of the trackbed had been washed away in western Tasmania's extreme weather and many of its bridges had collapsed. The revived railway opened in 2002, and now has all four of the old line's surviving locos.

NEW ZEALAND

New Zealand's many bush tramways were home to some weird and wonderful lokeys, as they were called locally. A common feature was a surprising number of wheels to cope with their lightly constructed track. Many lokeys were geared, but this 3ft 6ins gauge loco (Davidson 25/1920) was an economy chain-driven model. She worked first at Stratford & Blair's sawmill at Paroa, moved later to Ogilvie at Gladstone and ended her working life in 1942 with Donaldson at Redjacks, where she now stands on a short section of their tramway. All these concerns operated close to South Island's west coast, not far from the loco's birthplace at Hokitika. 30 October 2015.

The 3ft 6ins gauge New Zealand Railways' no 608 *Passchendaele* (Addington 163/1915) was the first of their celebrated Ab class Pacifics. With 149 members, they were the country's most numerous steam locos, and several lasted until the twilight of steam in the late 1960's. They were equally at home on passenger and freight work and could run almost anywhere. In 1925, no 608 became NZR's First World War memorial loco. Here she sets off from Waitati, on the east coast of South Island, bound for Oamaru with her train of period coaches, on 27 October 2015. The loco now belongs to Steam Incorporated, an enthusiast-led group based at Paekakariki, near Wellington, as do most of the coaches, though the leading vehicle, a baggage van, normally lives at the Glenbrook Vintage Railway, a heritage railway near Auckland which is also run by enthusiasts. It was built in 1913 and was withdrawn by NZR in 1978. The coaches' paintscheme is known as Midland Red amongst New Zealand's railwaymen. It was introduced in the 1920s and lasted for the remainder of the steam era and beyond. It is believed originally to have been sourced from the LMSR in the UK.

A little later, these sheep race past the flax to get a better view as *Passchendaele* climbs through the hills near Warrington. Steam Incorporated maintains its locos and coaches in authentic historical condition. They frequently operate steam specials, and New Zealand's railway enthusiasts are very fortunate to be able to enjoy their superb trains in action. The fourth vehicle in the train with the curved sides, no Aa1618, is one of five steel-panelled vehicles built as sleeping cars between 1925 and 1927 and was later fitted with a kitchenette. Along with two others she was rebuilt with conventional seating in the early 1970s for use in suburban service and she entered preservation in 1982 as a buffet car. The other four wooden-bodied passenger carriages were all built between 1909 and 1912 and were withdrawn from regular service in 1976 and 1977.

Journey's end! On 29 October 2015 *Passchendaele* and her train ran through South Island's mountains on their way to Greymouth on the west coast. The weather was atrocious nearly all day, but the clouds parted as the train came to a halt at Greymouth's attractive period station just before sunset.